ASCENT

The Mountaineering Experience in Word and Image
Edited by Allen Steck and Steve Roper

SIERRA CLUB BOOKS • SAN FRANCISCO

Published simultaneously in Great Britain by Diadem Books Ltd.
ISBN 0-906371-70-8

Cover photograph: Seen from the depths of a chimney, a climber jams a crack during the first ascent of the Supercrack, near Canyonlands National Park. *Ed Webster.*

Back cover photo: Sunset on the Tatina Glacier; Mount Jeffers rises on the right. *Mike Graber.*

Library of Congress Cataloging in Publication Data
Main entry under title:

Ascent, the mountaineering experience in word and image.

1. Mountaineering—Addresses, essays, lectures.
2. Mountaineering—Fiction. I. Steck, Allen. II. Roper, Steve.
GV200.A83   796.5'22   80-13855
ISBN 0-87156-240-5 (pbk.)

"Climbing Aconcagua" is reprinted from *After Such Pleasures*, by Frances Mayes (New York: Seven Woods Press, 1979).

"The Conquest of the Riffelberg" is excerpted from *A Tramp Abroad*, by Mark Twain (Hartford, Conn.: American Publishing Co., Chatto & Windus, London, 1880).

Text and illustrations of "The Great Match" originally appeared in *Alpinisme* (1930); reprinted from *Appalachia*, Vol. XIX (Boston: The Appalachian Mountain Club, 1932-1933). Opening illustration from *L'Opera de Pics*, by Samivel (Paris: Arthaud, 1944).

Jacket and book design by David Broom.

Printed by Dai Nippon Printing Co., Ltd., Tokyo, Japan.

10 9 8 7 6 5 4 3 2 1

A young mountaineering author has of course the courage of his convictions; but he should also have the courage of his emotions. If he is to be read by human beings, he must write his adventures exactly as he himself humanly saw them at the time. General or objective description, such as satisfied the slower timing of the last two centuries, now reads too slowly, and is dull. . . .

. . . An artist of mountains will devote his whole skill to painting them as they are. A writer has a greater opportunity: he can picture them not only as they are, but also tell of their effect on man.

Let him take courage, and write himself *into his story. He is not writing a lifeless scientific treatise. Wherever human beings are concerned, as they are in mountaineering, the writing, if it is to be true at all, must be human and personal; or it will soon die of dry detail, and be forgotten.*

Geoffrey Winthrop Young from "Courage, and Mountain Writing," an article in the 1955 Mountain World.

CONTENTS

INTRODUCTION

In the Sierra Club's early years, its membership consisted mainly of Californians who were closely involved with mountaineering and mountain-related pursuits. Later, as a leader in the burgeoning national conservation movement, the Club gained a far broader constituency. To reflect this new focus, the Club's leaders decided in the mid-1960s to bring out a monthly magazine devoted almost exclusively to conservation topics. This logical step, however, resulted in the Club's decision to cease publication of the annual *Sierra Club Bulletin*, "that model of all mountaineering periodicals," as Ronald Clark called it in *The Splendid Hills*. For more than seven decades, the *Bulletin* had published hundreds of informative articles about mountaineering in western North America, and many climbers mourned its demise.

Among them was Allen Steck, who became concerned that there no longer existed a publication devoted to the total mountaineering experience. True, the *American Alpine Journal*, published by the American Alpine Club, provided dutiful coverage of ascents, but its style was conventional and its format inadequate for quality photographic reproduction. And, as Geoffrey Winthrop Young wrote, the mountaineer need not be writing a "lifeless scientific treatise." Steck wished to create a distinctive publication committed to the more human aspects of climbing.

His emerging vision was invigorated by the timely appearance of *Everest: The West Ridge,* a Sierra Club Exhibit Format book distinguished by an eloquent text and marvelous photographs. It was in every way the opposite of a scientific treatise. Impressed, Steck decided to approach the Club with his idea: a large-format periodical which would graphically depict the sheer visual delight of mountaineering, and, using cartoons, drawings, and satirical articles, offer the reader an insider's view of the whimsical side of climbing.

Fortunately, the organization's sagacious leaders reacted with enthusiasm and in 1966 authorized Steck to begin work. The following spring he and co-editors Joe Fitschen and Steve Roper brought forth the first issue of *Ascent.* Now a collector's item, the forty-eight-page magazine sold for one dollar, and its vivid writing and innovative photography garnered instant critical acclaim. The Sierra Club accountants were less pleased as they pondered the red ink in their books, but during the following years the ink slowly blackened, thanks in no small part to the donated labors of the original editors and others who came and went: Edgar Boyles, Glen Denny, Dave Dornan, Chuck Pratt, David Roberts, Jim Stuart, and Lito Tejada-Flores.

By the end of 1972, Volume I, comprising 312 pages, was complete. Volume II, totaling 288 pages, included the issues of 1973, 1974 and the combined issue for 1975/76, which marked the first time *Ascent* appeared in softcover book format.

The hiatus of four years that preceded the present volume (Volume III) resulted in part from our desire to shift the emphasis of the magazine-turned-book toward writing of less topical—and thus more lasting—interest. There are presently several magazines in North America and Great Britain which cover subjects that *Ascent* alone once reported; some of these magazines, in fact, reflect the influence of past issues of *Ascent*. This increased stress on creative graphics and writing has been a positive force in mountaineering literature. But as times change, we think *Ascent* should continue to experiment.

For example, we have long been aware that fiction, as a form of mountain literature, generally has been ignored. Although there are countless examples of excellent personal narratives about climbing, mountaineers have been reluctant to imagine what goes on in the minds of others. But we are gratified to find the situation changing, and in the hope of encouraging this trend, we have included several fictional pieces in this book. Foremost among these is David Roberts' *Like Water and Like Wind*, the first novella with a mountaineering theme to be written by an American climber. Although its occasionally earthy language and bizarre ending may jolt the sensibilities of some mountaineers, we believe the story excitingly and accurately conveys the flavor of modern climbing.

Our other original work of fiction is a haunting and lyrical piece by John Daniel entitled "The Way of the White Serpent." We have also included two previously published works of fiction: "The Great Match," a satirical view of climbing competition; and "The Conquest of the Riffelberg," Mark Twain's tongue-in-cheek account of his initiation into the mysteries of Alpinism.

Interspersed among the fictional pieces are articles dealing with specific climbs or areas. The reader will reach the top of the Eiger's dreaded north face with Ron Matous; explore the remote Cathedral Spires, "Alaska's Yosemite," with Mike Graber; share Jim Balog's terror in the Black Ice Couloir of the Grand Teton; cling to rotten, overhanging rock with Tom Higgins on the volcanic crags of Pinnacles National Monument; and accompany Dick Shockley on a "routine" ascent of El Capitan.

Two other articles focus on opposite ends of the climbing spectrum, from the traditional to the "lunatic fringe." David Roberts discusses what is good and (often) bad about expedition books and gives a list of his favorites. Jeff Long investigates the phenomenon of urban climbing, sharing fascinating accounts of the human flies of the 1920s as well as his own experience on the recent attempt to scale San Francisco's Transamerica Pyramid.

The work of several photographers and artists are included in this volume, continuing *Ascent*'s tradition of dramatic graphics. Two color-photo essays reveal the startling diversity of mountaineering: climbing on the sunny, wind-etched sandstone of the American Southwest contrasts vividly with the chill blues and whites of Alaska's Cathedral Spires.

We wish to thank all the authors and artists who submitted their work to the Sierra Club for this first *Ascent* of the 1980s. We trust our readership will be large enough to justify the biennial publication of *Ascent* in book form, and we are ready to begin laying the foundation for another volume in 1982.

THE EDITORS

MAN MEETS MYTH
A TRUE FANTASY

Ron Matous

Pilgrimages are not easy to come by these days. In a mobile and icono-clastic society there are few places or objects that retain both the mystery and the historical value necessary to be worthy objects of a pilgrimage. Traveling thousands of miles to stand in awe of some revered relic is no longer considered a socially useful act. Our myths are no longer universal, shared and cherished by entire nations and dealing with themes of creation and ancient history; they have become more modern and secular, focused on shorter periods of time and events of purely provincial significance. Only erudite people now know the story of Prometheus or Ulysses; but who in this country does not know of Abe Lincoln, Mickey Mouse, or the Franken-stein monster? And for climbers, there is the Eiger. . . .

Were it not for all the tales of terror and epic struggles that have ema-nated from its undesirable flanks, I would never have been drawn to the Eiger. And if it had not been so obscured in the mists of hyperbole and climbing history, I would have known better just what I was getting myself into that spring day when Mike Munger, possessed by a wild lust nurtured by such epics as *The White Spider* and *I Chose to Climb,* asked, "Would you like to do the Eiger?"

I quickly and truthfully answered yes, although the meaning of that affirmation was closer to "I would like to have done the Eiger" than to "I would like to try it." Still, how could a climber in search of his heritage, reared on stories of Edward Whymper and the Creagh Dhu, go to Europe without at least looking at the Eiger? There was some consolation, too, in the knowledge that the weather was usually too poor even to attempt it.

One does not go to the Alps for a wilderness experience. They are the most heavily used mountains on the planet, and have been for centuries; they were the birthplace of this strange activity we love so much, and figure prominently in mountaineering's mythology. By going to the Alps, Mike and I were engaging in a pilgrimage, indulging our curiosity, escaping the rapid flux and competition of the climbing vanguard. We were retreating to dig among our roots. The climbs we had in mind were not the modern technologi-cal horrors of the "Seventh Grade," but rather the classics whose names had existed so long in our minds that quite definite (and usually incorrect) pic-tures of their nature had accreted around the germinal facts.

June and July saw us in the Dolomites and at Chamonix, enjoying ourselves, doing a lot of climbing, not really thinking about the Eiger except as a place we would get to sometime during the summer, when things felt right. Every day revealed the inaccuracy of our preconceptions about Europe, but nothing tarnished the idyllic nature of what we were doing. We were simply having a good time.

As the first days of August approached, then, we were feeling very satisfied with what we had seen and done. It was time to take seriously our promise to ourselves. All that would be required to make the summer perfect was an ascent of the original route on the Eiger's north face. Not much to ask . . . but I was still in the grip of legend, full of thoughts of the Hinterstoisser party, of rockfall, frozen ropes, sudden storms, and irreversible sections.

Facing page: The upper two-thirds of the north face of the Eiger. *Toni Hiebeler.*

When you go to climb the Eiger, you do not go to climb a mountain but rather to vanquish a myth, to scramble upon the stuff of legend, and to discover firsthand what you know that everyone before you had discovered—that you do not really want to be there except to make that discovery. To learn for yourself. . . .

I will not attempt to unravel the labyrinthine tangle of motivations that lead anyone to climb, least of all myself. Too much inconclusive, turgid prose has been printed on the carcasses of too many majestic trees to justify still another attempt. But what I do want to understand is not *why* but simply *what* I was feeling in the shadow of that mile-high symbol which, from the vantage point of our tent, underwent a constant metamorphosis of size, shape, color, and import, depending on the time of day, weather, and the state of my lower intestine. Because obviously it was the myth, not the reality, that was the living thing here; it was fascinating to watch the slow transformation of the one into the other as we waited, watched, and finally climbed.

After two days of hitchhiking to cover a mere hundred miles, I arrived in Grindelwald in the midst of a rare week of perfect weather. That is, it was perfect everywhere in Europe except at the Eiger, where it was raining. So already the stories were proving true: the Eiger was living up to its reputation of having the worst weather in Europe. The face itself was still hiding; I thought I knew approximately in which direction. My imagination was working overtime trying to peel back the clouds, and all the while fragments of truth gleaned from photos and books were falling together into patterns that made sense, at last, like a revelation.

All summer long the knowledge that I intended to have a go at the Eiger had been festering in the back of my mind, accompanied by the most extreme mixed feelings. There was no question that I wanted to see firsthand the Icefields, the Death Bivouac, the Traverse of the Gods, the Spider, the summit icefield. But I knew myself well enough to realize that this desire would be satisfied only by an honest attempt, and the reports I had heard of the objective dangers on the Eiger made me feel as if I were willfully throwing myself into the whimsical hands of fate. Only two weeks earlier, I learned in Kleine Scheidegg, two Germans who had successfully climbed the face were killed while descending the west flank. What was I committing myself to?

A myth. I was committed to discovering the truth behind the myth, to peeling back the onionlike integuments of human fabrication to see the face in all its stark, raving, immense beauty. I wanted to decipher the myth, undiminished even after forty years' worth of ascents.

Many climbers are in the habit of belittling the achievements of their predecessors with comments that betray a gross misunderstanding of the significance of the first ascent. To climb at the current high standards, it is first necessary to climb on the shoulders of earlier visionaries who, in turn, were accomplishing a precarious balancing act. It is a beneficial exercise in humility, when doing an established climb, to imagine what it was *really* like for the first-ascent party. I had heard plenty of disparaging remarks about the Eiger: that the ice was only fifty-five degrees, the rock only 5.5, the first 2000

A classic preoccupation at Kleine Scheidegg: tourists search the Eiger's face for climbing action. *Ron Matous.*

feet were third-classable, the face was festooned with pitons and fixed ropes, and so forth. Now, although these comments came from people who had never set foot on the face, I did not doubt the veracity of their secondhand information. But I still suspected that they were missing something, some factor lost in the analysis of the whole into its technical parts, that accounted for the ascendence of the climb into the mythological realm. That factor, as it turned out, was the numinous aura of its history, which hangs palpably over the black face like an eternal storm.

My first view of the *Nordwand* (which, to perpetuate the myth, German climbers call the *Mordwand*) was by full moonlight, after the first night's rain had cleared away. It was instantly recognizable from the photos I had seen, yet it bore no resemblance to my expectations. They had been blown up out of all proportion to produce a frowning monolith four miles high, black as pitch and inhabited by lightning bolts, which overhung its base by 300 feet and occasionally disgorged bits of climbers with a satisfied belch. In reality, however, this looked like an actual mountain, with snowfields, ridges, and a summit; the rumblings emanated solely from the regurgitating cows surrounding my tent. There was even a light on the lower face, a sight as comforting as a mother waiting up for her son. No headlamp was that bright, so I concluded it must mark the "railway window" I had heard so much of. (No feature of the north face causes so much perplexity among armchair mountaineers as these so-called railway windows. They have figured in many accounts of attempts, rescues, and attempted rescues, but I had always scratched my head and wondered just what the hell a railroad was doing up there, anyway? Certainly there was nothing in my experience to compare to it; for me the windows had been an anomaly best glossed over while I went on to the more comprehensible parts of the Eiger legend. I will not add to the confusion—or diminish anyone's imaginative fantasies—by an explanation here. The point I wish to make is that, on location, it was the work of a second to rectify several years' worth of sloppy conjectures.)

On the following day, now that I was aware I was facing reality instead of my preconceived notions, the north face assumed more understandable proportions. It was with great optimism, therefore, that I strolled the short distance to Kleine Scheidegg to meet Mike, just up on the train. It was difficult to keep a straight face as I passed the time watching the tourists thronging around the legendary telescope outside the hotel. (I kept looking for Clint Eastwood . . . reflecting that only since the advent of cinematography have we been able to enjoy the luxury of modeling the world after our fantasies, rather than vice versa. Here I was laughing not at the popularized portrayals of Kleine Scheidegg, but at how closely the reality resembled them. I was giddy because something was backwards here; there was some kind of cosmic practical joke being played.

During the ensuing two and half weeks there were numerous times when the Eiger briefly shed its Olympian façade and condescended to join the ranks of more mundane geographical features. That long spell of unsettled weather—it rained a little each day, and sometimes for two or three days without a break—gave me an unsurpassed opportunity to oscillate wildly between every conceivable attitude and perspective my subconscious could create. Nor were these thoughts within my conscious control; by the very act of arriving at Kleine Scheidegg I had relinquished any responsibility for the final outcome.

Clouds drift across the lower flanks of the Eiger. *Toni Hiebeler.*

We would remain until we could wait no longer, and if the weather and conditions allowed, we would try it, and simply climb to the best of our ability toward success or failure. We did not doubt that when the time came either to leave or to start climbing, the moment would impress itself upon us with an insistent salience that neither rationalization nor argument could alter. In order to sustain any chance at all of doing the climb, we had to relinquish control to the ambiance and symbolism of the place; otherwise, even a moment's rational consideration would have sent us packing, off to go swimming in the sunny south.

If the mountain occasionally forgot its reputation and shone in the rare light of a sunset breaking through the afternoon's accumulation of mist, there were days when the place was as uninviting as we could imagine, and it seemed that no amount of blue sky could entice us to venture into that shadowed, treacherous world from the sunlit meadows where we lay among the blueberries. Looking up at the wall from the warmth of our tent as the first rays of a clear morning burned the night's frost away was like looking at an illustrated article on the moon from the depths of a fireside easy chair.

One day, when returning from a morning's foray into Grindelwald to restock our supply of body fat, we saw the clouds part theatrically to reveal they had not been idle during the night. The entire face was moving in slow motion, as rivers of fresh snow poured down gullies and over cliffs, down icefields and into space, creeping with infinitesimal slowness down the immensity of rock and ice. It was the first demonstration we had actually had of the true scale of things here, to see what we knew were good-sized avalanches moving inexorably downward like a slow drift of dandelion puffs.

In retrospect, the chain of events that finally drove us onto the face was as carefully orchestrated as a Shakespearean comedy, and I wonder just how much of it we could even take responsibility for. On Thursday, August 19, fifteen days after our arrival, the afternoon storm clouds drew aside briefly to show us the most depressing sight our vigil had yet produced: fresh snow down to the level of the talus, a mere hundred meters above our tent. It seemed unlikely that the increasingly shorter days, even without the clouds, could produce enough afternoon sunshine to get the face back into the kind of condition we wanted for the climb. And we had been impressed enough with tales of the difficulty of retreat to be very reluctant to go up in conditions which seemed less than ideal. Unfortunately, the great fallacy in our reasoning was that the Eiger, almost by definition, is never in good condition. With little snow on the face, one is forced to climb on rock that breaks off under one's boots and rains down from above like an aerial bombardment. If there is enough snow to hold the loose rock in place, then there is enough to fill the cracks with ice and make protection and climbing difficult. In cold weather one climbs over verglas; in warm, through waterfalls. Only one thing was obvious that Thursday afternoon: we didn't want to climb while the face looked like *that*. We calculated that even with perfect weather beginning the next day, it would be two or three days before the snow consolidated enough to climb on, after which we would want three good days on the wall to be sure of

success (we hoped to climb it in two, but some margin seemed desirable). This meant we were asking for six consecutive days without storms, a seeming impossibility.

So it was with a wide spectrum of emotions that I packed my gear that night in preparation for leaving on the morning train. I was free of the burden of commitment: we had put in our time, and if the opportunity to climb had not presented itself, it was no fault of ours. On the other hand I was greatly disappointed, for a lot of energy had gone into anticipation, and our long period of waiting was to no avail. But rationally I had known that our chances of climbing the Eiger on this visit had been slim. People as determined as Don Whillans had been thwarted countless times; another Englishman I spoke with had been on the face eight times, turned back by everything from rockfall to the discovery of a severed human hand. That night I fell asleep to the familiar sound of rain, confident that our decision to leave in the morning was irreproachably correct.

Imagine my dismay, then, to awaken to the clearest morning we had yet seen in Switzerland. The haze that had obscured the horizon each morning, foreboding rain, was gone; not even the wispiest puff of vapor marred the sky. By an amazing display of mental gymnastics, we dismissed within seconds all the careful reasoning of the night before in favor of the argument that, having arrived at the end of one spell of fine weather, we would never forgive ourselves for leaving at the beginning of the next. No other course of action was possible: we had to stay.

The afternoon brought a few clouds, of course, but no rain, and that was novel. We agreed to consider this day as the first of the requisite six and slept that night with renewing hopes and fears. Fortunately, we were quite used to such rapid and massive shifts of attitude, and so slept soundly despite the excitement. I wasn't ready to believe anything until I saw it.

The length to which emotions had been stretched might be measured by an event of the previous night, when we had converted a bottle that had been saved as victory wine into a bottle of consolation wine. We had also tried hard to eat the rest of our food, not wanting too heavy a load while hitchhiking. So on Friday afternoon I once more made the long trek to Grindelwald to stock up again on bivouac food, and to avoid thinking too much.

By the next morning the fact was being pounded into my consciousness: good weather. Another clear day. Our reconnaissance the previous week—we had taken advantage of a fine morning to scramble up the lower 1500 feet of the face to the Difficult Crack and back—had settled us on the strategy of an afternoon approach and subsequent bivouac on a fine ledge at the base of the Difficult Crack as the most logical way of doing the climb. It was the least committing, gave us the greatest head start, and offered the best chance of being beyond the Third Icefield by two o'clock, when the afternoon sun hit the top of the face and the stonefall began. We could use the rest of the afternoon to climb the relatively sheltered Ramp. If we failed to cross the icefield by two o'clock, we would be forced to waste valuable time sheltering in the protection of the Death Bivouac.

The next question was, which afternoon to start? The longer we waited, the more ice and snow would melt out of the Exit Cracks, which we knew from our reading would be very difficult in poor conditions. But the longer we waited, the greater would be the chance of being caught in the inevitable next storm. It became obvious that we might as well begin that afternoon, Saturday. By the time we expected to reach the Exit Cracks, on Monday, they would have had three sunny days in which to clear off.

Coming so soon after our unequivocal decision to return to Chamonix, this reversal of our situation was incredible. The decision to climb fell upon a mind already so numbed by two weeks of waiting and gyrating emotions that I could do no more than mechanically pack my gear, then sit down and read a book to pass the time until two o'clock, when we figured on starting. Why sit on a ledge all afternoon when we could lie in a meadow all morning? Besides, it still might rain.

No such luck. That evening found us perched upon what was to be the finest of three bivouac sites, watching the slow decline of a brilliant day. A steady curtain of meltwater pattered off the protective overhang to splash at my feet, maintaining the proper degree of moisture in the mud floor of our little cave, lest it get uncomfortably hard. I was silent and stoic, wondering with detachment just what the following days would bring. They held a magnificent potential for the profoundest ecstasy or despair; but though somehow I felt that the fate of our attempt was already ordained, with only the motions to be gone through, I was vouchsafed no clue as to what it might be either by the events of the day or by the infinitely impersonal and tranquil scene before my eyes.

We had strolled along the meadows to the base of the climb with a funereal gait, not wanting to work up a sweat or get to our ledge too early. Despite the unmatched opportunity for contemplation, I avoided it, instead disappearing into the first phase of an egolessness that my subconscious deemed essential to the success of this climb. To have allowed the face in all its domineering presence full access to my mind would have been to invite demoralization; to succeed, a businesslike attitude was required, dealing with each pitch or problem as it arose, because unlike the monstrous whole, no single one of them seemed insuperable.

A surrealistic note of undivined significance crept into that first afternoon, when we passed the railway window near the Shattered Pillar. A wooden door set into an oval cement frame faced us incongruously like a gateway to some other world. Inside, a short passage revealed the railway tracks slanting steeply upward parallel to the face and a scant ten feet within. On the wall next to the track an electric bulb illuminated a placard reading not "Abandon hope, all ye who enter here," as I half expected, but "Open All Year Round" in four languages. For our benefit, or the passengers'? I'll never be sure. The line dividing fantasy from reality became even thinner.

As we slowly pieced together the climb over the next two days, one pitch at a time, the last traces of our quotidian existence disappeared, and each

The famous pitch known as the Ice Hose calls for steady concentration on steep ice. *Ron Matous*.

A climber follows the first
section of the Ramp, the
diagonal ledge that slices up the
wall above the Third Icefield.
Ron Matous.

ropelength occupied our entire consciousness. As we climbed higher and farther from the possibility of retreat, we must have become slightly mad, seeing nothing but the next difficult step, knowing nothing but a need to go up as going down became more improbable. At our second bivouac, high on the Ramp, we were at least a day's journey in either direction from safety. Yet sitting there on a small ledge, I could hear the cowbells below us as if they were again just outside our tent.

So far the weather had been excellent, and we had encountered nothing to make us despair of success. At that point, in fact, we had to succeed or die trying, for it seemed it would be equally difficult to reach the summit or the bottom safely; this saved us the trouble of thinking about retreat. Exhaustion and dehydration actually saved us the trouble of thinking at all; we had elected to save weight by not taking a stove, but had been unable to get close enough to any of the afternoon drips to replenish our water supply. Eating snow was not enough to slake our thirst, and a liter bottle of packed snow, slept with, produced a measly third of a liter of liquid for breakfast. We consoled ourselves with optimistic thoughts of being free from suffering in only one more day.

Conditions on the climb turned out to be vastly different from anything we had been led to expect. The preceding two weeks of storms had plastered the wall with ice and hard snow, which made the icefields a romp but the rock pitches extreme. If there were fixed pitons, most of them were buried, and so were the cracks. The Hinterstoisser Traverse was an eighty-degree wall covered by three inches of ice. A nagging fear occupied us: the Exit Cracks might be even more difficult than we were prepared for.

As it happened, they were. A third bivouac was needed only two pitches from the summit icefield, among a discomfiting proliferation of clouds. As the sun set, we found ourselves in a forty-five-degree ice gully capped by over-hanging rock. The route above looked dubious at best and ridiculous to attempt by headlamp. We set to work chopping a foot-wide ledge in the ice on which to spend the night; in the process the pick of my axe snapped cleanly off, leaving me aghast but not terribly chagrined. I still had my North Wall hammer and knew that no more steep ice lay ahead. But the Eiger had given us a glimpse of its unforgiving nature and it had more to show.

The afternoon clouds had been thicker than usual, but as darkness fell they seemed to disperse, and the stars felt close. Despite my fettered position, I slept for a few hours. A strange vision woke us around midnight: a helicopter flew in slow passes over the meadow far below, using a searchlight beam which must have illuminated a square mile with the brightness of the sun. Had some of the sacred cows escaped? We were at a loss otherwise to explain this bizarre activity at such an absurd hour. After half an hour it disappeared over the horizon, still unexplained.

I dozed for a few more hours, but awakened finally to see, with bitter, deep despair, the thunderless play of lightning on the predawn horizon. Wouldn't it be getting light soon? In a heavy storm I knew it would not matter, for we would not be able to move. I heard Mike shifting position and knew he

Facing page: Mike Munger on the exposed snowfield known as the White Spider. *Ron Matous.*

Right: Surrounded by afternoon mists, Mike Munger follows an ice-encrusted pitch in the Exit Cracks. *Ron Matous.*

was also watching.

For a long while neither of us spoke a word, feeling like a couple of kids caught stealing candy. We should have known. How could we have expected to get away with a fifth day of good weather?

Again I had the sensation of being in a movie, so carefully orchestrated was this dramatization. After an hour or so the lightning, which had slowly been drawing closer, simply stopped. I thought I detected the first graying of dawn; there were stars too; a clearing.

Then, unexpectedly, it started to snow. Dense, round pellets of graupel tapped on my parka. Lightly, then it stopped. Lightly again, then heavier. I took out my cagoule and pulled my bivouac extension up to my shoulders. It snowed harder, and after five minutes I began to hear snow slithering down our gully in a dry stream. Piling up against our backs, it began forcing us off our ledge. Quickly I stood up, brushed off my ice ledge, and sat again. After that I had to arise every few minutes if I wanted to retain my perch. The snow kept funneling down, pouring over us. It was getting light enough to see, and across the upper face I could see the snow torrents that we had watched with such smugness from the valley not long before. We were thankful to be so high, near the top of this avalanching face, and glad our gully was topped by an overhang.

I would have been much happier, though, if we had not been there at all. If only we had made it up those last two pitches of the Exit Cracks the day before; if only it was not so obvious that we were stuck, quite indisputably, at least until the end of the storm. The Exit Cracks had produced the most difficult climbing we had yet seen. The rock was coated with ice, the cracks were filled with snow, and fixed pitons (if the tales were true) were buried until spring. Now the last two pitches, which looked harder than anything

On the summit icefield.
Ron Matous.

After completing the summit icefield pitches, moderate ridge climbing leads to the Eiger's summit. *Mike Munger.*

below, had been converted into snow chutes for the summit icefield to shed its load. Having sat through two weeks of stormy weather in the meadow, we found little reason for optimism about the length of this storm. I sat there, still warm and dry but with the snow pouring around me, thinking only of the struggle ahead.

With the stage so carefully set, with our emotions so precisely manipulated to a perfect tragic pitch, the punchline was delivered. The snowfall stopped, the clouds parted, and our reprieve was granted. Although the day was not clear, it was without immediate threat. Light usurped the place of darkness. We sensed that the storm had been obligatory, but not malevolent. To have climbed the Eiger without encountering a storm would have been close to sacrilege. We gathered the remnants of our wits, shook ourselves off, and slowly undid our elaborate bivouac preparations. This was no easy task: imagine two people on a one-by-four-foot ledge, putting on boots (oh, think of the consequences of dropping one!) and crampons. The rope had been thoroughly soaked by the soggy snow of the preceding afternoon, and now it held its shape quite stubbornly. We bent it into a coil of sorts that would fit into Mike's pack and removed the still-dry nine-millimeter rope to use on the remainder of the climb.

One never gets away with anything in the cosmic perspective. Those last two pitches took us as many hours, and even having arrived on the summit icefield Mike couldn't rest his nerves: he was faced with an imaginary belay on two inches of ice while I sweated up the last and hardest pitch with as much tension as he dared give. What comes next, I wondered?

What came next were waves, billows, a veritable *tsunami* of relief. Emerging from the top of the gully, I saw only the lower-angled snow that curved back toward the summit, five hundred feet above. With the suddenly increasing certainty of success (and, by implication, survival), the consciousness of my life and its joys came flooding back into a numb mind that for three days had repressed all thoughts not essential to the task at hand, pouring the salve of ecstasy over the jagged harshness that had become my world.

We took great care traversing the narrow summit arête and descending the sodden snows of the west flank. Our lives, for so many years taken for granted, had been revealed as fragile things, and like works of glass we guarded them carefully against even the minimal dangers of the descent. Much more awaited us in the meadows now than we had left behind.

There was no sudden revelation, no lightninglike flash that I could point to along the way as the moment at which it happened; nevertheless, the myth and I had each subsumed the other, and both emerged quite changed. The battle had raged not on the face, but in the unknown vortices of my own mind. The mountain, except for a piton or two we had to leave behind, was unchanged. But I had not been climbing on the mountain. I had been climbing on some vast accretion of stories, childhood fantasies, rainy-afternoon daydreams, and photo books. Never again could I see or think of the face in quite the same way, or read those accounts with uncorrupted innocence. Lying in the meadow the afternoon after the descent, I tried hard to revive the awe that had dominated me in that very spot just three days earlier. It was not possible. Despite all I had gained, there was also the feeling of something lost.

EIGHTEEN YEARS AFTER THE RIESENSTEIN HOAX
A HISTORY OF THE CATHEDRAL SPIRES

Mike Graber

God went nuts when He created the Cathedral Spires. Why else would He have crammed all that geological confusion into a sardine can of smiling granite teeth and glaciers? It makes no sense. Seeing the result for the first time, one gets the impression that the view is strangely distorted, that the vertical has been stretched at the expense of the horizontal. Buttresses are stacked alongside ridges; faces round into steep couloirs. There is too much to see here, and the fact that the range usually hides under a blanket of clouds only compounds its aloofness.

The granite spikes known prosaically as the Cathedral Spires rise from a tight maze of glaciers near the western end of the Alaska Range, in the area called the Kichatna Mountains. By Alaskan standards the peaks and glaciers are small—the highest mountain doesn't even reach 9000 feet, and the longest glaciers extend a mere six or seven miles. Yet within an area of twenty square miles, there are over a dozen faces higher than Yosemite's El Capitan. And although the quality of the granite may not be as good as that on El Cap, it is superb by any other criterion.

The area is not paradise, however, for its remoteness and abysmal weather make the nature of the climbing exceptionally serious. Conventional radio communication from the standard base camps is usually impossible, with the exception of chance, line-of-sight contact with aircraft. And as in the rest of the Alaska Range, five- and six-day storms, along with tent-pole-breaker winds, are not uncommon. Waiting out a storm in a tent can be miserable enough; sitting out one on a wall can be a hellish nightmare. Climbers have learned to take advantage of the rare spells of good weather by climbing twenty-four hours a day, until fatigue or weather forces a bivouac. It is easy to see why the Spires remained untouched until only recently.

The first recorded mention of the Spires was by two geologists who traveled across central Alaska in 1898. They viewed some of the higher peaks from a point twenty-five miles to the south, near present-day Rainy Pass. The following year, while roaming near the headwaters of the Kichatna River, a man named Joseph Herron caught a glimpse of three spectacular peaks; he called them Gurney, Augustin, and Lewis, perhaps in honor of his favorite drinking partners.

There is no record of further explorations in the range until 1903, when the indefatigable Frederick Cook probed the headwaters of the Kichatna River during an attempt to find a pass described by Herron. Traveling alternately on horseback and on foot up the west bank of the Kichatna, Cook experienced typical weather conditions: "Up the valley of the Kichatna we saw continuous streams of great, fluffy cumulus and nimbus clouds drifting through the range to the arctic slopes beyond."

During Cook's 1906 expedition, his party attempted to cross the headwaters of the west fork of the Yentna River, immediately north of the Cathedral Spires. After two members of the expedition nearly drowned in the icy current, the attempt was abandoned.

View up the Cul-de-Sac Glacier from the northwest, showing two major summits of the Cathedral Spires: below the massive cumulus cloud is Kichatna Spire; to its left, displaying an imposing ice face, is the Citadel. *Ed Cooper*.

Above: Typical storm conditions in the Cathedral Spires: Grendel Spire from the Shadows Glacier. *Mike Graber.*

Facing page: A section from the USGS quadrangle Talkeetna B-6; many of the peak names have been added. Scale is approximately one inch to the mile.

For more than half a century after Cook's expedition, little attention was directed to the Spires; this was understandable, for explorers and climbers naturally were more interested in the gigantic peaks clustered around Mount McKinley. In the early 1960s, however, a series of events occurred that made the Cathedral Spires the locus of the most clever and successful hoax in the history of North American mountaineering.

Austin Post, a brilliant glaciologist and outstanding mountain photographer, was flying through the Alaska Range in the summer of 1961 taking photographs of glaciers to illustrate a book he was preparing. At the bush pilot's suggestion, they headed for an area in the western portion of the range where the pilot claimed there were fantastic rock formations similar to those found in McKinley Park's Ruth Gorge. Their goal, however, was blanketed by clouds when they arrived. But as the pilot began to bank the plane for home, the clouds parted, revealing a spectacular 3000-foot spike of granite. Post had time for only a few photos before the clouds again obscured the incredible mountain. Post recorded the photos in his notebook: "Unnamed peak, Cathedral Spires."

Later that year, Seattle writer Harvey Manning invited two good friends, Post and avalanche expert Edward LaChapelle, to his home for a get-together. Post brought numerous stunning photos from his summer's work in Alaska to share with his friends. Both Manning and LaChapelle recognized most of the photos—even the unusual views of famous mountains—but when Post flashed the photo taken over the Cathedral Spires,

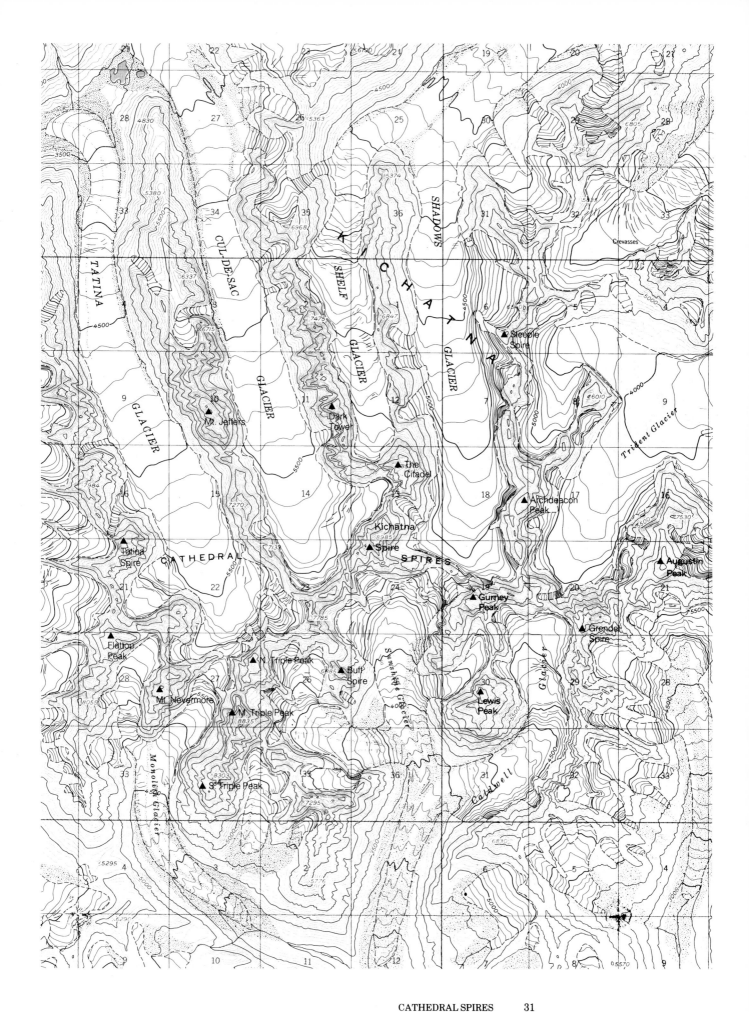

neither could identify it. As the trio admired the photograph, the trickster in LaChapelle stirred. Thinking it was time for a bit of chicanery, he began to mastermind the now-famous Riesenstein Hoax. After drawing a few fake "routes" on the photo, LaChapelle and Manning wrote an article describing the attempt of an Austrian scientific expedition to climb the "Riesenstein peaks of British Columbia." The purported author was to be a Canadian who had interviewed the Austrians before their departure to Europe. To give the author authenticity, Manning had a friend living in Calgary mail the article to the editors of *Summit,* a Southern California climbing and hiking magazine.

The playful deception had two primary targets. One was *Summit*'s Northwest editor, Dee Molenaar, a mutual friend of the hoaxers. The other target was also a good friend, the legendary climber Fred Beckey.

The northwest face of Kichatna Spire. The prominent buttress to the right of the large snow-field provided climbing of extreme difficulty for the party making the second ascent of the spire in 1979. *Alan Kearney.*

The editors of *Summit* published the photo—as well as an ambiguous map drawn by the perpetrators—in their June, 1962 issue. As the text was awkwardly written (the hoaxers had employed mock German-English), the editors shortened the article and printed an abbreviated caption—never suspecting a hoax and totally missing such subtle clues as one climber's name, Kronhofer (the brand name of a famous climbing shoe of the era).

When it comes to North American mountains, one can sandbag *Summit* some of the time. But to pull a fast one on Fred Beckey isn't that easy. He looked at the photo, then at the map; his encyclopedic memory of mountains told him something was wrong. Knowing that it was unlikely that British Columbia could harbor such a spectacular and as-yet-undiscovered peak, Beckey scrutinized the photo for clues. Studying the clouds, the crevasses, and the summit snowfields, he astutely concluded that the peak had to be somewhere in Alaska below 10,000 feet. One can imagine the fervor with which "the devourer of first ascents" examined maps of Alaska until he had narrowed the possibilities to a likely few.

If anyone could keep a secret about an unknown climbing area, it would be Beckey. He was the type of man who wouldn't mutter a word about the true identity and location of the Riesenstein until he was finished climbing there. And since Manning, Post, and LaChapelle had never intended to climb the mysterious mountain, they too kept the secret, gloating privately over the success of the hoax.

Meanwhile, somewhat less astute—but no less enthusiastic American mountaineers began planning expeditions and flooding the Canadian government map office in Ottawa with requests for topographical maps and aerial photos of the "Riesenstein peaks at the headwaters of the Klawatti River, British Columbia." The information from Ottawa caused confusion and frustration, for neither maps nor photos of this region showed the slightest trace of rock or ice.

It soon became obvious that *Summit* had been the victim of a practical joke. Yet the mountains were real. Where were they? And who was behind the hoax? Beckey? The editors of *Summit*?

Unable to pinpoint the exact location, Beckey lost interest over the next few years, and it was not until 1965 that the mystery was solved—not by Beckey, but by other mountaineers who had been fascinated by the enigma. New York climber Al DeMaria, with the help of Brownell Bergen, stumbled onto definitive information in the library of the American Alpine Club: the photo showed peaks in a remote and little-explored area seventy miles southwest of Mount McKinley. The topographical map published by the United States Geological Survey informed DeMaria that the rugged region actually had a name: the Cathedral Spires. He and five other strong and eager eastern climbers immediately organized an expedition to explore the area. Considering the team's collective experience on rock and in the Canadian Rockies, it seemed reasonable that the expedition could manage at least a few major peaks. It was not to be, however, and the men learned that two-dimensional renditions of unexplored mountains can be deceptive indeed.

Overleaf: Kichatna Spire, the highest peak of the region, rises to the left; the Citadel is seen on the right. *Ed Cooper.*

During the first ascent of
Mount Jeffers, a climber moves
up slabs forming the left wall
of an immense dihedral.
Royal Robbins.

In June, 1965, the famous bush pilot Don Sheldon transported the group to a major glacier on the northern side of the range. It did not take the six men long to discover two significant drawbacks to climbing in the Cathedral Spires. First and foremost was the abominable weather. Severe winds, sleet, and whiteouts were the rule rather than the exception, and the men spent a disproportionate number of days inside their tents. The second problem concerned their failure to find a safe route out of their enclosed glacial basin; future climbers to the Spires would often encounter this same frustrating anomaly regardless of which glacier was chosen for a landing. The 1965 explorers wasted ten precious days trying to escape from what became known as Cool Sac Glacier, a corruption of Cul-de-Sac Glacier. Although the region's highest peak, Kichatna Spire, loomed above the group's base camp, it seemed far too intimidating to even attempt. Other major peaks lay only a few miles to the south, but because the men were unable to leave their claustrophobic glacier, these goals too were absolutely out of reach. In spite of the bad weather and their entrapment, the climbers reached several minor summits, learned something of the range's convoluted topography, and returned to civilization raving about the huge, alpine walls. As DeMaria and Pete Geiser wrote in the 1966 *American Alpine Journal,* "it still remained the opinion of all members of the party that these were the most challenging peaks any of us had ever seen."

The experiences of DeMaria and his friends sparked curiosity, and in September of the following year another expedition flew into the Spires. Dave Roberts, Art Davidson, Rick Millikan, Dave Johnston, and Pete Meisler landed on what they soon named Shadows Glacier, a body of ice two miles east of Cool Sac Glacier. September is an extremely cold month in which to practice Alaskan rockclimbing, yet despite this handicap, two of the men finally stood atop Kichatna Spire after an impressive nineteen-day siege. Four other peaks fell during the course of the thirty-five-day expedition. As if making five first ascents wasn't enough, the group snowshoed and trudged across three more unexplored glaciers, eventually arriving at a tiny airstrip near Rainy Pass, some twenty-five miles south of the Spires.

Although no expeditions visited the area the following year, there occurred an event which was to have a profound effect on the future climbing development of the Spires. Dave Roberts' fifteen-page article in the June, 1968 issue of *Summit* served as a most informative and accurate guide to the area's remaining prizes and undoubtedly saved every subsequent expedition countless headaches. (Ten years after the article appeared, its author regretted having written it; he could not have imagined in 1968 the explosion of climbing activity that would soon make the area a crowded *Klettergarten.*)

By the end of the 1960s, rumors of remote Alaskan walls as large and as steep as those on El Capitan began to filter through the California climbing community. If there was one person in those days who couldn't resist the chance to prove that the Cathedral Spires weren't as horrendous as they were reputed to be, it was Royal Robbins, one of the world's finest rockclimbers. Don Sheldon deposited Robbins, Joe Fitschen, and Charlie Raymond on the

Overleaf: Kichatna Spire from the south. Gurney Peak is at right. *Ed Cooper.*

Tatina Glacier—the long icefield just west of Cool Sac Glacier—in July, 1969. The men's primary goals were three awesome mountains which Dave Roberts had referred to as the "Triple Peaks." During the usual gloomy weather, the Californians succeeded in establishing Grade IV routes up three 8000-foot peaks (including South Triple Peak) and in nearly reaching the top of North Triple. Like their predecessors, the Californians left the Spires soaking wet and tremendously impressed by the climbing potential. Robbins later wrote prophetically: "After the first ascents of these mountains, the story of their great ridges and faces will begin, a tale which promises to be long and exciting."

The tone of the Californians' approach to Alaskan climbing was to serve as an example to future expeditions. Their style of climbing—developed in Yosemite—was built on the belief that it was nobler to attempt a peak without fixed ropes and fail than to siege the peak and succeed. By means of this example, subsequent climbing in the Cathedral Spires was guided by an unwritten code: sieging the peaks was no longer the most stylish or practical approach. (The term "sieging" can be defined as using a greater number of ropes than a party would normally take up the wall with them. For example, if a party of four planned to use four ropes while climbing the wall, they could justifiably fix those four ropes before committing themselves. Fixing more than four, however, would be considered sieging.)

Dave Roberts returned to the Spires in June, 1970 with Hank Abrons. The first two-man expedition ever to visit the region planned to attempt the north side of Middle Triple Peak. Three weeks after their arrival, having been plagued by unmerciful weather (Roberts described "a porridge of white-out, drizzling snow, and insincere patches of blue sky"), the pair tramped south toward Rainy Pass. One morning, while the men were cooking breakfast alongside the Kichatna River, the weather cleared, revealing an unusual panorama north toward the usually cloud-covered Spires. To his surprise and pleasure, Roberts recognized the exact outline of the three peaks that Joseph Herron had seen and named in 1899. What Roberts was looking at were his "Triple Peaks," yet the government's map designated three different peaks several miles to the east as Gurney, Augustin, and Lewis. To Roberts, this mistake simply confirmed what he already knew: the area remained a barely explored wilderness.

The first year that two separate expeditions visited the Cathedral Spires was 1972. William Katra's small group set up base camp on Shadows Glacier and proceeded to make first ascents of two striking 8000-foot mountains: Gurney Peak and Peak 8520, later called Citadel. The other team was let off on Tatina Glacier: Al DeMaria—drawn back to "his" area—and two companions attempted the north face of Middle Triple Peak but were stymied by technical problems. This seductive summit thus remained the highest unclaimed point in the area.

Mountaineers were unexpectedly absent from the Cathedral Spires during the next two seasons. Meanwhile, however, an equipment breakthrough in the lower forty-eight states was to have far-reaching consequences. It had

The west face of Middle Triple
Peak. *Charlie Raymond.*

long been known that goose down, though the finest possible insulation when dry, was virtually worthless when wet. On high peaks, where only snow fell, down was the preferred filler for jackets, gloves, and sleeping bags. But those who depended on down in the lower ranges, where the precipitation comes in the form of rain or sleet, were begging for not only a thorough soaking but possible hypothermia. To bivouac on a sheer Kichatna wall was to risk death from exposure, and climbers chose their routes accordingly. In the mid-1970s synthetic fibers were used in mountaineering gear for the first time. Although this material could not insulate as efficiently as down did, it also did not act as a sponge and thus preserved many of its insulating qualities even when saturated. This development paved the way for more daring ascents of rock walls in every range on earth, for now climbers could bivouac in outlandish places with some measure of security.

In 1975, three separate expeditions made plans to attempt the magnificent unclimbed west face of Middle Triple Peak. One group never left California, when its organizer, Peter Barton, was tragically killed at the base of El Capitan. A group of five Alaskan climbers, Gary Bocarde, Peter Sennhauser, Paul Denkewalter, Clancy Crawford, and Charlie Hostetler, landed on the

Tatina Glacier a few days before the arrival of the second expedition, composed of Hooman Aprin, Dave Black, and Mike Graber. Constant avalanche danger kept both groups from making serious bids for Middle Triple; nevertheless, much climbing was achieved. The Alaskans climbed three peaks by excellent alpine routes; the second expedition succeeded in climbing the region's first Grade VI's: the southeast face of Tatina Spire and the west face of South Triple. During the descent from this latter peak, the climbers came close to dying from hypothermia despite their new "miracle" gear. In such wild mountains, this group learned, equipment will never substitute for experience.

Word of such big climbs spread, and in the next few years the range was overrun with climbers. Four expeditions visited the area in America's bicentennial year. Rik Rieder and Jack Roberts made the first ascents of Lewis Peak and Peak 7300+ (Archdeacon). Russ McLean and Charlie Porter won the "race" to the top of Middle Triple Peak by climbing its enormous west face in a bold ten-day effort. Dave Black, Andy Embick, Alan Long, and Mike Graber did the East Pillar of Citadel and—unaware of the Porter–McLean success—made the second ascent of Middle Triple, via the north-side route tried by DeMaria's group four years earlier. (Oddly enough, this was a route which had been marked on the "Riesenstein" photo which had appeared in *Summit* fourteen years earlier.) Royal Robbins and Joe Coates tried two routes—the southeast ridge of Kichatna Spire and the south ridge of Citadel—and managed to get up three others, including the second ascent of Archdeacon.

After the two ascents of Middle Triple Peak—especially the ascent of the awesome west face—climbing fever cooled somewhat in the Cathedral Spires.

Right: Alan Long on the summit of Middle Triple Peak. *Mike Graber.*

Facing page: Jeff Thomas follows a pitch on the awesome, still unclimbed, couloir route on the northwest side of Kichatna Spire. *Alan Kearney.*

But to those aficionados who had studied the area carefully, one of the most magnificent lines in North America remained untouched: the gigantic east buttress of Middle Triple Peak. In June, 1977 Embick, Long, Graber, and George Schunk skied from the Tatina Glacier across a pass which led to the western lobe of the Sunshine Glacier. The four men managed to climb and descend the twenty-eight-pitch route during an eight-day epic which so impressed the climbing community that it was included in the book *Fifty Classic Climbs of North America*. After Embick flew out to fulfill his medical-school obligations, the remaining climbers enjoyed three first ascents: Flattop from Tatina Glacier; Augustin via its 4100-foot west face (the largest face in the area); and Peak 7370 (called Miranda), which was skied to within a hundred feet of its summit.

During the same summer, a group from New Mexico spent several weeks on Shadows Glacier. After one member took a long fall on Kichatna Spire, the group concentrated on less ambitious and more enjoyable climbs, including the first ascent of Steeple Spire.

In 1978 alone there were the same number of expeditions to the Spires as there had been during the entire first decade of its climbing history. Many climbs were accomplished; a few stand out. In early May, Peter Sennhauser returned to the Spires with Richard Ellsworth to make the first ascent of North Triple (the first of the Triple Peaks to be attempted and the last to be climbed). Andy Embick, Andy Tuthill, Rob Milne, and Bryan Becker spent several weeks working out of the Cool Sac Glacier and built an impressive list of first and second ascents. The most significant route done by this group was the beautifully sheer and direct line up the 2400-foot east face of Mount Jeffers. Alan Kearney, Jeff Thomas, and Ed Newville also added a few first ascents to the Cool Sac area, including a Grade VI route on Dark Tower. Newville later recruited Chris and Arthur Manix and accomplished the first ascent of Grendel Spire, a complex and attractive peak at the head of Trident Glacier.

The Triple Peaks as seen from the upper Tatina Glacier. *Charlie Raymond.*

Facing page: Ed Newville leads an early pitch during the first ascent of Dark Tower. *Alan Kearney.*

Surprisingly, only two expeditions visited the Spires in 1979. Steve Pollack and a partner climbed Peak 7295 (a mile east of South Triple) and put up a new route on Buff Spire. Andy Embick, on his fifth expedition to the area in as many years, and Jim Bridwell made the second ascent of Kichatna Spire via its northwest face in a six-day blitz.

It is impossible to guess the future climbing activity in the Spires beyond the shallow assumption that it will continue to grow more popular among ambitious mountaineers. Although nearly all the major peaks have been ascended, there are enough untouched faces and buttresses to keep climbers occupied for many years. The weather will continue to cause problems, for technology still hasn't developed waterproof clothing to keep a person comfortable during a four-day downpour. If the Spires were located in a more climatically benign area, the free-climbing possibilities would be unlimited. But then, of course, the Cathedral Spires would simply be another Yosemite instead of North America's finest alpine climbing area.

THE
CATHEDRAL
SPIRES

Top: On the summit cornices of Grendel Spire. *Ed Newville.*

Bottom: The leader nears the top of the Citadel. *Alan Kearney.*

Right: Through the mist rises the east face of South Triple Peak. *Mike Graber.*

Preceding page: Gurney Peak after a storm. *Alan Long.*

Top: On the first lead of the east buttress of Middle Triple Peak. *Mike Graber.*

Bottom: Following steep ice on the immense, still unclimbed couloir route on the northwest side of Kichatna Spire. *Alan Kearney.*

Facing page: An avalanche roars down the west face of Archdeacon Peak. *Mike Graber.*

Facing page: Ed Newville jams
cracks near the bottom of Dark
Tower. *Alan Kearney.*

Sunset on the Tatina Glacier;
Mount Jeffers rises on the
right. *Mike Graber.*

Alpenglow on Gurney Peak.
Alan Long.

THE WAY OF THE WHITE SERPENT

John Daniel
Illustrated by Alison Salisbury

I have always looked to the mountain. I have watched it loom against the stars, darker than night, or gleaming faintly with moonlight. I have watched the soft glowing colors of the new sun stealthily emerge on its flanks and die in the blaze of day. I have seen the mountain angrily summon the clouds to its heights and casually dismiss them, a proud and powerful man. I have seen it lift and lower its snows with the turning of the seasons, a beautiful woman changing her robes. Often, fishing in the stillness of the very new light, I have touched the water of the river and wondered how long ago it was the mountain's snow, and where beyond our valley the mountain was sending it, and if it carried back the spirits of our young ones who have gone to the mountain and not returned. All my seventeen turnings of seasons, since my eyes first perceived forms in the world, I have looked to the mountain, wondering and hoping. . . .

It is the ancient teaching that the mountain was created by the Chooser at the time of the Dawn, numberless seasons ago, when the world was filled with the light of ten thousand suns. The Chooser drove the first of our people to the valley and imposed the curse, making the mountain for His own dwelling. There He sends down the river that gives us life, and watches, for our own well-being, that we do not wander from the valley; and there we send our young ones under the stern scrutiny of His wisdom. When the time comes that we are fit, He will remove the curse and depart, His dwelling will crumble into nothing, and the people will be free to go forth into the world.

But Eran, my teacher, says there is no Chooser, only the mountain itself. It was here long before the Dawn of our people, he says, and long before the deer and hawks and fish were here, before the forests and meadows, before even the valley itself. . . . Eran says the mountain has been here since the time the very substance of the world was drawn together by the Power that binds. Only the wind came before it, and only the wind will remain when it is gone.

For many seasons, ever since it shrugged him from its side during a Choosing long ago, Eran has journeyed to the mountain. He speaks of his visits only to me, for it is strictly forbidden to approach the mountain unless one is called to a Choosing. Transgressors are given the Darkness. The people are fearful of offending the Chooser: fearful that in anger He will harden the curse, stripping our seed of women altogether; fearful that He will never restore us to the time of legend, when it is said that a woman was born for every man.

Eran is an Old One, a member of the Council. He is well familiar with the teachings, but still he has gone to the mountain. The teachings are illusion, he says, the mountain truth. He speaks of it with love and reverence, as one might speak of a woman and great teacher in one. He speaks, and I listen: for the mountain has shown him a secret, and he has shared it with me.

It was only five seasons past, though the path from then seems much longer, that the girl called Natahla came to womanhood, passing the sacred blood. Great excitement stirred the people like wind in the trees, for it was said no girl of her beauty had ever before walked in the valley. Like the other young ones, I knew her only from stolen glimpses. None but her mother are

allowed near a ripening girl: the guardians, the men who are not men, ever surround her with their spears. But I have waited high in a tree while the sun traversed the entire sky, on the hope she would pass beneath. . . . I have seen the hair that flows even below her waist, the color of the last deep light of the old sun—I have seen it flash as it shifts across her back with her walking. I have seen the lightness of her step, the proud tilt of her head, the trembling of her breasts as she moves. And more than once the sound of her laughter has risen to my hiding place, the song of her joy piercing me with the pain of longing.

The day the Council of Old Ones assembled to select the six for the Choosing, the young ones ran games in the meadow. We laughed, we made play, but in each of us the fires of hope and fear blazed fiercely. The Darkness claims most who are called for a Choosing, but the Darkness is preferable to the unhappiness of never knowing woman. For those who are not called, and those who are called but rejected by Chooser and Darkness both, the paths are few and sunless. Many live out their seasons in the ways of youth, fishing and hunting, running games and drinking the aged berry juice, squandering their seed in fruitless couplings with other men. Others, that the torment might be relieved, have the pouch of seed removed and take the rigorous training to become guardians, pledging their lives to the protection of our ripening girls and paired couples. There are some, the renegades, who forsake valley and people, going to live as animals in the hills: they are taken by the madness of loneliness, howling in the night of strange objects and other peoples in distant places. A very few strong ones, such as Eran, are able to hold their seed and turn their longing within, eating the mushroom and exploring the hidden pathways of the spirit. These are the ones of wisdom, the teachers; but to a young one burning for woman, their path is as empty as the others.

Two things gave me hope that I would be called: that my father, before he was given the Darkness by the renegades who carried off my mother, had spawned a girl, showing our line to carry the female seed; and that my name as a fisherman was known to all the people. The Council selects for a Choosing only those who have proven their power, and while others were great hunters or trappers, and still others danced more skillfully or ran games with greater strength, I exceeded all in my way with the fish. So I hoped. But doubt still possessed me, and when my name was called among the six it came like cool water to a punishing thirst. We were led into the great stonelodge of the Council to listen, standing in a row before the fire, as the Speaker pronounced the ancient words:

"The Chooser calls six to His dwelling. Upon one He bestows His grace. The Chosen One will be paired with woman, to make a home with her and care for her. He will give her his seed, that she might bring forth the new ones. He will be blessed among the people of the valley. The Chooser, in His wisdom, for the good of the people, will decide. So it has been since the Dawn. Now look upon the one to be paired."

On the far side of the fire Natahla was brought forth, fair skin aglow, hair and proud eyes glinting, and with a trembling warmth spreading through me I vowed I would have her or not live.

For a full turning of the moon, under Eran's instruction, I ran by the river and climbed tall trees to build my strength and wind. With his help I sewed pelts into wrappings for my hands and feet and a great robe to keep my warmth in the mountain night. From deerhide I made garments to preserve my skin from the abrasion of rock and ice, and a carrying bundle to strap on my back. I fashioned a stout sapling into a staff, lashing a spear point to the lower end for piercing the crusted snow, boring a hole in the upper end and tying through a loop of hide to wear around my wrist. From long spear points I made handclaws for biting into ice. I dried fish, baked flat cakes of grain, made a water pouch of skin sealed with pitch. . . . By day I watched the mountain, at night I could see only Natahla.

Eran shared with me his knowledge of the mountain. He counseled me to beware, on the ice rivers, of the great fissures that were often concealed by a treacherous covering of snow or spanned by snow bridges ready to collapse . . . to climb the high chutes while the sun was very young, before the mountain loosed its rain of rocks . . . on the heights, to move slowly, with rhythm . . . to hold the eyes half-closed against the blinding glare of sun . . . to refuse the embrace of sleep, which in the cold of the mountain night promised warmth but delivered one to the Darkness.

"Your eagerness will destroy you if you do not restrain it," he warned. "One error can mean your ruin, for the mountain's paths are unforgiving. It is a strange world, a frightening world. Foolish paths will appear sensible. Unreal visions may come to your eyes. Do not be deceived. Remember the things I have told you, and look for guidance to the stillness within."

"Is it not the Chooser," I asked, "who hurls down the stones and collapses the bridges and sends untrue visions?"

"The mountain is a living spirit, like the streams and winds, a spirit of great power and many moods. But it bears neither friendship nor malice toward our people. The stones it sends down are not cast in anger; they are only gestures of its endless dance of power. The mountain knows nothing of our curse. It cares nothing for who succeeds and who fails."

"I will master it," I said fiercely. "I will be first of the six to the highest place."

"So also did I vow," Eran smiled. "But your heart is great, fisherman. It will take you far, whatever your path."

By the new light of the appointed day, the six of us left the valley with our watchers to assume the starting places of the Six Ways. A casting of stones in the Council determines the assignment of the Ways. Each is different, but none is gentle. The mountain's flanks are mild in only one place, on the side facing the old sun, where one can walk from a camp in the forest to the highest place and return in the light of one day. Even as we set out for the mountain, the delegation of the Council were ascending this mild side with the carven wood idol of woman: on the bed of stones at the highest place they would leave it, beseeching the Chooser to grant it to that young one who would spawn girls. And the Chosen One, bearing the idol that proved his success, that meant the greatest happiness for him and the greatest despair for any others who survived, would descend this side to the camp where the delegation waited to escort him back to the valley, to Natahla.

We journeyed that day and the greater part of the next, at first following the river and then leaving it to climb gentle slopes, the mountain screened from our eyes by the forest. On the second day our group diminished by twos as watchers split off with their charges. It is the duty of the watcher to deliver his young one to the beginning of his Way, seeing that he does not steal an early start and that no one assists him. My own watcher led me far around the mountain, through silent forests of great trees, across narrow rushing streams of the coldest water, finally turning directly up the steepening slope as the trees became small and twisted, unlike any I had seen. A cold wind began to sing. Glimpses of a great whiteness came to me, until at last the trees were mere bushes scattered among rocks and the mountain rose clear before my eyes. The ridge on which we stood formed one bank of a vast ice river that flowed steeply, greatly cracked and shattered in places, from a source high in a darkness of rock: and above, a thin white streak wound upward through the stone towers into the sky.

"The snow path is my Way?" I asked.

The watcher nodded. "The Way of the White Serpent."

"And where the Serpent ends is the highest place?"

"The highest place is beyond sight, up further snows and rocks, but the upper reaches are mild. The Serpent is deadly. It is said that the ice river snarls, the Serpent attacks."

"The mountain does not frighten me."

"The Chooser is the teacher of fear," the watcher replied coldly. "All who visit Him learn. You begin at the new light."

We waited the night in the shelter of a small growth of trees, sleep hovering near me but never touching, forever dancing away on the wind. Natahla's face and the mountain were a single fire within me, fiercely burning but empty of warmth. At the first trace of light, staff in hand and bundle on back, I descended to the ice river and turned my steps upward, grateful to be underway at last, alone with the task. The wind had lulled, leaving the gentle crushing sounds of my footsteps alone in a vast stillness. The mountain, alive with the soft colors of dying coals, did not seem so immense: I dared to think the highest place would be mine in one light. My spirit surged and my legs lifted eagerly.

But the mountain grew as the sun traveled its path. The upper reaches, the Serpent, seemed to recede even as I approached them. The bank of rock disappeared and the ice river swallowed me into its shattered flow. Great crevices barred my way, some without bottom, and from the depths of blue ice and darkness I thought I felt a cold sucking breath. *A living spirit. . . .*

62   ASCENT

Delicately, scarcely breathing, I stepped across sunken spans of snow, balancing with the staff, gently digging in my toes, frigid emptiness pulling on either side. . . . My progress crawled, as even the crevices themselves lost individual form in a monstrous chaos. Where the river made its steep cascades, blocks and great towers of ice reared wildly, sprawling against and upon one another. I was no longer walking but clawing my way, a wingless hawk, using the staff with one hand and an ice-claw with the other, gouging out steps for my feet. My path became a thread worked by a madman. There was no mountain, only the bluffs and gorges of this fractured vastness of ice, only my clumsy insect strugglings, only my fear . . . but too, in this world strange beyond dream, a faint pull of recognition, as if I had been here before, or perhaps always been here.

The sun, a fire too large, blazed upon my back even as the ice stung my hands and feet through the furs. The river was speaking now: long groaning rumbles from deep in its bowels . . . sharp cracks, like trees snapping in the wind . . . the giant footfalls of snow bridges collapsing into the depths: sounds of power, sounds that quickened my breath and brought trembling to my limbs. *The ice river snarls.* . . . As I clawed up a steep block , a huge tower to one side groaned and shuddered like a great beast in agony, then collapsed with the splitting sound of thunder. The block shook: I clung, waiting to be thrown into the abyss and crushed, but the quaking subsided from the ice, remaining only in me. I listened to my breathing for a time, seeking the strength of the inner stillness, and bit higher with my claws.

The sun was turning old as I mounted the ice river's highest slope and looked into the chasm formed where it split away from a wall of black rock. Wet and broken, the wall rose almost straight up to the height of two tall trees: and there, bulging out through a gap in the stone, dripping a trickle of water as if in cold mockery of my hopes, hung the icy lip of the White Serpent. I sat to rest, rubbing my burning feet, my heart struggling. The wall towered darkly, no clear paths up its fractured surface. There would be places to grip and step, but one slip. . . . *Fear is a trapped beast,* Eran's word echoed. *It will suck the strength from your blood for its nourishment, then strangle you in its frenzy. Do not feed it. Do not confine it. Let it escape through your breathing.* . . . I ate a piece of fish and drank deeply from the water pouch, then lashed the skins tightly around my feet and looped an ice-claw to each wrist. The staff would stay: it had done its work, and would only hinder me on the rock and the steepness of the Serpent.

There was a place where the chasm appeared to narrow sufficiently that I could stretch across the rock after lowering myself down a distance. A bottomless depth of darkness I entered, a home of frigid vapors and faint voices, never lit by sun. I stabbed the ice, lowering my weight from claw to claw, feet finding no grip . . . until at last, the strain tearing at my arms, I could span the gap. A foot, a hand, and I was clinging to the seeping wall, stiff and shuddering in the cavern's icy breath. Then, one movement at a time, one small fearful reach after another, I was climbing. My limbs began to loosen, my trembling slackened, and as I rose out of the chasm into sunlight the spirit flowed back into me and my heart grew large. One hand, one foot . . . lightly I climbed now, reassured by the sun's warm hand on the back of my neck, lifted by the brilliance of sky. A piece of rock tore loose as I stepped, but my hands held fast, and the sound of the hurtling stone only brought laughter to my throat. Pausing to look behind, I made out a small white form shimmering in haze where earth met sky—another mountain, at the far shore of the world.

One hand, one foot . . . the lip of the Serpent was not far above, only a few reaches and steps. But now the rock bulged outward, pushing me away, forcing me to grip fiercely. No milder way opened itself on either side. My legs tremored violently as the void tried to swing them away from the rock. Breath surged raggedly in my throat, without rhythm. *It will strangle you.* . . . One hand lunged for a higher crack, almost loosening me with the loss of its support. My fingers scratched, gouged, finally caught, but even as they did I felt the mountain's trap falling like a deadweight: I was frozen. To move a hand was to fall. My head turned from side to side, the frantic seeking of an animal at bay, fear coiling within me like a snake . . . a rising roar filled my ears . . . feet groping blindly for the stance not there, strength leaching from my rigid, useless arms. . . . Something seemed to be pulling my awareness out of my body: I visioned myself falling, slowly as in a dream, down the sunlit rock into the black maw of the chasm. The roar was thunderous now, a waterfall, and there came over my eyes a dim veil that I knew to be the shadow of the Darkness.

A fierce and helpless cry tore free from my depths and suddenly I was watching my still-clinging form from a distance behind, watching with the brilliant clarity of a hawk's vision. On silent wings I hovered, poised for a lifelong moment between return and release, knowing for the first time that the flesh was only my lodge, that I was something else, something the old ones call the *spirit that soars like wind.* In a lightning rush I was in my body again, stepping up on a tiny knob my toes had touched but feared before, reaching a hand higher, every slight detail of rock standing out with perfect clearness, each necessary movement unfolding itself in sequence, until I was over the bulge to milder rock and a dripping hollow beneath the snow of the Serpent.

I sprawled for a time, spent and trembling, but calm within. I had heard the old ones speak of the hawk spirit flying from the body when the Darkness was near. The body, if it felt its path was not done, could sometimes call the spirit back . . . and if it returned it brought a marvelous power from the place beyond knowing, lifting for a moment the body's limitations, which exist only because we believe in them. I had succeeded where I might have fallen, because my heart had cried out; but I knew also that the fall was truly as real as the triumph. Eran's words came back to me: *Every moment is a branching of paths. The body walks one only, but the spirit walks all at once.* . . .

Crawling to my left, I reached a place where the Serpent's lip receded, opening a way upward. I dug in my claws and climbed on, mounting the snow stream into its winding, steeply tilted canyon. Rock of many colors towered on both sides: where it was broken I used it to climb, half on rock and half on snow; where it was smooth I kept to the snow, carving steps for my feet. Bits of ice and stone rained down with whirring insect sounds, stinging my face; at times a larger rock would fall, a diving bird, and I would press myself flat until it passed. But after the unforgiving wall, the Serpent was a friend: its snows cradled my hands and feet securely, its steepness was as nothing. Within me flowed the certainty that the Chooser or spirit of the mountain or whatever life dwelled here had assaulted, grappled, and given—and now its heights were open.

But the sun was turning under. Perhaps I could climb through the dark, by the light of the stars. . . . *Foolish paths will appear sensible*. With eyes that felt full of sand I searched the walls for a place to await the new light. Then a sudden rumbling above, thunder before the storm. Down the Serpent, hurtling from wall to wall and high out into the air, a torrent of stones was rushing toward me, each as large as a man's head. I heard in their growing din the deadly laughter of the mountain. I lunged to the nearest wall and flattened myself under an outcrop, knowing it was not protection enough, the laughter deafening now, then a pain like fire in my leg and a scraping blow across my back and I was falling, arms clawing wildly . . . then hanging on a sharp spine of rock, the rumbling fading away beneath me and the air filled with the smell of struck flint. *The Serpent attacks. . . .*

I pulled myself to a small standing place. The leg burned and bled, but took weight: the wound was not deep. One claw had been ripped away and the bundle was gone, stripped from my back. I sagged against the rock, hands sticky with blood. Already a cold wind was groaning up the Serpent, sounding the mountain's claim of conquest through the last gray light. The dark was coming and I had nothing to keep away the cold, no water, no food, no place to wait. My eyes burned with a little one's tears, the tears of smallness in a world of forces beyond control. I cursed the mountain and its whimsical moods, its warm yielding and furious rock-hurling, its delight in lifting the spirit to the sky and dropping it like a dry leaf from a branch . . . and in a flare of energy I was moving again, up to the place where the stones had assaulted me and higher, climbing with the recklessness of hatred.

All light had long departed when I felt an opening in the wall on my right. A narrow gully, filled with a mire of loose stones that shifted with each movement, led to firmer rock and then to a mildly sloping ledge, broad enough for many. I crawled in against the steep rock at the rear and lay still, soaking from my refuge the warmth it had hoarded from the sun. Sleep, an enormous current, drew me down.

My shaking awoke me to cold moonlight. I was not alone. Stumbling to my feet to warm myself, I saw his huddled figure in an alcove at the far end of the ledge. For an endless moment we beheld each other without word or movement. Then I understood. I went to him, kneeling to gaze at the hollows that had been his eyes and the pale skin shrunken down tightly over the curvings of skull. The hawk-spirit stirred its wings inside me: we were no different, this one who would climb no higher and I who still breathed, two forms of the same being, two futures of the same path. . . . *"You came far,*

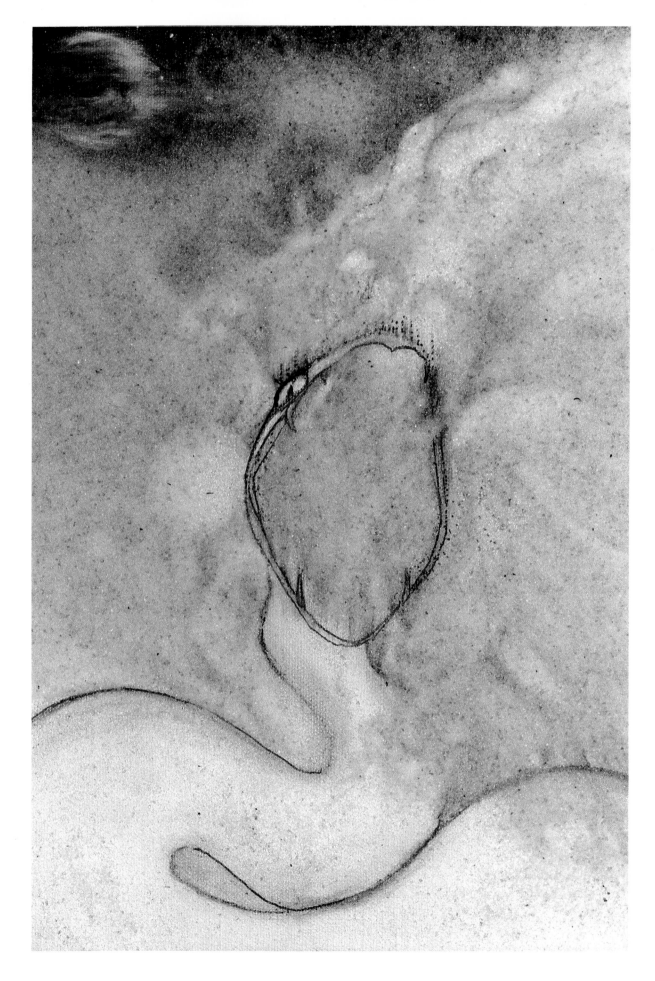

brother," I whispered, tracing my fingers slowly across his forehead, feeling beneath the chill of the Darkness the warmth of passion he had brought to the mountain. His water pouch was empty, food gone, but he made me gift enough. I slipped from his withered shoulders the robe that no longer warmed him and laid him gently on his side, finally to rest.

Dancing, I held the cold at bay . . . too weary to dance, I sat and sang my river songs . . . too weary to sing, I watched the moon and stars. Sleep is a woman: she steals up softly, gently stroking one's eyelids, murmuring warmly, asking why one resists her. . . . *She lies!* Eran shouts from a far valley of my mind. *The cold sings a song of warmth* . . . and I lurch to my feet, singing and dancing, welcoming the goading pain of my hurt leg. I had slept and returned once, but I would not be so fortunate again. My will was dried, cracked, but still of a piece, still urging. Yet it was changed: the day's path had wound long, leaving the past in the distance of dream. Five others, if still they breathed, were clinging to the mountain's cruel shoulders, keeping vigil through the same dark, watching the same stars. Each could ruin me, but I could not wish them ill. I would climb to outrace them, climb for Natahla, but I would also climb now for the mountain itself: for my hatred of it, but too for something I can speak of only as love . . . for a reason hidden deep beneath my knowing, the reason the winds blow. It is a thing difficult to express to those who have not been on the mountain.

As the very first light opened the dark I was moving up the Serpent. The mountain held back its deadly rain, held its very breath. There was only the biting of my claw and the huge surging of my wind. I was aware of no progress beyond the awkward lifting of my body from one carved-out track to another. My injured leg was stiff, a wooden thing, but moving. Thirst had driven away all other feeling: piece after piece of ice it consumed, flaring up savagely after each, demanding more, and more. . . . The sun grew, the blazing snows seared my eyes, clouding them darkly. Resting, I held them closed, and visions swam in my mind: the valley, impossibly green, the full-flowing river. . . . I lifted myself on. The mountain waited, holding still. There was no passage of time. There was only movement.

A gentler slope, softer snow. I could thrust in my hands, kick my feet. For each step gained I sucked chestfuls of empty air that gave no strength. I saw a fish of many colors gasping on the moss of the river bank, the deep clear water curling below, just out of reach. . . . The rocks were gone and I was wading a blinding field, sinking far in with each step, fighting a slow current that wanted to pull me down . . . the field rising to meet me, offering rest, the current ceasing. Always an echo of words lifted me on: *Your exhaustion and pain are your life. Do not trade them for deceitful promises. Think only this: climb until there is no higher place.*

Eddies of wind whistled around me, mocking the weight of my legs, the toil of my breathing. The snowfield extended endlessly into the blue-blackness of sky. A plunging step, the rushing of my angry wind, a step. . . . Within me the green-bordered river flowed, and I could not tell its moving from mine, its rolling murmur from my own breath. A voice shouted, faint with distance. Now the river was dissolving my ponderous weight: I gave myself to the warm weave of its current, seeing all colors, approaching understanding of all questions, but something was holding me back. . . . The murmur became a laughter, light and resonant . . . *hers,* at last, my struggles finished . . . my fingers stroked her breasts, trailed down the gentle swell of her belly, drew us together in a cloak of soft-pressing warmth, the first, forgotten warmth. But a familiar voice shot across a vast distance to pierce me like the cry of a hawk—*no higher place*—the voice becoming a pain of light, spreading from a single point into a blinding radiance, ten thousand suns, the Dawn. . . . I was on my back, facing the blaze of sky. Memory swept off its mask: I had rested on the flat rock for only a moment. . . .

The bog of snow gave way to the firmness of stone. My steps had new life: still a caterpillar's pace but in rhythm with my breathing now, one leg following the other of its own will. Entranced, my burning eyes held fast to the lift and fall of my feet. Wind and rock, an openness on each shoulder, the broad ridge rising mildly . . . then openness ahead, only a shadowed mass of sloping sides and level top, *no higher place,* wanting to run but legs turned to water, stumbling and scraping against the rocks, caring only that there was no higher place, the bed of stones was before me. . . . I clambered wildly, groping, turning in frenzied circles, joy suspended on a strand of web . . . *rocks.* I hurled myself at them, ripping the bed apart, then stopped at a sound from below, straining troubled eyes. Far down the snows of the mountain's gentle side, a figure was moving. Even as I saw him I recognized the sound as the hunter's song of success, and I knew what he carried in his hands. The drift of his song wound slowly through my mind, circled slowly like a hungry vulture, and descended in a rush of darkness.

Someone was rubbing my feet. A bitter wind raged. I lay among rocks, covered with a strange robe. My eyes were on fire . . . all was gray and dark. The rubbing stopped, a shape moved, a water pouch was at my lips. I sucked like a new one until the pouch was pulled away.

"More. . . ."

"Later, fisherman. You must not have too much at once."

"*Eran.* . . ."

His hand touched my forehead. "I rejoice that you live, young one."

Memory flooded back with his words. I struggled to rise and collapsed in his arms, despair pouring shamelessly from my eyes.

"Fisherman, you were chosen to live," Eran said softly. "That is much, even without woman."

"The mountain betrayed me," I sobbed bitterly. "It gave the idol to another."

"His Way was not as severe—none is as difficult as the White Serpent. Drink now."

The wind screamed its vicious laughter. I closed my eyes, drifting downward like a pebble in water . . . then Eran was shaking me.

"The sun is gone and the wind brings a storm, young one. We must start down. If others still breathe, they will not see the next light."

"There is nothing to go down for," I whispered.

He gripped my shoulders and lifted my face close to his. "Only a little one grieves for himself," he said harshly. "Your path came close to success, turning away at the last—so it is. But the gift of life cannot be rejected. There are things in this world beyond anything you know, powerful things, things that make us small. If you have the heart to walk the path that is opened to you, you will learn them. Now we go down."

He bandaged my eyes and put strange coverings on my feet, stiff and heavy; others, soft and warm like furs, he placed on my hands and over my head. The robe bundled around me, smooth and light almost as the air, held off the bite of the wind. Eran tied a length of heavy line between us, and we started: myself first, staggering in blindness over rock and snow, him following, calling out instructions against the wind and holding me on the line when I lost my feet. With each fall I wanted only to lie still forever, but Eran coaxed me on. At times I imagined I was still climbing, driven by the memory of his words. It was a dream, happening to another. I recall only the falling and struggling up, the wind and at times an icy rain; then the protection of the forest, no longer snow but firm earth underfoot, and finally the arrival at some kind of shelter. Eran made fire and I slept.

The shelter was our home for many days as we waited the return of my strength and vision, passing the time in talk. Eran had built it many seasons past, soon after his own trial on the mountain. It was here his secret journeys from the valley had taken him, to be alone, to reflect, to learn. He had spent the lengths of many suns wandering over snowfield and ridge, absorbing the ways and moods of the being that so deeply stirred his spirit. When the mountain drove him from its flanks in that Choosing of long ago, he too had been crushed and bitter, he told me. But he had also been implanted with a seed that grew into an attraction like the love of a man for a woman, the mountain finally opening itself and yielding the secret long buried in its snows, the secret he promised to soon share with me.

The day the other young ones and I had reached the starting places, Eran had come to the shelter, with a hope the mountain might spare me. Concealed by night from the delegation of the Council, he had ascended the mild side even as I was dancing off the cold in the canyon of the Serpent. And he had hidden himself in the rocks, watching as the other came first and carried off the idol, watching as I stumbled up the final ridge, not revealing himself until I had reached the highest place and my struggle with the mountain was finished.

One day after the light had returned to my eyes, he brought out the robe and coverings that had given me warmth in our descent, looking on as I marveled at them. All but the foot coverings, which were mostly of hide, were made of substances I did not know: smooth to the touch and almost without weight, colored with the brightness of the turned-under sun or the open sky. There were other things, too: the long and supple line, a back bundle, claws for

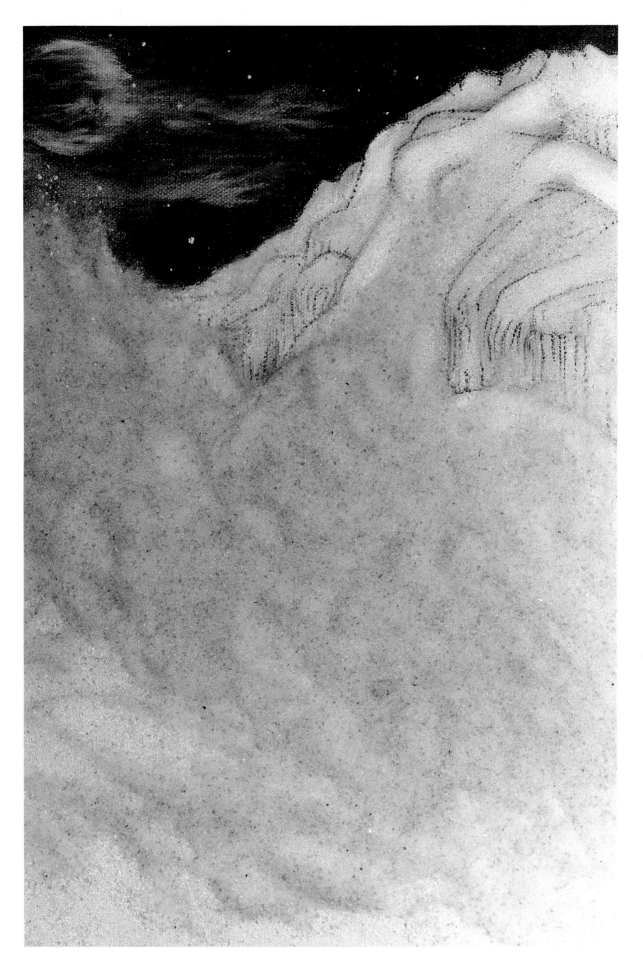

70   ASCENT

the feet of a substance harder and smoother than stone. Eran smiled at my questions, saying only that the things were gifts of the mountain and that I would learn more when I was stronger, leaving mystery to swim darkly through the reaches of my mind.

My flesh regained life from the greens Eran collected and the dried meat he had cached in the shelter, but my spirit would take no nourishment. I had little interest in the path ahead, little wish to return to the valley. Even now, I knew, the celebration of the Pairing was in progress: feasting and dancing by light of sun and fire, the traditional casting of grain, the solemn incantations to make the new pair fertile with woman. And in the warm haven of the Chosen One's lodge, the seeking caress and fevered embrace, the little cries of passion, penetration. . . . *If you meant to deprive me why did you open your heights to me?* my writhing spirit cried out. *Why did you give me life with nothing to live for, an empty vessel, no home for my seed? . . .* In answer came only the wind: the voice of a thousand moods, the voice that had raged and gloated on the mountain now offered from the trees a song of peace, easing my angry pain as the river smoothes a sharp-edged stone.

When almost a full turning of the moon had passed, Eran prepared a bundle one night by the light of the fire; and by the light of the new sun I was following him through the forests of the lower slopes of the mountain, around the mild side and further, ascending eventually to an ice river vaster by far than the one below the Serpent. Eran gave me a strange mask that shaded my eyes from the glare of sun and led me up the gently-sloped river, moving carefully around the crevices that lay in our path. The sun was nearing its highest place when he stopped. A great fissure yawned before us. Removing from the bundle a robe for each of us, Eran lowered himself into one end of the chasm and cautiously descended a steep pathway of steps carved into the ice. I followed. Far down inside, the left-hand wall opened into a small cavern. Eran stopped, motioning with his arm. At first I saw nothing in the dim blue light, then shapes . . . two bodies, chipped free of the ice.

"Young ones," I whispered.

"No."

I moved closer. A current of trembling swept through me—the feet were bare, one wore a bright robe.

"The things came from them?"

Eran nodded.

"But *who* . . . two men. . . ."

"Only one, fisherman. Look closely." He gestured at the one still robed. I leaned over the body. Without willing it my hand reached to the smooth skin of the face, the long, stiff, sun-colored hair.

"She is beautiful," I murmered.

Eran took my arm. "Let us return to the light."

I was still shaking as we sat among the warm rocks and he spoke of the ones below. "I found them eight seasons past, while studying the fissures. They loomed in the ice, terrifying—I fled, but when my fear slackened I

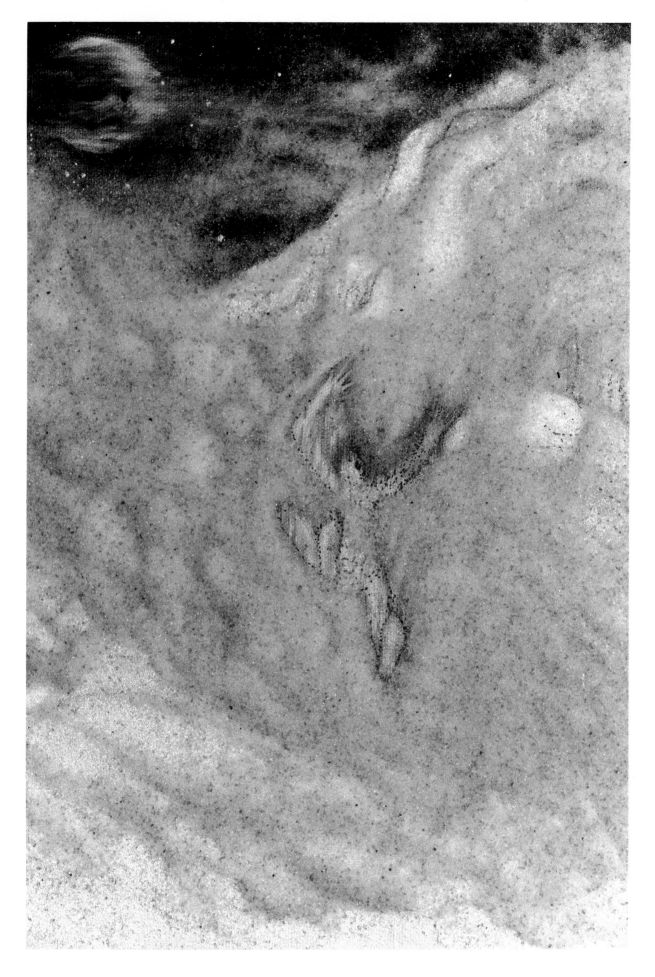

returned and carved them free. I took the foot coverings, the line that connected them, the back bundles, all the things you have seen . . . I studied and used them, telling no one."

"But who *are* they?"

"The ice river slows the current of time to a creep. They must have been lost countless seasons ago, high in the snows of the river's upper reaches."

"But why was a woman on the mountain?"

"I have thought much of that," said Eran, gazing out over the ice river. "Their people walked different paths, their things were different from ours . . . their seed was also different, I believe. I can understand it no other way. In their time men did not climb the mountain to be chosen for woman. There were women for all."

"The time of legend, before the Dawn . . . but why would they climb, if not for a Choosing?"

"A mystery, young one. They may have climbed for a reason we cannot know. It is possible they climbed for no other reason than the mountain itself. What has drawn me to the mountain, again and again? And you, what drive gave you the heart to master the White Serpent, beyond the drive for woman alone? You told me yourself there was something more."

We sat in silence for a time, listening to the breath of wind as if for an answer. My thoughts turned and twisted, straining to open themselves to incomprehensible distances. Finally a feeling shaped itself into words.

"Their appearance is much like ours . . . are we *of* them?"

Eran nodded. "The differences do not conceal the underlying sameness."

"But their woman, their things. . . ."

"I have no explanation. Here my thoughts lose form and scatter in the winds. But the image of the Dawn haunts me. . . ."

"The light of ten thousand suns, the beginning—"

"We call it the beginning, but what do we truly know of it? For these others, if indeed they lived before it, perhaps the Dawn was not a beginning but a death, or a change—a change even in their seed, that female new ones became rare, the numbers of their people declined, scattered. . . ."

"If they lived here and climbed the mountain we would find signs, their *things*."

"They may have journeyed great distances to climb the mountain. We know little of what lies beyond our valley, young one. The renegades babble of strange ruins, other peoples."

"We are of them. We would remember."

Eran was silent a moment, his eyes wandering over the ice river, over the rocky heights and blazing snows of the mountain. "These two have passed seasons beyond count in the embrace of the ice," he said at last. "The mountain remembers, and speaks through them, but our power is not as great. The teachings have taken root in our minds, fisherman, and recollection has dwindled under their shadow. The path of time is long and full of turnings. Even as it advances, meadow and forest are overgrowing it. One who turns to trace it back soon becomes lost in the trackless silence of the wilderness."

Eran is old. He feels the shadow of the Darkness upon the path of his body and stays apart from others, preparing himself for the last flight of his spirit. He knows this to be proper, like the turning of the seasons, and he looks ahead with peace. I too look ahead, but I am still young. I fish and dance and run games as I used to: at times I laugh, and at other times, lying awake in the dark, my loneliness rises and I cry. Often, pretending to be fishing at some distant place in the valley, I go to the shelter on the mountain. Using the things of the ones in the ice, I climb and wander, looking and learning.

When the wind carries the clatter of falling rocks, I remember; but no longer do I feel a malevolent spirit in the mountain. When my heart is struggling, when my sorrow engulfs me, I lift my eyes to the heights. The same mountain that deprived me, rising above the world like a figure of dream, like the silent expression of all possibilities, fills me with the breath of courage. Soon I will travel further, to other valleys and other mountains, seeking the pathways of those who lived before . . . and those who perhaps still live. The fisherman will become a tracker. There will be signs.

At night I lie in the shelter listening to the wind, the voice that murmurs of all things and tells nothing. A part of me, beneath the lodge of words and thought, understands the language it speaks. I feel it flowing across vast distances of time, out of seasons and seasons past . . . through all the generations of my people, through the Dawn and the day of the ones in the ice . . . from a time before hawks soared the openness and fish plied the streams, before the hillsides were robed with forest, before the valley and the mountain and the world itself were even born, from somewhere deep in the endless black pool of sky. . . . I lie in the dark and listen.

THE RIBBON OPTION

Jim Balog

This was no measured, rhythmic climbing such as I was used to; instead it was a hurried, struggling attack, driven on by a dangerous nervous tension. I could hear the noisy thumping of my heart; and as I gained height, the sense of insecurity, whose origin I could not fathom, grew and grew.

TONI HIEBLER

Boulder, Colorado
September 2, 1976

Dear Justin,

Early summer was a rough time for climbing in the Tetons. Not that the weather was bad or anything (in fact, it was great most of the time); it was just hard to find partners to do any good routes. While I was there, the most talked-about climb of the season was the Exum Ridge (the *upper* Exum, to be sure). You know how much I wanted to do the Black Ice Couloir on the Grand Teton and then head for Canada, but time started sifting away fast, and it was two weeks before I met anyone seriously interested in it. At that point I ran into this guy Mick (from Texas) who said he'd like to give it a go. There's not much to say about him. He was a quiet, intense guy—and strong. That's nearly the sum total of what I remember; even after all we went through together, he's not much more than a silhouette framed against Valhalla Canyon. Oh, and also, he had never climbed ice before! Crazy, going with a beginner on that thing, but I figured it was better than soloing if and when the famous rockfalls came down. That's a helluva dumb and selfish way to pick a partner for something like the Black Ice Couloir, but so it was. I wound up leading the whole climb. Belay anchors were either terrible or nonexistent, and since I was constantly thinking Mick would fall, I never had a moment's peace. With the 20/20 vision of hindsight, soloing would have been better.

The sun dissolves to incandescence in a cloudbank. An eternity away, the Grand Teton flares to molten gold as two dark figures scuttle across its massive western flanks. They stop, then prepare a bivouac at the foot of a clean sheet of granite. The wall above them glows like an orange skin and radiates warmth. The two men doze while the wind shrieks around a nearby ridge and stars dapple the night.

Well, chief, I don't mind admitting that by the time "rosy-fingered" dawn washed across the buttresses of my old buddy Mount Moran, I was plenty nervous. Couldn't even eat Tiger's Milk bars, in fact. You know as well as anyone how I like and need that stuff, but I had no stomach for them this time. It looked like anxiety and adrenalin would get me up. So away we went across the Valhalla Traverse—steep, frozen snow, then some 5.7 in crampons. Finally, I found some good pins welded into cracks at the start of the ice couloir. It was encouraging to fantasize that some demigod (Donini? a Lowe? Chouinard?) had whaled those babies in with a healthy dose of fear coursing through his arteries.

THE RIBBON OPTION   75

On the third pitch of the Black Ice Couloir, the leader rests on a small rock outcrop while calculating the next series of moves. *David Sweet.*

The two figures confront a white gash in the dust-brown west face. Above them, the couloir is filled with ice: blue water-ice; brittle, air-filled gray ice; névé; and rotten, honeycombed, frozen snow. The wall of the Enclosure towers above, an even-handed spectator in the unfolding drama, for it is both a giver of shelter and a prime source of the couloir's notorious rockfall. Small bubbles of human emotion—trepidation and confidence, terror and delight—may be seen floating through the quiet vacuum which surrounds the face. They burst, and are lost on its impassive shoulders.

Ah, Jimboy, this is it at last. Not too bad, eh? Cake: up it quick. Not so cocky there: rockfall and the jinx of counting it done before it is. Yeah, yeah, but you've soloed things harder than this. Wait. . . .

One figure advances rapidly up the couloir. His pace is smooth, rhythmic. After he is some distance above his companion, he stops and spends a long time groping in the rocks which form the gully walls. Finally, after a repetitive exchange of phrases, the second figure begins to ascend. At first his motions are slow and awkward, but their efficiency soon improves. He joins his partner after a time. The first figure advances again, and the two-headed caterpillar that the roped team has become creeps up the couloir. Progress gradually slows.

Not so great, this bite-the-bullet diet, eh? Great stories for climbing books; not much for climbing. Speed up, waterfalls there. Godalmighty, when're the rocks gonna come down? This can't last. Almost rather have some to see what they're like, than wait in suspense.

Inexorably cranking higher into the sky, the sun soon burns into the couloir. Ice reverts to water, and the tomblike hush is replaced by the cadence of rivulets streaming from the Enclosure. The first figure advances again, only to pause at a rock rib jutting from the couloir. The passage around the rib's left side is a continuation of the main line of the couloir. To the right, a two-foot-wide ice ribbon snakes up a groove between the Enclosure wall and the rib. Nearly a ropelength above, this ribbon almost reconnects with the couloir; only an aerial view reveals that a rock wall prevents continuity. The leader chooses the ribbon option. He creeps upward, but stops near the top of the ribbon, just below the rock wall. Crampons can be heard grating on ice of concrete consistency. The rope glides in a long, unbroken curve down to the second figure, who is perched uncomfortably on a small rock horn and attached to the gully wall by pegs driven a short distance into rotten cracks.

Oh yes, wanted to do it so badly? Your Big Climb? You're in deep now, pal. Some shortcut, fool. But it was out of the rockfall. Yeah, yeah. Go back. Christ, can't move. God, why? Terrorized a little, eh? You've made it this far, turkey. Climbing you always wanted to do: heroic, like pictures of Scotsmen. Bet they were scared too. Tough luck. Ice like a rock. No handholds. Whining, boy, calm down. Shit, get out of here, forget it, no more, ever. West Ridge, so inspiring— "up and over . . . no retreat." Great stuff—in the living room. Here it is now, bozo.

The west face of the Grand
Teton. The Black Ice Couloir
lies to the right of the
prominent snowfield in the
middle of the face. *Leigh
Ortenburger.*

Quivering, the upper figure inches a crampon up the ice; blunted points scrape uselessly. He struggles to stem a flaring groove, but appears to be grossly off-balance and ready to fall.

God, I can't believe this. Readi-Whip muscles. Head swimming a little? Butterflies? Yeah, shutup. Get a hand . . . nubbin there . . . swing. Lord, bouldering in crampons. Not like city-park bouldering, nossir. Different game. Can't . . . gonna fall. Swing, you jerk. Shutup. OK, swing.

After the two figures are reunited, their pause is long. They drink, and ingest bars of various shapes and sizes. Since the sun no longer bears directly on the couloir, the waterfalls cease and early morning silence falls again. As the pyramid of sun-washed rock which is the upper west face slowly shrinks in size, the confines of the couloir become imperceptibly more violet. Finally, the figures proceed yet again. The couloir funnels into a long, steep, and continuous cascade of blue ice belching from a cleft in a near-vertical rock band.

So anyway, Justin my friend, we climbed the Black Ice Couloir, but it was one royal burn-out. Pulled onto the top late (don't want to tell you how late!) that afternoon, dehydrated, hungry as wolves, and smelling like cows from anxiety and hard work. Needless to say, it was an incredible relief to flop down at the Upper Saddle and relax and feel like I was finally attached to the earth.

At that point, all I could think of was how much I hated the climb. I suppose parts of it were fun, but there was always the worrying: about Mick, about rockfall, about our anchors. I really lost it in there for a while. Now that it's all over and I'm a few months removed from the whole business, it seems like a good thing to have *done,* but a lousy thing to *do.* I can't understand how anyone can really enjoy a climb like that. It's just crazy. You could die from forces completely beyond your control as easily as you could come through alive—and God knows the Black Ice is a lot safer and easier than many other climbs. I'm beginning to wonder if the real reason people do such things is to experience the rush of success; perhaps nobody really enjoys such climbs.

But I'm not sure I can really buy that theory. Seems like there's too many climbers doing hard mountain routes for them all to be out there only for the success rush. Maybe some of them are genuinely crazy and lack the basic survival instincts we're supposed to have. But, again, I wonder how many real crazies climb. More common must be those guys who are dumb and unimaginative, who can't even see a dangerous situation.

That may sound a bit strong, but think back on all those hotshots we met in Chamonix. Remember how incredibly thick-headed some of them seemed? And here's another example: I was rappelling down the Higher Cathedral Spire in Yosemite with this British guy who was a wildman (he had been on the second ascent of Changabang). Remember the tremendous exposure on most of those rappels?—one mistake and you're dead. Well, this turkey was so dumb that instead of actually rappelling, he went hand-over-hand down the rope. Even if you *are* the Incredible Hulk, that's got to be a stupid thing to do.

With crampon front points biting securely into the ice, a climber starts the fifth pitch. *David Sweet.*

Yet, when you think about it, being dumb might be helpful on a dangerous climb: you could go fast because belaying wouldn't seem worthwhile. You wouldn't get freaked by "minor" things like rockfall; and, in this guy's case, you wouldn't waste time messing around with anything so trivial as a *descendeur*. Pure and organic, maybe even as holy as (dare I say it?) Our Father Who Art in Ventura.

Though most climbers aren't as dense as my friend on the Higher Spire, I suppose none of us see reality too clearly. We love to think we can analyze some climbing problem and then—by virtue of heaven-sent wisdom—decide if the risk is acceptable or not. Ridiculous.

But you know from your little adventure on the Walker Spur that if you get driven enough you can't even *let* yourself see danger. If you do, you're a lost cause like I was in the Black Ice. I suppose that's no great revelation, but it ties into the crux of the issue: fear keeps you from fulfilling your self-image as Climber. And that means FAILURE in bright letters. It's just a short step from there to thinking you're generally inadequate. It's a real macho sort of thing; I've never thought of myself as macho, but since I saw it in so many of my friends, I finally realized I must be like that too. Why else do something you don't want to? How many times have you seen people shuffle off to a climb hating even the thought of it?

Maybe some climbers aren't at all macho and are perfectly tuned into reality—if that's possible—and consciously decide a climb is worth dying for. Then, they can unwind and accept a climb for what it is, and somehow enjoy it.

Facing page: Protected by an ice screw, the leader encounters steepening ice. *David Sweet.*

Left: The tubular ice screw is a favored tool of the ice climber. *Jim Balog.*

That must be how heroes from Audie Murphy to those guys in Chamonix do what they do: they don't care if they die or not because it's all worth it. I believed that jive when I was younger and imagined striding into the Climbing Hall of Fame as a martyr to a great route. But now, at the advanced age of twenty-four, I just can't buy it.

Who knows? Maybe I'm missing the boat entirely and everyone else has the key that's eluded me. Whatever it is, I wish I had it, because when I arrived at the Upper Saddle, I swore I'd do nothing but easy routes ever again. How many times have you heard that one? Out I went, three weeks later, onto the west face of Snowpatch Spire. Sick, sick, sick—but that climb was one of the finest of my life. Perfect rock, perfect movement, perfect weather, perfect place. I pray I don't keep trying to rediscover days like that and wind up getting killed. One thing for sure, though: I am never, ever going to climb the Black Ice Couloir again. No way.

Take care,

Jim

CLIMBING ACONCAGUA

Frances Mayes

For Vera Watson

In the sudden storm
we lost ourselves, the white
darkness settling on us
neither blind nor seeing

There was no east, no ascent
only the rope of wind
pulling me in deep, deeper

Ahead, the swirls
of their bodies thickened
The four rucksacks turned
to a flurry of blue
vanished and I was left
dumb, my legs instinctive

———

When my body wanted
to turn to snow
the storm stopped
I found myself near
a rock wall sheeted with ice
where I saw clearly
 a woman's boot
her leg bone in it
clean and frozen

A black boot, a bone
something so simple
Held as when I was
a child and kept
a violet in an icecube
all summer long

Is this the way

my parka a red jewel
glowing through ice
my backbone printed
in ice
a fern leaf from when
this earth was warm

Is this the way

not my father
tucked in the earth
with the bronze angels
or my friend swallowed
by the tide, her limbs
unraveling into microscopic
threads of green and brown
inseparable from algae

not grandmother
home from the crematorium
in a cardboard box
her fine body
changed to porcelain
less than one of her teacups broken
when we emptied her into a blue
silk scarf and buried
it in the garden, wrapped
so small, a bird
torn by the cat

ice
a wreath of white
who
was she
The field sloped up
to a pale green sky
where I saw three suns
without surprise
then, in a clear place
sheltered by rocks
I pitched this tent

When I woke it was too dark
Someone was near
Even in my sleep I heard
the ring of a piton
splitting into my ear

A moment
of cruel happiness
waiting for the face
to break the dark
Nothing   air
ringing in the ice
shale falling, not footsteps

I am breathing fast
demanding more from the thin air
My body in its down cocoon
is warm, returned
Slowly I have melted snow
stirred in brown cubes of soup
With my face close to the low steam
I sang all the songs I know

Now by flashlight I am writing
like all survivors
I have thought of those
south of here who tossed
their gold watches into the ice
to free themselves of one more burden
who lived on penguin bones
they thawed in their teeth
and of her
outside
suspended in ice

My shadow is thrown large
against the tent
I am that close
to my own life

At this moment I am with no one
in my past   even the wind
is blowing somewhere else
Inside me I feel
something willing
I want to write it here
but it is beginning too far in
to reach this way

I am closer
to the black Andean night, closer
to the stars below me
glittering and distinct:
a ring of animal eyes
looking up from the odd world

THE GREAT MATCH

Etienne Bruhl

Mountaineering has been competitive from its inception. Bitter rivalries surrounded the first attempts on the Matterhorn, and the race to be first up the fearsome north wall of the Eiger is well known. In the following article (first published in a 1930 issue of the French magazine Alpinisme*), Etienne Bruhl speculates what climbing competition—abetted by commercialism—will be like in the then-distant year of 1954.*

Most prophetic works contain elements which prove accurate, and some of Bruhl's predictions are remarkably prescient. His vision that climbing would become so specialized that its participants would require several different sets of footwear has come to pass: today's Yosemite climbers flash up imposing jamcracks with one brand of shoe on one foot and another type on the other. Bruhl imagined that speed-climbing competition would take place in the Alps and in Great Britain; he did not guess that this controversial activity would take place eventually only in the Soviet Union and its satellites. The French author's comment that some climbers would be unwilling "to embark upon an adventure of excessive risk for a too uncertain profit" has also proved accurate, and many mountaineers worldwide now embark on dangerous climbs in anticipation of the book contracts and lecture tours that await the successful.

Bruhl believed that the "spiritual factor" in climbing would vanish in the future, and that few mountaineers would still attempt serious climbs solely from "love of sport." Although older climbers of each generation have routinely echoed this refrain, one wonders if modern practitioners would agree that the sporting aspects of mountaineering have diminished.

But one should not seek deep sociological insights from this half-century-old article. It is clear that Bruhl—and the well-known French illustrator Samivel—enjoyed letting their imaginations run wild. This English translation, somewhat condensed from the original, first appeared in the December, 1932 issue of Appalachia. *Climbing historian Chris Jones brought it to our attention several years ago.*

THE EDITORS

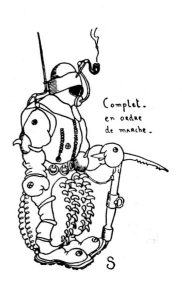

Complet. en ordre de marche.

The contract was signed May 24, 1954, in the parlor of the Hotel du Cheval, at Chambéry. The signatories were, on the one hand, the French alpinists Duverdier and Raucourt, on the other their Italian confrères Facelli and Porra, and thirdly the promoter of the meet, M. Peironnet, director of the Chamonix Casino and President of the Chamber of Commerce of that town.

The news, published that same evening in the papers, produced a marked sensation in the sporting circles of the entire world. Everyone knew of the rivalry between the two famous teams which, for several years past, had each been performing prodigious feats in the Alps. It was in 1951 that this rivalry had assumed a particularly acute form. At that time a leading Italian paper, the *Gazetta delle Vette*, conceived the idea of opposing the two parties by having them try simultaneously the same great mountaineering problem. It was a question, in a word, of a particularly difficult route up Mont Blanc, on the Frêney side.

The idea of such a competition was not entirely new. It was recalled that in 1943, following a challenge, two parties had come to grips on the face of the Aiguille du Dru. This encounter had had a tragic end, and the French police had even considered it their duty to forbid any performances of this kind. However, regular races were now gotten up in the Eastern Alps, particularly the Dolomites and the Kaisergebirge, as well as in certain rock-climbing districts of Great Britain. The competitors set out at intervals of a quarter of an hour, and their times were taken by chronometer to a fifth of a second.

But the suggestion of the *Gazetta delle Vette* had not been carried out. It had had no other result than to let loose a violent controversy in the papers of the day, each side accusing the other of being actual, if unavowed, professionals and so unfit to compete. After the negotiations had definitely failed, some gossips claimed that the chief reason for their lack of success was the insufficiency of the purse that was secretly offered the alpinists. Two years later M. Peironnet was to show that these gossips had not been entirely wrong.

With the fine audacity that had made his reputation and his fortune, M. Peironnet in fact took up the suggestion of the *Gazetta delle Vette* in the course of the winter of 1953-54, but he offered the alpinists such substantial sums that he counted upon overcoming the scruples they had so often proclaimed to the world. When the figures became known the general opinion was perfectly unanimous in holding that M. Peironnet had lost all sense of proportion and was perpetrating a folly. But the impresario was unmoved by the criticisms, scoffings, and insults that came to him from all sides. Reckoning on the worldwide reputations of the competitors and the lively polemics of which they had become the object, he felt certain of realizing a considerable profit, both for himself and for the trade of Chamonix in general.

M. Peironnet had shown a talent bordering on genius in his selection of scene for the encounter. He had fixed his choice upon the famous north face of the Grandes Jorasses. This colossal wall, of ice-coated rock, was still unclimbed at that period; it was universally considered the greatest problem still awaiting solution in the Alps. The papers recalled to mind that the face had been tried many times along about 1930, when what was called "the heroic age of mountaineering" still reigned. At that period a goodly number of adventurous young men were still to be found who attempted great feats from pure "love of sport." Since then the attitude of mind among climbers had undergone much evolution. The spiritual factor had decreased in proportion as technique had been coming to perfection, and no one was willing any longer to embark upon an adventure of excessive risk for a too uncertain profit.

Having come to an agreement on the principle of the meet, the promoter and the competitors had to argue a long while before they could settle the details of the contract. Each side sought to protect itself against a possible default by the others. M. Peironnet had to promise a sum of five hundred thousand francs to each of the parties before they would start at all. An equal sum was to come to the teams which passed beyond a height of thirty-eight

hundred meters. They were to collect two hundred thousand francs more for each additional belt of one hundred meters that they crossed. Finally, the winners would have a prize of five hundred thousand francs to divide. Furthermore, the alpinists were to pocket a substantial percentage of the movie rights and those of the radio broadcast of the contest.

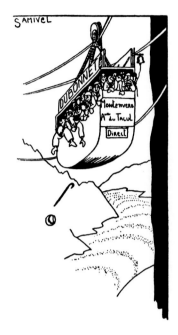

The two parties both intended to try the ascent by the buttress which projects from the Pointe Whymper, but they had chosen, upon this great rock rib, two routes which were entirely distinct, though very near each other. The competitors could thus start simultaneously and the competition, becoming a genuine race in line, promised to offer a highly spectacular attraction.

The meet was set for July 24. The start was to be made at eight o'clock in front of the bergschrund.

Before we begin the account of this historic contest it will perhaps be necessary to describe the state in which mountaineering was at that time. At this period the old "mountaineering with guides" had finally died out. The rôle of the guide, who had had his hour of glory, was little by little losing its importance and coming to be confused with the former function of "porter." The alpinists made more use than ever of the services of native professionals, but this was in order to effect the transport of the considerable apparatus which the development of technique had made necessary. Toward 1950, in fact, the implements of the climber had reached a very advanced degree of perfection. One no longer set out on a climb without having at his disposal a complete set of crampons (for hard snow, for glare ice, for snow upon ice, for verglas, etc.), a series of all the ice axes in current use and, finally, a good assortment of special footgear (rope soles, cloth soles, soles with great friction for smooth slabs, high boots of soft leather for narrow cracks, etc.). On long climbs, also, it was necessary to carry bivouac equipment and, especially, sleeping bags with electric heating. At the base of each new pitch the alpinists asked their guides for the instruments which they thought it best to use. Certain facetious old men, survivors of the "heroic age," readily grew ironical about these new methods. They compared the alpinists of the modern school to golf players followed by their caddies.

To tell the truth, something more was often asked of the natives: they were always ready to give information on the best route to follow and even to take the lead to cut up an ice slope. They could thus hope to earn some little additional gratuity. But such methods were not considered quite regular, and the alpinists who made use of them took care not to boast of it. It was thought, in fact, that the climbers ought to effect the ascent entirely through their own resources. When they had overcome a passage they fixed a knotted rope or a flexible ladder which enabled their auxiliaries to rejoin them quickly.

After the middle of July the excitement at Chamonix became extreme. Dense groups argued endlessly before the large cafés and at the street corners. The bookmakers were already doing a great business. On the twenty-third of July, the evening before the great meet, the crowd began to move in masses into the district of the Grandes Jorasses. The spectators detrained by hundreds at the Trélaporte station, which then formed the terminus of both the

left bank railway and the automobile road. Caterpillar tractors thence transported them across the glacier up to the aerial railway of the Aiguille du Tacul. That evening the new hotel, erected upon the summit of the aiguille, was absolutely full. Other spectators, meanwhile, were taken by vehicle up to the Mont Mallet Glacier, which they then climbed *on foot* up to the upper plateau. There bleachers had been constructed at great expense by M. Peironnet, as well as temporary but comfortable barracks which offered an agreeable shelter for the night. It was the general opinion that the winners would need at least two days to reach the summit.

The fans who had not the means to treat themselves to tickets for the privileged precincts had to be content with less advantageous positions, on the Mer de Glace or in the region of the Couvercle. These "popular" places, nevertheless, still cost dearly enough. An imposing police force gave chase to the rogues who tried to work themselves into the reserve sections by trick. However, certain groups of people were pointed out perched upon the ridges of the Grépon or the wall of the Dru.

Of course, all had provided themselves with aerial field-glasses which magnified the image several hundreds of times. Those who had neglected to bring such instruments could, however, procure them on the spot. In order to avoid dangerous traffic jams it had been decided to prohibit private airplanes from entering the basin of the Mer de Glace. The only machines allowed to follow the ascent were those of the officials in charge, the newspapermen, and the movie organization.

As the National Bureau of Meteorology had announced more than a month ahead of time, the weather on the morning of July 24 was absolutely glorious. The crowd pressed up to the edge of the bergschrund, which for the season was already very wide, in order to see from close at hand how the competitors would cross this first obstacle.

A little before the time set the two parties lined up at the starting point, greeted by enthusiastic cheers. It was observed that the Italians were provided with a considerable outfit, which was carried by twenty-seven young Piedmontese. It was clear that Facelli and Porra counted on using all the resources which the most advanced technique could offer them. The French seemed to have adopted a quite different set of tactics. Seeking light weight and ease of movement, they had reduced their equipment to the minimum and were accompanied by only eight porters. The view at once spread that only reasons of economy had led the French thus to decrease the size of their personnel. The Italians instantly moved into the place of favorites, while the two teams had until then been considered practically equal.

At exactly eight o'clock, in the midst of an impressive silence, the two parties set about crossing the bergschrund. As had been foreseen, the Italians at once made use of a series of elaborate instruments which made it possible for them to cross the obstacle swiftly; and soon Facelli could be seen upon the upper lip of the crevasse, while Duverdier was still struggling with a bad ice-crack. But no one was surprised in the sequel to see the Italians lose all the advantage of their lead when it became necessary for them to bring up one by one their twenty-seven auxiliaries. During the first hours the climb continually showed the same character. The Italians led the field at each difficult passage, but they were rejoined by the French before they had been able to reassemble all their followers. A little after noon Facelli and Porra seemed to become aware of the error which they had committed. They sent back ten of their men after having loaded them with considerable equipment. This change of tactics, coming in the middle of the contest, made a very bad impression. The stock of the French rose rapidly.

In the afternoon the competitors attacked a formidable rock step. Raucourt accomplished marvels in climbing this passage and toward six o'clock the French party was considerably in the lead and progressing at a good pace.

But down among the spectators M. Peironnet was pointed out nervously sizing up the official enclosure. Upon his face was to be read a lively anxiety which occasioned not a little speculation. It was soon learned that he had been cruelly disappointed in the size of the official gate. Undoubtedly the spectators were numerous, but the promoter had reckoned on a crowd at least twice as large. Was he heading for financial disaster?

Talk was going on in this way when, about seven o'clock a serious incident took place. While the Italians were crossing a great couloir a terrible stone-fall occurred. A rope of porters was swept away by the avalanche and, hurled down many hundreds of meters, smashed up on the glacier. The spectators had lost no detail of this catastrophe, the news of which was at once spread throughout the whole world. Immediately hundreds of automobiles, airplanes, and special trains rushed from all quarters toward Chamonix, so that on the following day the most outlying districts were literally filled to overflowing.

Meanwhile, at the approach of night, Duverdier and Raucourt had attained a good lead. They had now become great favorites, especially as the two porters to whom the accident had occurred had carried down in their fall complete assortments of special ice-axes and crampons with which their employers could ill dispense.

The alpinists now seemed to be looking for bivouac sites; the first day's work was practically finished. Driven away by the cool of evening the spectators began to take refuge in the barracks, giving up their observation until

SAMIVEL

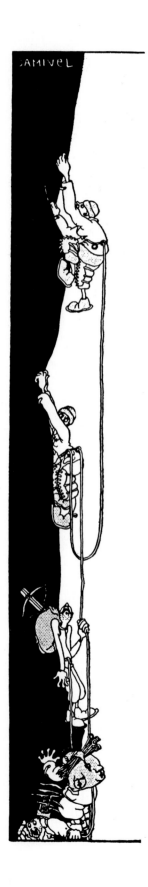

dawn of the following day. Toward 10 P.M., however, when people were finishing their dinner in the immense cafeterias, a strange rumor suddenly spread round. People rushed outside to see bright lights sparkling on the great, somber wall. The loud speakers soon gave the explanation of the mystery. The Italians had had the foresight to provide themselves with powerful searchlights, by the aid of which they were able to continue the ascent during the night. This news produced a great sensation. The Italian spectators expressed their joy loudly while the French protested against this proceeding, which they characterized as unsportsmanlike and irregular. Fights broke out in many quarters. As for the betting odds, they were again upset. The shrill voices of the bookmakers were heard in the midst of the general hubbub.

Facelli and Porra went on all night, contenting themselves with two brief halts. At sunrise it could be seen that they had not only made up their loss of the day before but had even gained a very considerable lead. The French had not moved during the night. However, it soon appeared that the Italians, misled by the darkness, had engaged upon a bad route. They were shortly seen to turn back and redescend a part of the ground won during the night. When they could resume climbing up again their lead over the French had become insignificant. Besides, their work during the night had very visibly tired them; while the French, after a good restorative sleep, appeared to be in excellent condition.

On the other hand, it could be seen that the manpower had diminished in each camp. The night had been a hard one for both and many porters had had to be sent back as a result of serious frostbite or illnesses due to the cold. The contest was proceeding, however, with extraordinary bitterness when a very serious accident took place, which seemed as if it must put an end to the struggle. Duverdier, who was then leading his rope, could not avoid dislodging a loose stone. This fell and struck Raucourt, breaking his left forearm. The valiant champion, thus put *hors de combat,* had to come back down, supported by two porters.

Duverdier, far from allowing himself to be vanquished by his bad luck, at once resumed work with admirable persistence. But the rules prohibited him from roping himself with a professional and, forced to continue the ascent all alone, he could have no hope of conquering his redoubtable adversaries. From this moment, indeed, the Italians increased their lead considerably. People thought for a moment that they could reach the summit before the end of the day, but it was evident that they were feeling great fatigue. Their progress appeared to become all the more laborious because they had just reached the beginning of a region of extreme difficulty. Now that the battle between the two men had virtually come to an end, attention was concentrated upon the struggle between man and the mountain. Facelli and Porra constantly relieved each other at the head of the rope; they were making a desperate effort, as if they wished above everything to avoid a second night on the wall. Farther down, much farther down, Duverdier was heroically continuing the climb, alone, without hope; a true sportsman.

But a new misfortune was about to strike the Italians. Towards six o'clock, at about thirteen thousand feet of elevation, five of their porters slipped in an ice couloir and went down to be crushed at the foot of the gigantic wall. Their disappearance was disastrous for the team, for their packs contained all the equipment for the night: the searchlights which would have made it possible to finish the climb after sunset, and the self-heating blankets which would have made a bivouac supportable. Facelli and Porra continued their way not the less courageously until nightfall. They then made camp at about 120 meters below the summit.

The next morning the spectators were astonished to see the Italians remain for a long time motionless at their bivouac site. Then it was observed that a large group set about descending. Exhausted by his efforts of the preceding days, Facelli had been unable to endure the rigors of the night. Shivering with fever and suffering from serious frostbite, he was no longer fit to finish the climb. Three porters were in the same condition. Porra had to detach five more good men in order to safeguard the descent of the sick ones. He had at his own disposal only two porters with which to finish the ascent, and during this time Duverdier was savagely pursuing his way. Up at the first light of dawn, he had at once resumed his slow but regular advance, followed by the two porters who remained with him also. His handicap diminished bit by bit and a new hope, still very feeble, began to be born in the hearts of his partisans.

Porra undertook the ascent of a great vertical chimney. From the glacier all the spectators could see that this chimney had no exit. It was obstructed in its upper section by enormous overhanging rocks, impossible to surmount. Being right at the chimney, without a good view of it, Porra could not realize this. He was seen to jam himself in the crack, then to raise himself slowly, painfully, by unheard of efforts of all his muscles. After twenty minutes of superhuman labor, Porra perceived the obstacle. For a long while he continued to struggle in the mad hope of surmounting it just the same. Then he realized that he was wasting his last bit of strength and descended again to the foot of the chimney in a state of absolute exhaustion.

From below people were anxiously following Duverdier, who was continuing to ascend and now found himself very near his rival. The struggle became agonizing. It was a genuine drama which was developing before the eyes of the public.

Reclining upon a great flat rock, Porra sought to regain his breath and strength. His mind was a prey to gloomy thoughts. After forty-eight hours of painful struggle he had come to within 100 meters, only that, of the goal, but these 100 meters he felt he could not make. His muscles, his heart, his lungs were done up and now refused to serve him. With Facelli he would have been certain of triumphing; alone, he was conquered. The two men who still remained with him were also exhausted. Their morale had fallen so low that they were insisting upon abandoning the attempt. Porra did not dare propose to them a new effort for the summit; he feared a downright refusal.

Suddenly he heard puffing and panting, the raucous breathing of a man

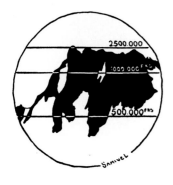

struggling desperately. Turning his head he perceived two hands on the edge of the flat rock; then a head, red in the face, appeared; and in a final effort Duverdier pulled himself up on the rock by his side.

Duverdier remained motionless for some seconds, surveying his prostrate adversary fixedly. Then he held out his hand to the Italian, who seized it, and, with a voice shaken by emotion as well as breathlessness, he asked:

"Then the pitch won't go?"

Porra contented himself with sadly indicating a negative.

"I, too, am at the end of my strength," resumed Duverdier. "I do not feel able to finish alone."

"I have tried," confessed the Italian, "but it is impossible. I have just decided to give it up."

Duverdier remained silent for some moments. Then, with great emotion, he began again to speak.

"Porra," said he, "we have struggled against each other loyally and with all our energy. Each of us has lost his companion. Now we've come to the same point. The contest has been an equal one. We can consider it finished. Porra, let us rope together. Two of us, we can succeed. Oh, yes indeed, I, too, am thinking of the objection . . . the public . . . the newspapers. . . . Oh well . . . what of it? The contest would have been a draw. We have proved that we are of the same strength. Why need there be a victor if the two adversaries are equal? Why make it look like a supremacy if no supremacy exists? Come, Porra, let us rope up together."

With his right hand he presented the Italian with a loop of rope. Porra hesitated a few seconds; then, getting up abruptly, he seized the loop, placed it about his waist, and tightened the knot. He had remained silent during these preparations. When they were all finished he seized Duverdier's hand effusively.

"Duverdier," said he, "you are a man!"

Below, upon the glacier, the crowd had viewed this extraordinary scene with amazement. When the new rope was seen to get in motion and attack, with Duverdier in the lead, one of the first cracks, numerous protests went up. Then, suddenly, there were enthusiastic cheers. To tell the truth, the public, completely puzzled, did not itself know what it ought to think.

Now Porra was in the lead for the ascent of a very steep, ice-covered slab. After this pitch Duverdier was preparing to take the lead again when he heard himself addressed by Porra.

"Duverdier," said the Italian, "Duverdier, I think we're fools."

And, as the Frenchman regarded him with astonishment, "Yes, fools, if we proceed," continued Porra. "We have each of us already won a fine sum of money. Let's descend and next year the contest can be started all over again. Then we can get three times as much."

"But the public?"

"The public has lost interest in the contest since we joined together. They came to view a competition rather than an ascent. You may be sure that they'll be greatly disappointed at our reaching an understanding."

"People are going to be astonished at seeing us give up so near the end. They're going to raise the cry of scandal."

"Not at all," replied the Italian. "The spectators will be delighted to see the problem remain unsolved. They'll continue to ask themselves who will be able to solve it, the French or the Italians. Don't you think, yourself, that the success of a mixed rope would be heart breaking?"

"But anyway," cried Duverdier, "it's now too late. We've been seen going together."

"What does that matter? We'll say what we choose. That we were exhausted, both of us, or that we couldn't agree on the management of the party."

Porra's perception had been correct: the public had ceased to enthuse for the spectacle when the two adversaries united for the final effort. When the alpinists were seen to stop so near the end and set about the descent, people were certainly very much intrigued by this new bit of surprise, but no feeling other than amazement was shown. There was no protest, no anger, even no disappointment. Soon the loud speakers proclaimed the official reasons for the abandonment of the attempt and the crowd began to move away slowly, commenting on the events of the contest. True, no positive result had been gained, but the show had been an extraordinary one. Everyone had the feeling of having had his money's worth.

A week later the newspapers announced that a new contract had been signed among the different parties. The historic encounter was to be repeated in July, 1955. The exorbitant conditions exacted by the alpinists had at once been accepted by M. Peironnet. The latter, however, reserved the right to engage new teams, one for each nation. The contest might thus be transformed into a magnificent world's championship event. Interviewed shortly afterward, the famous adversaries all declared the experience of 1954 would be profitable to them and that they were certain of winning in 1955. Very quickly public opinion turned from the recent past to consider only the distant future.

But on August 14 following, when sporting circles were beginning to look forward eagerly to the competition of the following year, an event unexpectedly occurred which smashed this beautiful dream. Three facetious young men, Oxford students with a love of practical jokes, left the climbing hut a little after midnight. Acting with the greatest mystery, they ascended Mont Mallet Glacier and attacked the famous wall. That same evening, toward seven o'clock, their silhouettes stood out from the pale blue background of sky upon the summit of the Pointe Whymper.

This curious ascent has generally been considered, since that time, as the last manifestation, the final outburst, of the former school. Before disappearing forever the old mountaineering of our ancestors turned round upon the verge of its disappearance and, at the modern age which had come to supplant it, maliciously addressed its thumb to its nose.

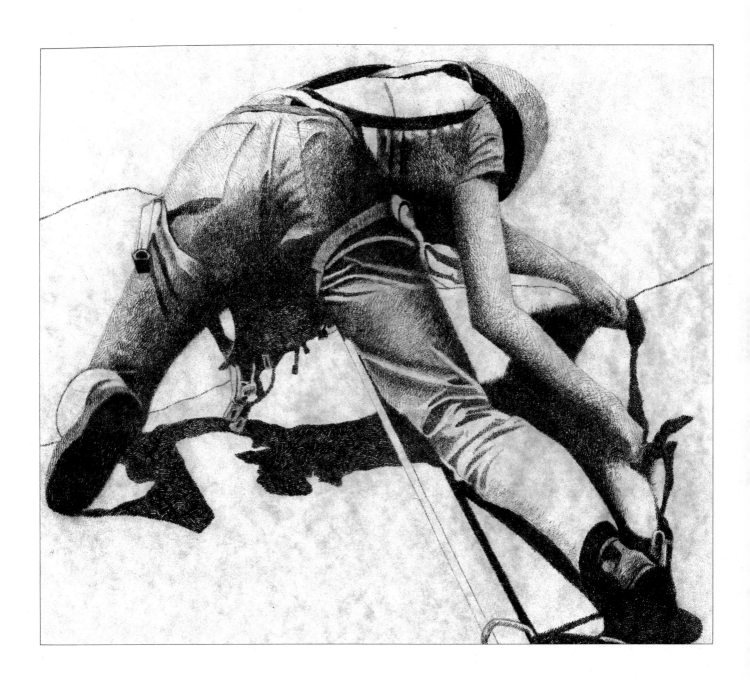

LIKE WATER AND LIKE WIND

A Novella by David Roberts

Myself when young did eagerly frequent
Doctor and Saint, and heard great argument
  About it and about: but evermore
Came out by the same door where in I went.

With them the seed of Wisdom did I sow,
And with mine own hand wrought to make it grow;
  And this was all the Harvest that I reaped—
"I came like Water, and like Wind I go."

Edward Fitzgerald
The Rubáiyát of Omar Khayyám of Naishápúr

Far north in Scythia, beyond the Arimaspians, we come to the "Ripaean" Mountains and to the district which on account of the ever-falling snow, resembling feathers, is called Pterophorus. This part of the world is accursed by nature and shrouded in thick darkness; it produces nothing else but frost and is the chilly hiding-place of the north wind. . . .

Pliny
Natural History, Book IV

Pterophorus, *mtn., 9764', 61°37'30" N.; 153°51'20" W.; at the head of unnamed glaciers feeding Desolation and Tired Pup Creeks. Name found on anonymous miner's 1917 ms. map.*

Roth
Glossary of Alaska Place Names

PART I: AUGUST 1964

1

They were in their fortieth hour of bivouacking—afternoon of the second day—when Ed said, "Let's go down."

Victor shifted on the two-foot ledge and stared once more at the vertical ice-filled chimney that blocked out all speculation about the final thousand feet above. "Now? But—"

"It's not going to stop." The snow, indeed, had picked up in the last hour.

"If we go down it's for good."

"I'm too damned cold. This is getting scary."

For the hundredth time Victor cursed himself for the decision they had made when they had reached the ledge, forty hours before. He had wanted to attack the chimney—the apparent crux of the whole route—that evening. But it was late summer, with a solid six hours of darkness by now, and Ed's fussiness had won the day. Granted, it was a good thing they had spent that hour sorting and hanging the hardware, chipping the ice from their ledge, laying the rope to sit on; for neither of them had bargained for the storm that had sneaked in that night from the south, behind the mountain. Yet with a rope fixed on the chimney, they could have prusiked up and bombed for the summit, storm or no storm. Victor was glad now that Ed had wavered first; but that minimal pleasure was dwarfed by the outrage of failure.

"We could come up again," Ed was saying. "The plane's not due for a week."

"You know as well as I do. . . ."

After a while Ed answered. "Yeah. But this is getting dangerous."

"We're so close. Just to show those bastards down below—"

"We'd never get up the chimney now." Ed waved his hand listlessly. "Look at the rime."

Three days before, as the week of rain and hurricane winds had at last ended, Victor had roused Ed at base camp for a six A.M. start. Only Arthur, loyal as always, had bothered to walk with them across the mile of frozen névé to the base of the route. Chalmers, still taking codeine for his "broken" wrist, had not so much as offered a goodbye from his sleeping bag. Victor had heard the man moaning in the night, whether from pain or nightmare he was unsure.

Arthur had pounded them on the back and wished them luck. "We'll give it a whack, anyway," Victor promised, turning at once to the fixed ropes. Parting scenes embarrassed him.

By the end of the day, with the weather clearing steadily, they had reclaimed the tiny bivouac tent 2000 feet up, at the end of the highest fixed rope. The tent had been pitched there, on a down-sloping drift, seventeen days earlier by Victor and Arthur. Now it took Ed and himself an hour's digging to excavate the structure. Their sleep that night was cramped and fitful.

The next day had been the best of their climbing lives. On new ground the moment they scrambled above the tent, they were moving before the sun appeared in the cloudless northeast. Ed wanted to pack up the bivvy tent and take it with them, just as, in base camp, he had argued for six days' food rather than four. But Victor had talked him into lightness and speed.

The climbing was intricate and devious; the granite seemed most rotten at this height, and every hold had to be cross-examined. The decent angle- and bong-cracks of the first 2000 feet were distant cousins to the bottoming runnels and grooves up here. On the rock they retained their crampons, skipping belays about half the time. The series of ceilings and featureless walls on which Ed had performed his weeks of binocular scholarship kept threatening now to funnel them into a dead-end. Yet the back alley of their route, full of traverses and zigzags, wended its possible way upward.

Down below they could watch the insect forms of their colleagues creep about on timid loops around the colony of tents. It was the finest day of the month, but the lethargy that had settled over base camp seemed to dictate to the others only domestic chores—drying out bags, perhaps, or repitching the tents, or patching the igloo. Victor knew that some of them—Chalmers not least—were waiting only for salvation by airplane, a week hence.

They snacked while belaying, drank but a few sips of lemonade the whole day. By seven P.M. they had found the two-foot ledge beneath the crux chimney, with its vertical snake of ice, a yard wide all the way up to the brow of the known universe. Ed estimated that the day's climbing had covered the equivalent of 25 rope lengths, gaining 1500 vertical feet. If so, they were a mere thousand feet below the top. They had done only one pitch of aid all day; the rest had demanded nerve as much as technique, trust in deceitful knobs and flakes, a crablike scuttling on crumbly slabs, crampon points hooked on crystals of quartz. More than once it had been Victor's drive that had taken them across the dubious patches.

The evening was happy and warm. Victor held the stove on his lap and brewed up tea and soup and more tea. They dissected the wonderful day— better even than Hungabee, Ed agreed. They analyzed the crump spirit that had seized upon the others. They spent an hour scheming against the chimney above them. Ed was for staying in the ice; but Victor thought it was too steep to chop steps in, and that the key would be stemming and bridging. He offered to lead the pitch, and Ed did not demur.

Shifting from one haunch to the other in the middle of the night, Victor opened his eyes; the stars seemed dimmer than before, the darkness murky. Only moments later the gusts of wind began, and then the flakes of snow. Within an hour, full storm.

They spent the whole day in the bivvy sack. "It's just a flurry, or a series of flurries," Victor said more than once. They nibbled at gorp and cheese and Logan bread, and tried to stay warm. With a sinking heart Victor watched the rime ice form and build on the rounded edges of the chimney. The wind was the worst of it: it seemed to find all the apertures in their nylon cave, and sent draughts of chill into the clammy recesses inside their clothing.

They tried to kill the day with talk. Ed delivered soliloquies on gear. "We should have brought one of those French butane stoves. No gas bottles, no priming. You just turn the thing on . . . I really don't trust the manila ropes, even if they're five-sixteenths. I trust nylon. I trust the give." Victor nodded, uninterested.

"Are you going to stay at Hopkins?" he asked, just to change the subject.

"I guess. For another year anyway. I can't hack the dorm-mother bit, though. How about you?"

"The fall?" Victor stretched his stiff limbs. "I don't know. I haven't thought beyond the expedition. It's not real back there."

"Working in a climbing store's not real. Not after a few years of it."

"Spare me that shit," Victor said, vexed. The hours of uncertainty were merging with his darker fear, of failure. Nothing had worked out since Hungabee.

"Sorry, Lionel." Ed lapsed into silence.

The whimsical name jolted Victor out of his irritation. He looked over at his friend and felt a pang of nostalgia. But he saw in the blond patchy beard, the ascetic face, not the faint resemblance to Lachenal—it was the similarity of his own looks to Terray's, after all, that had spawned the whimsy, that and, after Hungabee, the sense of a destiny together. Instead he saw Ed as Vera saw him, the shy, frail-looking aristocrat. He wanted to respond in kind, to voice the "Louis" which would reassert that destiny. But all he said was, "Let's cook dinner."

"What do we have? The pork chops?"

The food warmed them slightly, but once he had turned off the stove the drifting flakes in the dusk seemed to Victor all the more inescapable.

"Wind's down," Ed said.

"Yeah. Tomorrow. Just wait."

There was a long silence. "Tell me about the trip with Vee last August."

"I already have."

"Not in detail."

Victor sighed. "What a wash-out. She was paranoid about bears from the first day, even though we never saw one. Then she got all psyched out about the plane not coming. Like our friend Chalmers." He snorted. "Here I thought the Brooks Range would be such a picnic after Foraker. I guess I was pretty hard to take, too. I kept going over everything that had screwed up on Foraker. Two fiascos in one summer, Jesus. If you'd been along it would have been different."

"So why couldn't you just relax and enjoy the scenery?"

"With Vee? There was this range of unclimbed peaks, up the Nigu about twenty miles. Easy stuff, Colorado style, but I thought we could bag a few. Not Vee. 'What if the airplane flies over to check while we're gone?' Christ."

Ed had his wry smile. "Always got to get somewhere else, don't you?"

"You know me."

"How are things between you two?"

"I don't know." Victor refastened his hood. "I really don't know."

He slept until the middle of the night when he woke suddenly from a bad dream. He found that he had started to slip off the ledge. His anchor rope had cut off the circulation in his left arm; he had dreamed it was frostbitten. Ed, evidently unable to sleep, was kicking his boots on the rock in a steady rhythm.

The morning was gray and windless. The snow showed no signs of stopping. Victor was alarmed that he could no longer see base camp in the white-out. He felt a surge of anger at Chalmers. He fumbled with the stove, noticing that his hands were clumsier than the day before. He was starting to shiver every now and then, and he could feel Ed shivering beside him.

They kept up the vigil with a minimum of conversation through lunch. Then, a few hours later, Ed broke the silence: "Let's go down."

Victor kept up the objections, but his heart was not in it. He tried his last debating point. "Look, Ed, there's no way we can get down to the bivvy tent before dark. One more night here."

"I don't know if I can take one more night. I didn't sleep at all."

"So where do we bivouac?"

"I don't know. We've got to move, I think. This is too much like that Frêney Pillar thing. The ones that didn't move died."

Victor stared once more at the ice-filled chimney. "I just can't stand the thought of giving up the summit. We're so close."

"There's no chance now anyway," Ed said wearily. "You couldn't get five feet off this ledge in these conditions. Try it."

"All right." Victor started to get to his feet. "We'll go down."

2

It took them two hours to pack up. Except for the strands they had been sitting on, the ropes were frozen into grotesque tangles. Ed worked the goldline back to suppleness with patient strokes of his mittened hands. Victor tried to cram the frost-heavy bivouac sack into the bottom of his pack. A corner had frozen into the ice; when it didn't respond to his tugs, he gave an angry jerk, ripping the seam and leaving a piece of fabric in the ice. "Take it easy," Ed said sharply.

At least the hardware had been racked before the storm hit. The slings were stiff with ice, though. One of them had been tied in the middle to shorten it; Victor pried at the recalcitrant knot with his fingers, then with the pick of his axe, until, in disgust, he threw the thing into the void. "Hey," Ed said.

"We can't fart around with things that don't work." But he felt ashamed of his petulance. As on Hungabee, in a situation like this it was he who stormed through difficulties with a Lachenal-like recklessness, Ed who grew methodical, double-checking everything like a man who couldn't see because he'd broken his glasses. At this very moment Ed was coaxing the dented pot inside its nesting lid. Through the heat of his impatience Victor felt a flicker of amusement.

The worst task was putting on their crampons. It was awkward standing on the small ledge to stamp their boots into the springy metal frames; their balance was bad, moreover, from two days of sitting. Victor's straps, too short to begin with, had to be stretched and clawed at to get the crampons on tight. He couldn't manage the job himself, so Ed knelt on the ledge and battled with the frozen leather.

In the first fifty yards Victor realized that the terrain beneath their bivouac ledge was in much worse shape than he had guessed. The rock was coated everywhere with frost feathers that had to be knocked loose before one could use a hold. There was no trace of their crampon marks from two days before, and a thin layer of rime disguised the patches of water-ice they had been able to circumvent on the way up. Once Victor, backing down without a belay, kicked a crampon through the rime and hit ice; his boot bounced off and he nearly fell.

It was alarming how little warmth he seemed to be gaining from the strenuous effort. The wind was up again, or perhaps their ledge had been sheltered from it. It seemed to be getting dark already. His watch was in his pocket—too much trouble to take off a mitten and fish it out.

The route had zigzagged so much that there were no possible rappels at first. Pitches they had moved together on two days before they had to belay carefully now. They leapfrogged downwards, traversing, climbing up short stretches, trying to stay on snow. The details began to confuse Victor. When Ed had joined him on a small platform he said, "Where the hell are we?"

"We're on route."

"You sure? It feels like we're too low. If we get into those vertical plates—"

"We're OK." Ed pointed. "Remember that prong?"

"No."

"You used a sling on it on the way up."

Good old Louis, Victor thought. What an eye for a route. He promised himself patience, but the dark weather in his mind was gathering. A sentence appeared behind his eyes, as if typed on a blank sheet: We could actually die on this thing. He passed an erasing wand over the sentence, but the black words were burnt into the paper.

They crept downwards, but with each pitch it seemed to Victor that they were moving more slowly. As he made his laborious way down the long tunnel of a couloir, hanging at times on the lodged pick of his axe, he cursed the dull, too-short front points of his crampons. The wind was gusting now—a possible sign, Victor thought, of the end of the storm. Meanwhile the sudden blasts of air threatened to wrench him loose from his awkward purchase on the world. Communication with Ed had dwindled to the briefest of belay signals.

He became aware that the gray sky full of storm had appreciably darkened. The watch in his pocket seemed as inaccessible as before. He hurried, nearly slipped again, forced himself to take his time.

Ed was wedged in a narrow fissure between a pillar of granite and a slab of ice. When Victor had joined him, he said, "I've got two pins in. We can bivouac here."

"Are you crazy? Standing up?"

"What's the choice?" Ed's voice sounded uncharacteristically listless. "It's getting to be night."

"There's hardly room for you here, let alone both of us." In Victor's mind the phrase ran its repetitious loop: We could die on this thing, and not even have made the summit.

"No worse than that one on Hungabee."

Victor looked hard at his friend's face. The complacency of the voice had alarmed him, and now he saw it mirrored in a strange sleepy calm about the eyes. Ice had caught in the straggly patches of Ed's beard. Victor tugged at his own with a mitten. "All right," he said finally. "Maybe we can hang our packs and sit on them."

An hour later it was dark. As he was trying to prop the stove on his pack and fill the reservoir with gas, Victor's feet slipped. His hand, swinging up to grab the anchor rope, knocked the stove off its perch. They heard it clank as it caromed off rock thirty feet below. Victor swore violently.

"It's all right," Ed said groggily. "I wasn't thirsty anyway,"

"Of course you are. We need water. Suck some snow. Goddamn it to hell."

"I'm all right."

We could die right here, Victor thought. We had it made, just a thousand feet to go, just the chimney and then clear sailing to the summit. We don't deserve this, not after a month full of storms. He cursed his clumsiness, and Chalmers, and the last two years of his life. He closed his eyes and picked at the ice in his hair. Suddenly a particular camp on the Nigu with Vera came to him whole, an image of paradise. Grayling cooking on a scrubwillow fire, Vee picking blueberries in the sunny meadow up the bank. He tried to picture her now, jotting down notes in the safe, snug library where she spent each afternoon. If I get past this thing, he promised the djin of his boyhood luckiness, I'll never take an easy day for granted again.

Ed was shivering. "Just hang on," Victor said. "Get through the night."

"Once we reach the fixed ropes we're all right." The voice was slow, with a trace of slurring in it.

"We've got to be more than halfway down to the bivvy tent."

"Less."

"Are you sure?" Victor asked, disheartened, for he knew Ed's calculations would be accurate.

"They're probably giving us up for dead."

"Arthur might come up."

"Not in the storm. Chalmers will talk everybody out of it."

"Fucking Chalmers," Victor muttered. His feet seemed to have gone numb. He tried stepping in place, but it was too crowded. The thought of getting out the bivouac sack and trying to fit it around them was too complicated to take seriously. In his exhaustion he almost fell asleep. A thing like a dream flitted through his mind: he was being made to walk along a seacoast somewhere, but his legs sank into a marshy ooze, and then he was crawling on his knees, his arms buried in mud . . . .

The cold brought him back to reality. Ed was whispering to himself. "What are you doing?" Victor asked.

"Counting things."

"What?"

"Nights I've spent in the wilderness. Girls I've gone out with."

"How many nights?"

"At least a hundred and thirty."

"How many girls?"

Ed snickered. "Not as many."

A little later Victor was jolted out of a stupor by Ed's rummaging through his pack. "Now what?"

"Getting my water bottle," Ed said. "We have to have water." Victor moved to accommodate the fumbling. "If we fill it with snow," he said blandly, "we can melt it with our body heat. I'll keep it inside my parka."

Well, Victor thought, it's another way to fill up time. His own thirst was maddening.

Just before morning the snow stopped. "Look," said Victor.

"I know." Ed shivered violently. "Christ, I'm cold."

"But it's over. The storm's over, at last."

"Maybe."

Because they had hardly unpacked the night before, it required little more than knocking out the anchor pitons to be off. The water bottle yielded only a sip or two apiece of slush. They did not bother to eat.

In the gray dawn light they could see out to the foothills in the northwest, bright with new snow, and even catch a glimpse of the tundra plain beyond, with its nameless braided river snaking westward. But base camp was eclipsed now by the series of sharp buttresses—the "Dorsal Fins," Ed had called them early in the expedition—which they found themselves among.

As the morning wore on, Ed's spirits rose steadily. Victor let his friend set up a series of rappel anchors, as he usually did, trusting in Ed's superior mechanical sense. And he gave himself over to the other man's routefinding, too. He felt that he was saving himself, coasting in Ed's wake, in case a new emergency should come. Gradually his own fear ebbed. We'll make it after all, he began to say to himself, just as we did on Hungabee. You can't stop Louis and Lionel.

Ed kept underlining the significance of the change in weather. "It means they'll be out looking for us. They'll probably go up the fixed ropes and meet us at the bivvy tent, or even higher. If they have any brains, they'll be brewing up hot drinks." Despite the compulsive talking, Ed's gear-handling remained methodical to an extreme.

Toward mid-afternoon they began to run short of hardware. Ed's over-caution with rappel anchors had depleted their supply almost without either man noticing. "My brain's going about forty percent," Ed joked. Victor nodded. The Dorsal Fins seemed more extensive than he had remembered. He was very, very tired, and a mood of vague apprehension was reclaiming his spirits.

Now Ed insisted on down-climbing three pitches it would have been easier to rappel. The afternoon hastened by; the sky kept its steely gray look, but there was no wind. Stopping on a belay ledge, Victor glanced across the glacier. It occurred to him that the rime-plastered pinnacles on the next ridge were beautiful, and with the perception came a stinging sense of loss. So damn close, he thought bitterly, just that chimney and then clear sailing.

"Almost there," Ed shouted from the lower end of the rope. Victor summoned the energy to retrieve his watch. The hands had stopped at 10:15. He put the watch back in his pocket without winding it.

An hour later they traversed around the last of the Dorsal Fins. Victor's eyes picked out the bivvy tent, covered with snow. Ed said, "Jesus Christ," in a low, numbed voice.

"What?"

"They haven't even left base camp."

Victor stared at the distant squares of tent, the tiny lump of the igloo. There were a few short trails plowed out around camp, but none that headed toward the mountain. There were no figures visible. "They think we're dead," he said.

"Let's yell for help."

"No," Victor said vehemently. A ferocious anger had taken him over. "Fuck the bastards. We'll do this all on our own."

"I was counting on them. I was already tasting the soup."

"Let's get over to the bivvy tent. We can sort it all out there. It's getting dark again."

It took them more than an hour to get the tent swept off and themselves installed within. Victor spent fifteen minutes alone getting his crampons off. "At least it's warm," Ed said at last.

The fury in Victor had not ebbed. "What are those bastards doing? Playing cards?"

"You know how it is. When you're cozy and it's storming out, you can't believe anybody could be climbing in it."

"But this is life or death." He shifted a leg; it seized up with cramp, making him howl as he tried to straighten it.

"How do you feel?" Ed said a little later.

"My throat's burning. I've never been so thirsty."

"Shall we try the water bottle thing again?"

A couple of hours later they were able to drink about a third of a cup apiece. Victor's anger was unslaked. In a stupefied half-sleep he had visions of going at Chalmers with an ice axe.

The darkness made the bivvy tent claustrophobic. When either man moved, the other had to adjust his own position and remold a pocket of stale air in front of his nose and mouth. Slowly the warmth ebbed away. But in place of the darker, life-giving dread of the previous day, Victor felt, now that only a chain of fixed ropes separated them from the glacier, a petty irritability that magnified each discomfort into a real grievance. The sense of failure gnawed at him. For two years, he thought, everything has screwed up, Ed or no Ed.

Impulsively, he spoke. "Let's get out of here."

"Now?" Ed asked. "In the dark?"

"Let's go on down. We can clip in to the fixed ropes. It's a cinch from here down."

"What's the hurry?"

"I'm fed up with this mountain. We're not going to sleep tonight. Besides, the thirst is dangerous. The sooner we get water, the better."

There was a long silence while Ed seemed to go over the logistics of retreat. "What about all this gear?"

Victor was incredulous. "Are you kidding? I'm not about to haul down the tent and stuff. Let the bastards come up for it. It's the least they can do."

Another silence. Victor tried to get a distance on his own impatient rationalizing. But Ed's decision came as a surprise. "All right."

"No shit?"

"Yeah. I've had enough, too. We should be able to go down the fixed ropes in the dark."

"All right, Louis, let's move. By noon we'll be drinking the Courvoisier. If Chalmers hasn't finished it off."

Packing was again a minimal chore. There was the faintest hint of light in the air—no stars in the sky, but a kind of afterglow radiating from the glacier below. It's funny, Victor thought, how it's never truly dark in the mountains. Not dark like in a cave. Once he had his crampons on, he clipped his waist loop into the manila line and started down, a hank of rope wrapped around his left forearm, his axe gripped in his right hand. "It's easy," he shouted up. Despite his utter tiredness, it felt good to be moving. At the anchor pin a hundred and twenty feet down he switched to the next rope, yelling up, "I'm off!"

After three pitches he stopped to adjust a crampon strap. Within minutes he heard the clanking of hardware, but it was only in the last twenty feet above him that he saw Ed dimly outlined against the gloom. "How's it seem?" he asked.

Ed's voice was neutral. "It's all right. This is the top of that crack system. Where we decided not to go left."

Victor laughed. "If you say so. It could be the New York subway, as far as I'm concerned. Want to go ahead?"

"Sure."

Victor watched his friend clip in to the rope, then cautiously wrap two handfuls around his mitten. The hardware jangled. Ed moved downward into the darkness. Victor waited impatiently, thinking about all the things to drink at base camp. There was a sound of rocks being kicked off below. Vaguely he remembered leading these pitches with Arthur, three weeks before. There had been some scary run-outs on the crumbly rock. How full of hope they had all been then—how even the hardships had had the purposefulness of discovery.

Ed was taking a long time on the pitch. In Victor's head was a tune that had been running through his mind, he realized now, for the last three days. Hurry up, Ed, he said to himself. It was strange that he didn't feel colder. Only the parched burning in the back of his throat . . . . He scooped up a mittenful of snow and put it in his mouth. At last he called out, "Are you off?" No answer. He yelled again, "Ed! Are you off?"

He reached down and tugged at the rope: it was loose. So Ed had been off for a while; either Victor had not heard the call, or Ed had forgotten to give one. He gathered up the line in his hand. Something was wrong. The rope was too . . . what? Too *light*. With a growing panic he reeled the fixed rope in. After forty feet he came to the end. He took off his mitten and felt with his fingertips the ragged fibers where the rope had severed. "Oh, no," he said out loud. Then he shouted, first timidly, then at the top of his lungs: "Ed!" ED!" He listened. The answer he did not expect did not come.

In the darkness he leaned against the rock, hearing himself groan. "All right," he said softly, "keep it together." He had to figure out what to do for himself. He still had the climbing rope, coiled on the top of his pack. If only they had stayed roped. But no; likely as not he'd have been pulled off with Ed. That sound of rocks falling: it hadn't been rocks. Was there a chance that—? No, not after 2000 feet.

All the hardware was gone with Ed. So it's clear, he told himself. You sit here and wait till morning, then yell for help. He forced himself to sit down on the ledge. He scrounged an extra carabiner and reinforced his clip-in. But the silence and the solitude were intolerable. He heard the rapid pounding of his heart. I could rappel this pitch single-strand, he thought, leave the rope, and count on fixed ropes the rest of the way. But he couldn't count on them, that was obvious. All it would take was another sharp edge, somewhere below. From two days before, he heard Ed's prophetic words: "I don't trust the manila . . . I trust nylon. I trust the give."

The urge to keep moving, to cope with the terror by forcing his way down, was powerful. But another part of Victor's mind kept warning, "What if you go and get killed, too? Then nobody will know what you did." He stood up. The blood rushed out of his head, dizzying him. All at once Ed's disappearance hit him, in a wave of grief that was like the longing of first-glimpsed love. The years of weekend climbs, the pilgrimage to the Rockies, the triumph of Hungabee, the two of them and his sense of luck—all negated now, made nothing in the arbitrary severing of a strand of five-sixteenth-inch rope.

I could shout now, in the middle of the night, shout for help. He opened his mouth, but no sound would come. An image of Chalmers' face arrived unbidden, deciding for him. With a grim attention to detail, Victor uncoiled the heavy goldline rope, moved along the ledge to the fixed-rope anchor, and tied a bowline through the eyes of both pitons. He flung the other end of the rope out into the darkness, wrapped the line in a Dülfersitz around his body, and started down.

It was morning by the time he unclipped himself from the lowest fixed line, just below the lip of the bergschrund. An hour before, they had seen him from base camp. Now all four of them were making a trail towards him; but they were still a quarter-mile away. Victor felt a ruthless pride that he had got off the mountain before they had been able to help him. He would have preferred to walk in to base camp unobserved; but at least now he could despise them without owing them any gratitude. The last few hours had been the worst. He had been plagued with aural hallucinations: of angelic choral voices tempting him to sleep, of car horns blatting and echoing from the granite walls. The swelling in his throat had given him the fear that he could not breathe freely. His toes were definitely numb. Overlying all had been the terror-filled anticipation of a sudden gift of slack each time he had hung on the fixed ropes.

He faced outward and staggered down the steep snowslope below the bergschrund. On the easy terrain he caught one calf with the crampon on the other foot and nearly fell. Panting, he stood still, then heel-kicked his way carefully downward.

Arthur was closest, a hundred yards away. Victor felt a sudden shyness. But there was Chalmers, just behind, his arm still ostentatious in its sling; and the anger washed away any self-consciousness. The other two were behind Chalmers. The gap closed.

Arthur held him under the shoulders. He shrugged himself loose. "It's OK," he said. His voice, scratchy and thin, sounded like another man's. "We had it. I'm OK, I can stand up by myself." There was fright in Arthur's eyes, a dull expectant look in Chalmers'. "I got down by myself," he lashed out. "Where were you bastards all this time?"

"Where's Ed?" Arthur asked.

"He's gone. He's dead. The fixed rope broke. Where were you?"

Arthur took him under the shoulders again. "Oh, Lord," he said, his voice twisting. "That's what I was afraid of. First that both of you, then when we saw just one this morning—"

"Do you have any water? I've got to have water."

A bottle was produced. Victor chugged from it, feeling the pain in his throat surge back into being.

"On the way down?" Arthur persisted. "How did it happen?"

"On the descent, yes. It just broke."

"Did you make the top?"

As if hovering far above the glacier, a prehistoric bird observing an inconsequential scene, Victor saw himself nod. No, a closer voice shrilled in his ear: take it back now, while you can. But the anger in him gave his mouth words: "We bagged it. It was beautiful up there. And we were almost down, and then the fucking rope broke. Last night, in the middle of the night."

There were tears in Arthur's eyes. In Chalmers', the dull look had a trace of pain. The others seemed almost sheepish. "I can't feel my toes," Victor said softly.

Chalmers spoke at last. "Let's get back to camp. We can go out later and look for the body."

Arthur's voice was charged with emotion. "Poor Ed. I knew we should have gone out looking. What an incredible thing you guys did. This will be famous."

3

Victor Koch and Ed Briles had met four years before, at the University of Minnesota, only three months after Victor had come to Minneapolis. The drive east with Vera had marked the first time Victor had crossed the border of his home state, Montana, and so the unsettling voyage had been for him full of the unknown. But what was known, certifiable, in his universe was that he could not live without her. If she had to go to graduate school, he would follow.

Asking her to marry him had been at first merely a means to an end; he was astonished that she had accepted.

They moved into a cramped apartment in student housing, surrounded by the wails of infants and the drone of TV soap operas through the walls. At the University Victor made a half-hearted start as a history major, getting just enough credits from Montana to put him in the sophomore class. He dropped out in late October to take a job painting the library. That ended in less than a month, with the first snows, and Victor found himself hanging around the apartment drinking beer, the unwatched TV on for "company." He fantasized about having a baby, not so much out of a desire for children as because he could think of nothing else that was supposed to happen after marriage. The boredom was like a quagmire. When Vera would come home from an evening class and choose a book about the Renaissance over going to bed early, he would sulk for hours. One day, exasperated, she said, "Look, Victor, you used to love sports and being outdoors. Why don't you join the outing club?"

He signed up for a beginning-level snowshoe hike. The day began with a four A.M. departure from the city. The talk in the car, all about stoves and bindings and numbers of miles accomplished on other hikes, profoundly depressed him. There were two women along, both homely, both incessant talkers. On the trail it took Victor a while to get the hang of the bowlegged waddle, but once he had, he could not believe how slowly the group moved, how the people pampered their bodies, stopping to make major surgical operations on incipient blisters, fussing like mothers over liquid intake.

By mid-afternoon Victor was half a mile ahead of everyone else. He stopped at a trail junction and waited for the leader to catch up. The man, a tall, beefy sort, admonished him between panting breaths: "Say, we'd appreciate it if you'd stick with the group. No chance of getting lost that way, right?"

"Sure."

"Great stuff, isn't it?"

Victor nodded so as not to offend the man. "Do you ever, you know, do anything different?"

"How do you mean different?"

"I mean do you just walk through the woods every time?"

The man laughed heartily. "Too tame for you? If you want some cheap thrills, we've got a sewering trip next Thursday night. Briles is leading it, and he's one crazy kid."

The first sight of Ed did not impress him. The sharp-featured face was the type Victor considered "Eastern," and the body looked thin and unmuscular. But as they sneaked into the basement of the Neo-Gothic church in St. Paul, Ed spoke with an air of unmistakable authority. "OK, if you get scared, don't lose it, just talk to me. It's not really sewers, it's steam tunnels. Let's see if we can hit the garage near Macalester. I almost worked it out last time."

Hours later, completely disoriented, Victor was astounded to hear Ed say, "We're near Summit and Fairview right now."

"How do you know?" he asked.

"You sort of keep making a map in your head. It takes practice."

Later the group went out for pizza. Victor managed to sit next to Ed. After two beers he got up the nerve to say, "That was fun. Do you ever go caving?"

"We've done spring-break trips to southern Ohio. It's not all that great unless you're really into it. Muddy and wet." He tore off a wedge of pizza and gave Victor an appraising look. "If you liked this, you ought to try climbing."

Thus the long relationship was born. On his first day at Taylor's Falls, Victor displayed the aptitude that had made all sports easy for him. Thirty feet off the ground, he felt the playground blend of fear and exhilaration that had coursed through his veins in grade school every time he prepared to do his famous front flip off the top of the jungle gym. Driving back from their third outing, the car jammed with beginners, Ed said quietly, "See? I told you."

"What?"

"That you'd be a natural. Shit, there's dubs here that in three years haven't gotten to where you're at."

Victor flushed with embarrassed pride.

"You use your arms too much," Ed went on. "And you're too impatient. Sometimes you don't stop and really look at the moves, and so you get hung up. But it'll come."

On the weekend trips to Devil's Lake Victor encountered the first playground gang whose inner circle he could not crack. Ed, by virtue of some gutsy leads, had worked his way to the fringe of it. But the politics of the elite were defined by the late-afternoon adjournment to Mr. Siffler's house, the ramshackle farm building nearby that the old man—who had taken up climbing at 45 and who now, at 53, was still soloing 5.7's, despite his recent shoulder dislocation—had bought and renovated. As he stood with Ed, contaminated by the outing clubbers they had imported with them, watching the heroes tromp off to the ritual "beer at Mr. Siffler's," Victor burned with a passion to belong.

One night he brought Ed home for dinner. Afterwards, snuggled up beside Vera on the sofa, he asked, "Well? What did you think?"

"He's good-looking, I'll have to admit."

"I didn't mean that," Victor said, both vexed and pleased. "Isn't he an interesting guy?"

"It was a strange evening."

"Why?" Victor moved a few inches away.

"I've never heard anybody talk so . . . so compulsively about something. Even you. All we talked about all evening was climbing."

"It's not just climbing, Vee. It's people and getting up your nerve and stuff like that."

Vera yawned. "He's so critical."

"You're not seeing him right." Victor brooded. "It's just that Ed's the kind of guy who doesn't take any shit."

"What I do like is how much happier you seem. You're even drinking less."

The next day, at lunch with Ed, he fished for the reverse appraisal. It seemed important to Victor that the two of them—his wife and, yes, his best friend—like each other.

"She seems like a good lady," Ed offered. "Damn good cook, too. She doesn't seem like the type who'll give you any crap about going climbing."

"No," said Victor, disappointed. "She's too busy."

"You should see Westerveldt. He has to call home collect the minute he's survived another weekend. Most good climbers aren't married. Or even really involved, as far as I can tell." Ed smiled quickly. "Look at me. How did you two meet, anyway?"

Victor launched into a half-hearted account of his past in Missoula, of meeting Vera at a dance, of how different she had seemed from the other women he had had, of her efforts to turn him into a plausible student, of following her career to Minnesota.

"She's older than you, then," Ed said. Victor nodded. Though he seldom did so, now he allowed his thoughts to wander back to the past, even before Vera, while perfunctorily answering Ed's questions. Up to a certain age—as late as the eleventh grade, he realized—girls had meant nothing to him compared to sports. It was sports he had lived for, because he was good, yes, but mainly because of his mother's mysterious prohibition, when he was only seven, of all rough and boisterous fun. The five years he had disobeyed her had given him, he sensed now, his first firm knowledge of how things worked in the world. His skill at sports depended on the charm of secrecy.

Then, when he was twelve, his mother had finally explained the prohibition, had told him about the single working kidney he had been born with, and that if he ever suffered a sharp blow on the wrong part of the back, he might die. "Why did you wait so long to tell me?" he had asked; his mother could not explain. From that moment Victor had learned two other basic facts about himself. The kidney was a thing to be ashamed of: his mother was ashamed of it. Like the surreptitious sports, it was a secret that had to be kept. Because it was clear that what he thought of as his "luck" was somehow only a congenital charm that made him different from others. It explained his skill at sports.

Now, with Ed praising his climbing, he felt a confessional urge. He wanted to share the secret with Ed; it would forge a bond between him and this new friend he admired so much. But the older superstition—that to tell anyone about the kidney would be to dispel the charm of his luck—prevailed.

His mind continued to roam back over the past, while Ed rambled on with outing club gossip. His mother had explained the medical situation to the junior high tennis coach, and Victor had gone out for the team, though without much enthusiasm. But he lived for the illicit weekend games in the park, time she thought he was spending with friends listening to records or watching TV. Brutal games of tackle football on the dead, patchy grass, baseball on the makeshift diamond with the rock-hard infield, netless-hooped basketball on asphalt courts. Five more years of success that depended on secrecy—until, in the eleventh grade, his tennis coach, hearing from another student about one of Victor's spectacular diving catches in the outfield, had rechecked his medical records and, without even informing him, had phoned his mother.

Victor had taken up women as if they were an alternative sport. With his souped-up '49 Chevy, a pint of rum in the glove compartment, in the piney pullouts off the logging roads south of town, he found it easy to maneuver his dates into the back seat, to persuade them to do the things they weren't sure they should. It was his good looks, he thought, his football build, and the cocky air that went with them. But more than that, it was the plain fact that he had no fear of rejection.

Yet the sex itself, undeniably "fun," had been less important to him than the looks of envy on his friends' faces the next day in school. It occurred to him now, as he watched Ed talk, how to explain what he had felt then: that in fucking there was no 5.9. When the occasional girl told him that she loved him, his impulse was to say "Thank you"; he had no idea what she really meant by the trite formula.

He had quit high school and moved out of his mother's house, ignoring her pleas, to seek the clean freedom he had felt only in the gliding flight after a potential triple in center field, the tackle-shrugging run down the sidelines. Because there seemed more challenge in it, he had started hanging around the University, preying upon college women instead of the too-easy game his own age. It helped, he found, to eavesdrop in the student union, picking up the kind of small talk that allowed him to pass for a collegian. Within weeks he had perfected the disguise of a sophomore economics major. It bewildered him that no one saw through his web of lies. With a bed in an apartment—in lieu of the back seat of his car—he found as many college women succumbing to him as had high-school girls.

Then he had met Vera at the dance, and when, after midnight, sitting on his sofa, she had pushed him away, laughing, "But Victor, I don't even know you yet," he had felt for the first time in his life the sting of rejection. He drove her back to campus in a tire-squealing rage. A few days later he had run into her again. She had said, "Let's go out again, Victor. You fascinate me."

By the fourth date, with her teasing intelligence, she had unraveled his recent imposture. She had had the look in her eyes of knowing so surely, that all his indignant fabrications had collapsed in a single spasm of confession. With his head in his hands, he said miserably, "How can you even stand to be around me now?"

She took his hand and held it. "Look, Victor, it's part of why you interest me. You have this intensity, and I know you're smart, and you have a funny kind of talent. Winning all those games and dares in grade school. Look at me." Shyly Victor raised his head. "So you've squandered the talent playing this silly game of pretend. But you could be something really good. An actor, maybe." Victor shook his head. The talent was not really his; it was the old congenital thing, the kidney. "You'll never know," she continued, "unless you go back to school."

Over the next weeks, with a sense of dread, of watching a bank on which he was standing erode away as the stream cut beneath it, Victor discovered what the business about love meant. The urge for other women vanished. Meekly he underwent Vera's campaign of rehabilitation, acquiring through correspondence courses the high school diploma, starting his laborious voyage as a history major. When Vera got accepted at Minnesota, he knew that he had to hang on to her, and the only way he could think of was to ask her to marry him.

Now, in the warmth of his new friendship, he had a yearning to tell Ed all of this, even the secret life that up till now only Vera had penetrated. But an old caution put a finger to his lips. Drinking his third cup of coffee, he gave Ed only a skeletal version of that past, and indeed, Ed seemed interested in no more.

That summer the two of them spent three weeks in the Needles of South Dakota. By the following September they were climbing as well as all but a handful of the elite at Devil's Lake. One day it happened. Digby, who had put up "Avenger," and whose "Limelight" was still unrepeated, turned that Saturday afternoon to Ed and Victor and said casually, "Why don't you guys pick up a couple of six-packs and come on over to Mr. Siffler's?"

The talk in the old farmhouse, for hours as the golden sunlight streaming through the windows dulled into dusk, rang in Victor's ears like ethereal music. Digby and Axelrod traded stories about rusty piton-eyes breaking off. Axelrod showed everybody how to reach for the hidden hold on "Isotope." McCarter bemoaned his difficulties getting the right party together for an expedition to Mount Foraker. Mr. Siffler took off his shirt and showed everyone his shoulder-operation scar.

Back at the University, the club held a special meeting to condemn Ed for his irresponsibility in leaving the beginners to fend for themselves all weekend. Ed listened for a while, then stood up and said, "Fuck you all. Get somebody else to lead the chubbers. I quit." Victor jumped up and added, "Me, too." Outside, they headed straight for the pizza place where, laughing and whooping, they drank themselves into joyous incoherence.

The next July they drove out to the Canadian Rockies. Ed had climbed briefly in Colorado and the Wind Rivers; for Victor it was his first trip to real mountains. They started with guidebook routes around Lake Louise and found them remarkably easy. In a tavern in Banff they managed to join a table of aspirants circled in rapt attention around Jimmy Bryan, the emigré Welshman who had become the arbiter of standards in the Rockies. During a lull, Ed found the nerve to ask, "What about that face on Hungabee? The one you see from Temple?"

Bryan squinted sharply through the cigarette smoke. "It's totally daft. Loose as the bejeesus. It's a splendid-looking thing, but some lads from Edmonton went up on it and came back all whimpering and sniveling." The man paused, scrutinizing Ed. "You blokes wouldn't be from California?"

They were five days on the route. On the fourth, in marginal weather, a helicopter flew by. Ed and Victor waved; it was only later that they learned that the chopper had been searching for them, that the pilot had never spotted them, that they were subsequently given up for dead. That same day Victor pulled loose a block, fell twenty feet, and landed on his back. He got up and continued the lead, but the pain in his back was in exactly the wrong spot, the place he had been warned about. He pushed grimly through the rest of the day, as the clouds closed back over them, up to the horrible standing bivouac. He was thinking to himself, at last it's run out, all the luck. He decided that, as soon as the crippling pain started, no, as soon as the blood showed up in his urine, he would tell Ed the secret that he had shared with no one since his mother's death, and then insist that his friend try to solo on to save himself. He wondered how bad it was going to be to die that way.

All through the sleepless, dreadfully cold first half of the night he reviewed his childhood. The last clear memory of his father was of the beating that had led to the discovery, the blood for days in his urine, the doctor coming to talk to his mother, her tears and her hysterical screaming at his drunken father, just before he had left for good. Victor had linked the doctor with his father's disappearance; in adulthood he had never visited a doctor. The blood in his urine was logical—when you were hurt there was usually blood, and his father hurt him regularly. The misery of his early years had left him with no particular fear of dying, any more than he would later fear rejection from a woman.

But in the middle of the night, when he had to urinate, the flow was clear, without a trace of blood. At last the dawn came. He climbed in a stupor all day, his back stiff as an old man's; Ed took the hardest leads until, in total blizzard, they stood on the summit. The descent took another day and a half, during which they nearly got swept off a rappel by an avalanche. The weather cleared in the middle of the last night, and by noon the next day they were giggling and napping among the wildflowers in the impossibly green meadows.

In Banff, Bryan was speechless but magnanimous. He invited them up to Robson, but Victor and Ed were flat broke. They cadged contributions from hitchhikers and barely made it back to Minneapolis.

From Hungabee came a sense of shared destiny, bodied forth in plans for a dozen summers, in the private allusions to Terray and Lachenal. But the next June, Ed, who was graduating, was offered a job teaching math at the Hopkins School on the condition that he catch up with some education courses over the summer. Victor, deeply disappointed, accepted McCarter's invitation to the Foraker expedition the man had finally put together.

Everything went wrong. A scared pilot landed the men thirty miles from the base of their route. Then he airdropped from 150 feet; losses amounted to forty percent. To Victor's immense impatience, McCarter insisted on a tedious fixing of ropes on low-angled snowslopes. By the time they had run out of food the party had reached their so-called "Camp V" at only 10,500 feet.

Victor met Vera at the Fairbanks airport. The three-week Brooks Range idyll he had planned went sour. The drab loneliness along the upper Nigu plunged him into an acute depression, while it terrified Vera. She resisted his efforts to clump off toward the unclimbed peaks, seeing no particular virtue in being *there* rather than *here*. She took a gardener's pleasure in the cinquefoil and fireweed and Arctic cotton, and spent hours gathering blueberries. Around the willow-twig campfires she would say, "Let's really talk, Victor. About us. Something's changed." But Victor's mind was on the Foraker fiasco. He missed Ed. It was during these weeks that he began, in the core of himself, to link the hunch of his lifelong luckiness with the presence of his friend; without Ed, the charm was broken. Back in Minneapolis Vera seemed to fade once more into her history books. Ed and Victor spent a restorative weekend at Devil's Lake and pledged the next summer to each other.

In February Victor gave Ed a call. "The outing club's lined up a slide show. Rex Chalmers."

"On Pterophorus?" Ed asked.

"Yes."

"I'll be there. Think they'll let us inside the club room?"

Chalmers lived up to his reputation as a poor speaker. He also came across, it seemed to Victor, as cold and arrogant. He freely admitted that he was touring the country just to raise the cash to pay off his helicopter debt from the previous summer. In a bored tone he ticked off the mountain's history, from its "discovery" by Blakey in 1959, the tracing down of the name to the miner's manuscript map, through the famous photo published in *Piton*, to the first expedition composed of Blakey protégés which, unable to cross Tired Pup Creek, never even saw the mountain. Despite the jaded narration, Ed and Victor sat breathless before the aerial views that flashed on the screen: the legendary upper plug of the mountain, like Devil's Tower in Wyoming but for the ice encrustations, looked as difficult as Blakey had prophesied. A little warmth crept into Chalmers' voice as he described his 1962 expedition, which had gotten nine hundred feet off the glacier on the southeast face; but it was mixed with obvious contempt for the weaknesses of his teammates.

It was then, Chalmers went on, that the mountain really acquired its status as a prize. When John Richards paired up with the Scot Ian McDougall, everyone guessed that the mountain had met its match; it seemed inconceivable that the pioneering Yosemite wall climber and the man reputed to be the best in the world on ice could fail. With gruff humor Chalmers recounted his bumping into Richards in a supermarket in Anchorage, where the Californian pumped him for information, his own sneaking over to Merrill Field where he called Talkeetna to cancel the pilot and immediately engaged a helicopter. It was Chalmers' hunch that a series of ramps, avoiding the prominent boiler plates, might afford a better route on the north face than the bottoming cracks of the southeast side. Camp was a gloomy, sunless niche on a strange, stagnant glacial tributary, actually depressed in altitude below the main ice stream it had once flowed into. By the end of July Chalmers and Arthur Bowen had reached a point 1500 feet up. The rest of the party, the man implied witheringly, were worthless. It was clear that he had spent the month animated by the fear of success on the opposite side of the mountain, and there was no concealing his glee when he mentioned that Richards and McDougall had turned back a pitch below Chalmers' own high point of the year before, or when he repeated the rumor (which Ed and Victor had already heard) that McDougall had been psyched out from the beginning.

Victor and Ed joined the gaggle of admirers after the show. Chalmers yawned ostentatiously, his eyes seldom fixed on his interrogator, as he answered questions. Victor's own pride kept him silent, but he heard Ed saying, "Do you plan to go back?"

"Yeah. Maybe." Chalmers cracked his knuckles.

"The north face again?"

"Probably. Not in July, though. Too icy still."

"With the same group?"

Chalmers allowed himself a thin smile. "Hell, no. Bunch of turkeys. Except Bowen, he's all right."

Victor was surprised, even embarrassed, that Ed kept playing the sycophant. But now Ed said, "That rime ice looked really shitty. We ran into the same-looking stuff on Hungabee."

Chalmers' eyes instantly focused. "You were on Hungabee? That face?"

Ed nodded. "With Victor here."

Chalmers picked up his slide trays, and in a way that clearly dismissed the others in the room said, "Let's go out and get a beer."

By the end of the evening Ed and Victor were part of the expedition. All spring they rockclimbed obsessively, so that by May they were putting in routes at Devil's Lake on a level with Digby's and Axelrod's best. A weekly correspondence with Chalmers in Denver kept them abreast of the filling out of the team; Bowen would go again, as well as some good young climbers from Salt Lake City. But there were clouds on the horizon. At least two other expeditions were headed for Pterophorus, one a group of relative unknowns from Oregon, the other led by Richards, who had talked some Yosemite Valley cronies into joining him. They were both slotted for early July, both for the southeast face. Chalmers considered jumping the gun on them again, but at last decided August was the only month for the north wall. He was going to head up to Anchorage in mid-July to handle the logistics himself.

Victor and Ed spent an anxious, newsless early summer, climbing every day and spending most of their free time together. It seemed to Victor that Vera had almost ceased to be a part of his life, or to be no more than the familiar warmth beside him in bed each night. Yet he had never been happier, except for the gnawing of anticipation.

At last, on July 25, the letter from Chalmers came:

They're out. Both parties. What stories they have. Richards has had enough, he says, never wants to go back. *Neither of them got more than 1500 feet up.* The Oregon party was established at base camp (our '62 camp) three days before Richards arrived. They had even fixed a few pitches. Get this. Richards ordered them off "his" route! And the poor buggers obeyed him.

So the Oregon party tried a hopeless line around to the left, sort of the southwest buttress. Got 1000 feet up, but quit when one guy (I think his name was Gervin, or Garman, or something—nobody famous) fucked up a rappel and bought the farm.

Meanwhile Richards, Cowell, and the young hot-shot Rich Bakamjian went for it on the southeast face. You know how Cowell wrote up in his big-deal *AAJ* article how he'd never wear a hard hat? Well, on the first day he got plunked on the shoulder, so he borrowed Bakamjian's helmet and never took it off, day or night. They managed to get five pitches beyond our '62 high point, and then they said the rock got really terrible. Cowell kept saying, "I don't like this, I don't like it at all." Finally they bagged it and came down. Bakamjian had not said a word the whole time. They get off the last rappel and Cowell takes a deep breath and says, "We're lucky to get off this thing alive." Bakamjian says, "You guys are chickenshit," and walks off!

So you two get on up here pronto. We've got a mountain to climb.

4

Victor sprawled on the ice-bench that served as seating inside the igloo. Arthur was working at the clumps of ice on his gaiters, while one of the others had a stove going. "There must be something else to drink," Victor said. Chalmers picked up a water bottle with his good hand and shook it; a piece of ice rattled inside.

It was warm in the igloo, deliciously so. Not even on the descent from Hungabee had Victor felt so utterly exhausted. A few minutes before, Chalmers had asked for details about the climb, but Arthur, in his fussy, maternal way, had said, "Later. Let's just get the man warm and comfortable, and look at his feet."

Victor was grateful now for the chance to remain silent; for, stabbing its way through the fog of his tiredness, a wholly novel sense of alarm was spreading its branches. What have I gone and done? he thought. It's still not too late to change everything; I could pretend I misunderstood Arthur's question. But it was like hesitating to jump onto a train that was pulling out of the station; with each second the gap grew larger. His thoughts turned instead to a more practical realm: what would he have to seem to know, when he did tell the whole story? His mind felt fuzzy, as if he were slightly drunk.

A voice came from the door of the igloo: "Guess what? Snowing again."

"Shit," Chalmers said. "This place . . . ."

"How's your wrist?" Victor asked. He had an instinct that it was Chalmers, if anyone, who could do him harm. Only Chalmers had seemed disappointed by the news of their success. "Do you think it's broken?"

"I'm pretty sure," the man said, averting his eyes. "I tried shoveling with it the other day, and it really swelled up."

Victor thought: it's not broken, you ass, you washed-up crump, it's just a convenient excuse to keep you out of action. Out loud he said, "We just missed getting hit by some big chunks of ice up high. Just like the stuff that got you." Chalmers nodded.

At last Arthur had removed the boots. He was holding Victor's bare feet in his hands. Victor watched himself wiggle his toes; there was still no feeling in them. "Well?" he asked Arthur.

"There's some frostbite, I'd guess. I don't think it's too bad. You should stay off your feet for a few days. And get lots of liquid." Arthur unbuttoned his own down jacket and pulled his sweater up, then placed Victor's feet against his stomach. "See if this helps," he said, shivering involuntarily.

"You don't have to do that," Victor said.

"Be quiet."

In the middle of the operation the nerve endings in his toes sprang all at once out of their slumber. The pain was sharp. Victor twisted on his ensolite seat, moaning. "Rex," Arthur said, "get the codeine, will you?" Chalmers sullenly left the igloo and returned moments later with the medical kit. "That's a good sign, that pain," Arthur fussed. "Here. Take one now and one later."

Within minutes the codeine spread its dull euphoria through Victor's bloodstream. Arthur kept forcing hot fluids on him, but the pain of swallowing made him reluctant to drink. Chalmers fidgeted morosely on an opposite bench. At last he said,"I suppose we should go look for the body before this snow covers everything."

"Can I get you anything else?" Arthur asked.

"I just want to sleep."

"I'll put you in my tent. Pete can move into the blue one."

The blue one, Victor thought, with a numbed sense of irony. Not "Ed's tent," any more, but, superstitiously, "the blue one." For the same reason, no doubt, Arthur was oversensitively trying to relocate him. "I'll stay where I was," Victor said.

"You sure? You probably should have somebody with you to look after—"

"I'm OK. I just want to sleep. Thanks, Arthur."

At last in his sleeping bag, Victor wrapped himself in the warmth and horizontal comfort that he had been denied for so many days. His mind was blurry with codeine and fatigue. He heard the clanking of metal things as the others got packs together to go search for Ed's body. On the tent roof there was a steady ping of snowflakes. He was half into sleep when Arthur opened the sleeve door.

"I'd be glad to stay with you," he offered. "I'm not sure you should be alone."

"I'm all right." Victor laughed softly. "What could happen to me here?"

Chalmers' head poked into view. "You say it happened on the third pitch below the bivvy tent?"

"Third or fourth. I can't remember."

"It could make a difference." The characteristic irritation was in Chalmers' voice. "We've got to figure out the fall line by sighting where the accident happened. Try to—"

"Leave the man alone, Rex," Arthur ordered. "Can't you see he's wiped out?"

Chalmers walked off. Arthur lingered for a moment. "It's been hell down here," he said conspiratorially. "I know one fellow I'll never rope up with again, not if you paid me." The genial face smiled ruefully.

"It's snowing like a mother, isn't it?"

"Yes, damn it. What a gloomy spot this is. See you in a few hours. Victor?"

"Hmm?"

"Suppose we do find Ed." There was a pause. "What should we do with him?"

"Throw him in a crevasse," Victor said groggily. He meant to add something about that being what Ed would have wanted, but it came out: "That's what I'd like, if it happened to me."

At last he was alone. Sleep lapped at him like waves on a beach, but he could not get all the way under. The snowflakes pinged and slid on the blue nylon above his head. What have I done? he asked himself. The alarm was running through his veins. He thought for a long while about how he could back out of it. There had been no conversation about the summit since that first meeting. Except that Arthur had twice repeated his remark about how famous the ascent would become, and Victor had not mustered the effort to contradict him.

He rolled over and tried to sleep. His toes tingled with a dull pain. All the muscles in his body were sore, and his head felt the way it did when he was coming down with a fever. All at once it became obvious that he had only one choice. It would be manageable after all. A matter of consistency and plausibility, no more than that. It would be like the months on the Montana campus, convincing everyone—almost everyone—that he was a sophomore economics major. Because at the heart of his lie, thanks to Ed's death, was the safe secret privacy of it: no one else had been there. They might ask if he had left anything on the summit. Of course not, just as they hadn't on Hungabee.

He began to compose the details of his story. The first day above the bivvy tent—he could get the dates straight later—they had indeed climbed 1500 feet and bivouacked on the two-foot ledge. The next day, after the storm had begun, instead of resting on the ledge, they had pushed on to the summit. The climbing had begun with Ed's brilliant lead, stemming and bridging up the vertical, ice-filled chimney. Above that, clear sailing to the summit. Only a few minutes on top, because of the storm. Then back down.

Back all the way to the two-foot ledge? No, that would be implausible. Back half the way; an uncomfortable bivouac in a wedge segmented out of a steep snowslope some 500 feet below the summit. A bad night, then an early start; a long day down past the two-foot ledge, picking up the rest of their gear, down to the standing two-piton bivouac. The one that had really happened. The rest was real also. It would be simple.

Just before sleep he sensed that his secret would be like a criminal's—with him every day of his life, a homunculus buried within his flesh, threatening to be born.

When he awoke it was still snowing. He was not sure whether it was the same day or the next. He sat up; the stiffness all through his body convinced him that he had been unconscious for a long time. He listened and heard the faint mumble of voices inside the igloo, twenty feet away. The dryness in his throat felt like cotton stuffed inside his mouth. Stretching, he looked around the tent. Next to his own sleeping bag lay Ed's greasy old Bauer, just as he had left it the morning they had gone up on the mountain. For the first time the truth of Ed's disappearance fully came home to him, sending a constriction all through his neck and shoulders. The business of the summit was not so important after all. Arthur was exaggerating; not many people outside their own expedition would care all that much whether a certain mountain had been climbed or not. But without Ed there would be no more afternoons at Mr. Siffler's, no silent drives through the night toward the Rockies, no more of Louis and Lionel. And no sedentary later years, as he had unconsciously promised himself was their due, to sip their beers and reminisce about the exploits of youth.

He dressed slowly, grief making the motions laborious and formal. His feet protested as he forced them into his half-frozen boots. Outside, he noticed that a lot of new snow had accumulated. He shivered as a gust of cold wind caught him. Looking up, he could barely discern the outlines of the mountain in the storm.

As he entered the tunnel door of the igloo, a voice inside broke off. He crawled in and stood up; they were all staring at him. Arthur rose to offer him his seat on the ice bench. "Morning," he said heartily. "Did you get some sleep?"

"I must have," Victor said, testing his voice like a long-unplayed instrument, "if it's morning." He smiled. The faces were watching him intently. He took Arthur's seat. "Do you have anything to drink?"

"Sure," said Arthur. "There's Wyler's in the bottle, and we're just brewing up another pot of tea. It's good you slept so long. You needed it."

"Did you find—?"

"No," Chalmers said with disgust. "It's hopeless in this white-out. We couldn't orient on the mountain at all. And I'm afraid the goddamn snow has already covered everything."

"Maybe it doesn't matter. I don't believe in afterlife, and I don't think Ed did."

Arthur went on, "We're going to have another look when the snow stops. And Pete and I'll go up and get the bivvy tent."

"Be careful when you do." Victor was surprised at himself; he had never been one to worry about others' safety.

Almost shyly, Chalmers asked, "Do you feel like telling us about the climb?"

"As soon as I get some tea." He thought: Well, this is it. Whatever I say this time has to become the truth. Someone handed him a cup of tea. He took a sip and looked up. The staring faces gave him a jolt; they had the look of *knowing*. There did not seem to be enough air in the igloo; perhaps the stove? He took a deep breath and spoke. "The first day, whatever it was—"

"The fifteenth," Chalmers said.

"I guess so. We got up to the bivvy tent." It seemed to Victor that his voice was quavering. He forced on. "We spent the night there. The next day was real long. We did all this zigzagging and traversing right. Ed kept track of the route. He figured out we gained 1500 feet. We stopped that night on a good ledge, right below this vertical ice chimney. We were really excited, knowing we were only a thousand feet below the top."

"That's the night the storm began," said Chalmers.

"Right. It wasn't too bad at first." He was talking too fast. He stopped and took a gulp of tea, scalding his tongue. The faces watched and judged. He avoided looking at Chalmers. "It was hard getting off in the morning, getting everything packed.We flipped for the lead, and Ed got it. It was the most amazing lead I've ever seen. This fucking chimney really was about vertical. Ed started up it, stemming and bridging, getting a couple of lousy Marwas in for protection, but staying off the ice itself. He could do this amazing kind of stemming, he was so loose and wiry. I don't know if any of you ever saw him—" Suddenly he was sobbing. His voice broke into high-pitched wails, and his eyes flooded with tears. He hid his face in his hands.

Arthur put his arm around Victor's shoulders. "It's all right," he said. "Go ahead, get it out."

Victor leaned against the other man's shoulder and wept. The treble voice he heard did not seem to be his own. After a minute or two he rubbed his eyes and peeked through his fingers, still sniffling. The others looked subdued, embarrassed, no longer distrustful. Chalmers was staring at the wet floor of the igloo. Victor closed his eyes and gave himself up to a new gust of sobbing. Arthur held him, murmuring, "It's OK, it's all right," rocking him slightly. At the hermetic core of his grief Victor recognized a curious liberation: he could cry as much for himself as for Ed, and no one else could tell the difference.

5

Arthur was right after all. The news spread quickly through the climbing grapevine, and the October issue of *Piton* used tabloid-style headlines: "Pterophorus climbed! Briles lost on descent, after summit dash with Koch." In the same month came requests for articles from *Alpinismus* and *Mountain*, and a few weeks later a telegram from John Richards: "Want you for featured speaker American Alpine Club Banquet Denver Dec. 4. Will cover air fare."

At the climbing store Victor found himself treated, even by his friends, with the careful awe normally reserved for celebrities. Digby called to offer congratulations and sympathy, and to invite him out to Devil's Lake. Victor made excuses. Climbing was not something he wanted to be doing right now.

Vera alone seemed unimpressed with the ascent. He had called her first thing from Talkeetna, only to have her burst into tears at the news of Ed's death. Although he thought it rightfully his own job, he accepted her offer to inform Ed's parents. Since then, Mr. Briles had adopted the practice of exchanging letters with Vera, not Victor, even though he had spent a whole Sunday composing a note of condolence.

One day in October Vera said, "You're the one who really should be answering these, you know."

"I'm no good at writing," Victor said. "I can't express myself on paper. I'm having a hard enough time writing this article for *Alpinismus*." He snickered. "Even though they're just going to translate it into German." He went to the refrigerator and got a beer. "Want one?"

Vera was in a bad mood. "You take it all so lightly."

"What? Their letters? Look, I only met them once."

"But they really exist, Victor. Listen. 'I don't know why they'—by 'they' I suppose he means climbers—'I don't know why they keep talking about this great achievement. All me and my wife know is that our son is gone.' What can I say to that, when I agree completely with him?"

"Say that it mattered to Ed." Victor took a long drink of beer.

"Why don't you say it, dear? At least add a note to mine."

"I've got to finish this article."

The look on Vera's face was one of exasperation. "All right, what should I say to this? 'We also want to know if there is still any chance of finding our son's body. It would mean a lot to me and my wife to see him at least have a decent burial.' "

"Tell him we looked for days. The blizzards covered everything."

"What about next summer?"

"By then he'll be down in the ice. As good a burial as you could want."

As December approached, Victor grew anxious about the Denver slide show. Arthur had sent him duplicates of all his best slides; but none of them covered terrain above the bivvy tent. The camera had been lost with Ed, which, Victor reflected, was a kind of blessing. But what would he show on the screen during all the climactic, crucial part of the telling? He had never in his life given a slide show.

Yet during these months the homunculus inside him seemed to settle into the dormancy of a dead organ, like his unused kidney. His luck had followed him beyond the obliteration of Ed.

One night in November he lay in bed beside Vera, sleepless as so often in recent weeks. "What's the matter, Victor?" she said at last.

"Nothing. Just this insomnia."

She put a hand on his chest. "It's something about us, isn't it? I feel it, anyway."

Victor had always feared her sensitivity. Now he countered, "We hardly ever make love any more."

"I know, dear. I'm sorry. When I work this hard, I get sort of asexual."

Victor turned over, his back to her. She hesitated, then put her arms around him. "I'm scared we're growing apart. It's been different ever since the climbing started."

"Or since graduate school."

"Both. But this fall you seem so unhappy. I know you're really upset about Ed. I can feel how you miss him. You walk around the apartment all restless, the way you did that first year here. Last spring you'd have called Ed and gone bouldering on the bridges or something. But now it's all locked up inside you. You're like a little kid who can't show his feelings because he has to be brave."

"I'm all right."

"Another thing. I'm worried about your drinking."

"Leave me alone." Her probing threatened him: a single needle might find the homunculus. "I'm handling it."

"But it's way up from before. Not just beer any more. How often do you go through one of those fifths of bourbon?"

"I don't keep track." But Vera had stirred up his old needful love for her. He *was* unhappy. He turned toward her, saying. "Come to Denver with me."

"Oh, hell, you know I can't. It's right before my orals."

"But it's my big moment."

"I'm sorry. Maybe next summer we can do something, when all this craziness is over."

The AAC meeting was held in a posh downtown hotel. Lonely and nervous, feeling underdressed in his borrowed tweed jacket with the elbow patches, Victor wandered along the fake Gold Rush corridors from registration to business meeting to lunch. There was no one there that he knew. The afternoon slide shows intimidated him with their smooth deliveries and stunning photos. At the cocktail party, along with everyone else, he put on a name tag. Now total strangers came up to him, peered at the tag, and immediately acted like friends; but the allusions to his climb were oblique: "I'm really looking forward to your show tonight." Victor's anxiety mounted, and almost without noticing he had drunk three strong bourbons. He was surprised not to have run into Chalmers.

Now a face familiar from photographs was approaching him. It was John Richards, trailed by a retinue of younger athletes. There was an open smile on the uncomplicated face as Richards offered a hand. "Congratulations, old man. Bitch of a climb. Sorry about your buddy, too." The onlookers stared enviously as Richards steered Victor toward the bar. "I'm supposed to introduce you. We have to sit up at the head table with the old farts. After the circus is over a bunch of us are going to hit Larimer Street. Come on out with us. I want to talk to you about something." Victor nodded numbly.

He could eat only a few bites of the rubbery banquet chicken. Richards had obtained a bottle of wine, and kept filling Victor's glass. As each after-dinner honoree—men in their fifties and sixties—got up to utter a few words, Richards gave Victor a thumbnail sketch. "This guy really is an old fart. So he raised a few bucks for the Research Fund. Big deal." Or, "This guy deserves it. We climbed his route on Keeler Needle, and it's still bitchin' hard." As his own time drew near, Victor realized that he was fairly drunk. The alcohol had calmed him somewhat, but now he was scared that he would slur his words. The carefully prepared summit dash was a scramble of details in his mind.

Richards had left. From a great distance he heard Pterophorus being described as "the toughest climb yet done in Alaska," heard himself being characterized and introduced. The applause prodded him toward the lectern. Victor fiddled with the microphone, coughed, and heard the explosion rattle through the huge hot room. He looked up. Hundreds of faces were fixed expectantly on his. There came a surge of pure panic. He opened his mouth and nothing came out. Finally a nervous whinny escaped, multiplied again through the room. He managed to blurt, "I've never done this kind of thing before." Currents of laughter lapped in the darkness, but he heard an edginess in them. "Can we start the slides?" His 's's sounded drunken to him. I can't go through with this, he thought, feeling his chest covered with sweat. When I get to the summit, they'll know.

He looked at the screen, away from the faces. There was the mountain. Somehow his voice began making words; when he could think of nothing else to say, he would plead, "Next slide," and an invisible hand would change the view. Then, all too soon, he was stuck on Arthur's single photo of the mountain from the glacier. He apologized, "We don't have any pictures from above here, since Ed had the camera." There was total silence in the room. He kept his eyes away from the people and recited. His voice was going too fast, running away with him, leaving him no air to breathe. But he was up the vertical, ice-filled chimney, onto the easier ground above, remembering details he had never known before—the bite that morning of his crampons into the rime ice, the taste of a lemon candy, the view from the summit. The descent went quickly, and as he approached Ed's accident, despite the deepening silence in the room, Victor heard his voice gain assurance. In a flat monotone he announced the death, and was aware of the sound of breaths drawn sharply in. Then it was over. To his surprise, the applause was thunderous; people were pushing back their chairs and standing up. In the triumph of the moment, Victor felt an aching sorrow, that neither Ed nor Vera could be here to share it.

An hour later Richards was buying the rounds, saying, "To hell with the audio-visual aids. Just put a battered old sod up there in front of the mob and let him tell what it was like. Palm of your hand, old man." Later, his head fuzzy from Jack Daniel's, Victor was aware of Richards maneuvering him away from the group, into a corner where the country-western band could be shouted over. "Where?" Victor tried again.

"Kichatna Spires," Richards shouted. "Three-thousand, four-thousand-foot walls. Good granite. Nothing's been done yet, one party in there. What d'you say?"

Victor was smiling, drunk and happy. John Richards was asking him to go climbing. He heard himself say, "Sounds good." But beneath the flattered ebullience of the moment, he sensed a disturbance. He was not sure he wanted to go on another expedition next summer. It would be so hard to get in shape all over again, to get psyched up. And up high, above the gleaming glaciers, chopping the ice away, he might well feel, yes, *afraid*.

In February the issue of *Mountain* came out with his article in it. The climbing store gave Victor a party. Vera came to it, and though it was not the same as Denver might have been, when they got home that night Victor felt the old sense that their lives were interlocked for good, the snug closeness that he associated with Montana.

He started climbing again in April. The first afternoons at Taylor's Falls he was appalled at how clumsy and weak he felt on familiar climbs. The sedentary winter had put ten pounds on him; now he started running to trim down. The first time he climbed with Digby at Devil's Lake, he looked up at the forbidding line and said, "I'm in shitty shape. You'll have to drag me up it." Drag him up Digby did; but Victor hoped the man had not witnessed the thrashings of pure fear that drained all his energy on the lowest forty feet of the single pitch. Within days, however, his competence began to return.

Late in the month he got a call from Arthur. The man was out of breath. "How are you?"

"Fine," said Victor.

"No, I mean how are you handling it?"

"What?"

"That double-crossing skunk. I'm writing them a letter today. I can't believe it."

"Slow down, Arthur. What is it?"

"You haven't seen *Piton* yet? Oh, no wonder."

"For Christ's sake. What?" Victor sat down in a chair, suddenly weary.

"It's Chalmers. He says he doesn't believe you and Ed made it. He's going back."

Victor felt he had to speak. "That fucking bastard."

"Nobody will credit him, Victor. I'm writing them a letter today. They didn't even call you to tell you this was coming out?"

"I have to get hold of the magazine. I'll call you back."

"The May issue."

It took Victor a full day—a day of dread so strong he found himself gagging every few hours—to locate a copy. When he did, he tore open the pages. The title read, "Was Pterophorus Climbed After All?" Victor's eyes skimmed through Chalmers' pompous prefatory remarks and seized upon the "evidence":

The gist of my claim that Koch and Briles did not make the summit lies in the following facts:

1) Throughout the last days of the expedition, Koch was extremely vague about where the fatal accident happened.
2) His description of the last thousand feet—"clear sailing" above a certain chimney—simply does not jibe with all the known photos of the mountain.
3) The time scale seems wrong. I don't think there was enough time for them to do what Koch claims they did.
4) It is hard to believe that anyone could have climbed at all on the 16th and 17th. At base camp we had difficulty even fighting through the storms to get to the base of the route.
5) At the Denver AAC show, Koch talked about the view from the summit. He told us they reached the summit in total white-out.
6) The thing that first aroused my suspicion was what Koch said the moment we met him, as he came off the mountain. First he said, in a sort of disappointed voice, "We had it." Then moments later he said, "We bagged it." I think the first remark was the spontaneous one, the true admission of defeat. I expected to hear, "We had it, and then the storms ruined our chances," or some such statement. But for some reason, Koch decided right then to claim the ascent.

The case seems strong and clear. I consider Pterophorus unclimbed and will be leading an expedition to the mountain this summer.

Victor's anger peaked in a spasm of pure rage. As it had on the descent, the image of attacking Chalmers with an ice axe flashed before his eyes. But in the same instant he began to check himself for wounds. How serious was the "evidence"? Could he stuff the burgeoning homunculus back into its hiding place? So the bastard had been in Denver after all, lurking in the corners, hoping to pick up some silly little slip. The summit view had been careless, but he could cover it: a momentary break in the cloud cover. The vaguenesses about route meant little: he had always been poor at routefinding; Ed took care of that end of things. The time and the weather proved nothing. But what about that remark of his? Had he said, "We had it"? Victor could not remember.

He tried to call Vera at the library, but could not locate her. As he walked back to the apartment, he forced himself to govern his rage and plan the dignified response. There was a note for him from Vera. "Call Ron Winston at the *Mountain Journal* collect. Urgent." Two numbers, business and home. So it was news everywhere. The thought of talking to Winston, the self-styled arbiter of American mountaineering, filled Victor with fresh terror. But as he sat there, staring at the note, it became clear that not to respond was to indicate weakness. He drank a large tumbler of whiskey very quickly and called the home number. Arthur, after all, had believed him, never doubted for a moment.

Winston was friendly, reassuring, talkative. He would be coming through Chicago in a week, on a trip West to gather material for a big summer issue. Could he meet Victor there for an interview? It would be the best way, Winston suggested, to clear his name once and for all, to relegate Chalmers to the oblivion he deserved.

By the time Vera got home Victor was dead drunk; but the call to Winston had given him new self-confidence. She read through the article in *Piton* with a frown on her face. "What an unpleasant fellow," she said. "But you can easily prove he's wrong, can't you?"

"Of course." Victor told her about the interview next week.

The frown was still on Vera's face. "So it's really just his word against yours?"

"So what? I was there. He wasn't. It's as simple as that. Let's go to bed." In the middle of the night Victor woke. He was shivering, covered with sweat; his arms were tight around Vera, the hands clutching at the bed sheets.

Victor met Winston in an austere, high-ceilinged hotel room. The man was ruggedly handsome, one of the smoothest conversationalists Victor had ever met. Although, to Victor's knowledge, Winston had ceased to climb about five years ago, he still spoke with a categorical air of authority about everything from bolting in Yosemite to the decimal ratings in the Shawangunks. An instinct of distrust crept over Victor; he would stick carefully to his version of the ascent.

For the next two hours he did just that, while the tape recorder spun away. Despite his encouraging nods, Winston seemed disappointed. At last he shut off the machine, stood up, and said, "Well, I'm sure that does it. Come on downstairs, I'll buy you a drink." Victor felt a surge of immense relief.

A couple of double bourbons later, Winston returned offhandedly to the subject. "So how do you figure Chalmers? What's in it for him to spread all these aspersions?"

Warmed by the drinks and Winston's friendliness, Victor answered, "Chalmers is through. He was psyched out from the beginning. He got a little bump on his wrist, so he walked around all month pretending it was broken."

"He wants to go back."

"He wants somebody to drag him up it. He couldn't stand that Ed and I did it without him. You should ask Arthur Bowen about Chalmers. He's like that German who keeps going back to Nanga Parbat."

"Breitkopf?"

"Yes."

"Have another."

"One more, maybe." The waitress went off.

"What about the weather business?" Winston went on.

"Sure it was bad weather. But Chalmers was so out of it, I'm not surprised he couldn't move his ass out of the igloo while we were climbing. They didn't even get up the fixed ropes to the bivvy tent to support us."

"Chalmers—"

"Chalmers is a washed-out crump."

"One last thing, Victor." Winston pulled a photo out of his briefcase. "I forgot this upstairs. How about marking in your route here? For the issue."

Victor's spleen was up. "See, that's the kind of bullshit Chalmers was pulling in *Piton*. And what the fuck does it prove? I could draw in a cute little dotted line here, or here, or here, and how the hell would you know which was right? Ed was the best damned routefinder you ever saw."

Winston wrung his hand, thanking him effusively. On the train back to Minneapolis Victor got his first sound sleep in a week. The next day he sent Richards a note: "Don't mind the bullshit in *Piton*. I've got an interview coming up in *MJ* that sets everything straight." In the return mail was a postcard. "No sweat. The guy's an asshole anyway. When we get together, remind me to tell you about Chalmers' first trip to the Valley. See you in July. I'm up for it.—JR."

Over the next month Victor's life seemed to return to normal. His friends at Devil's Lake believed him, it was clear, and when they realized Victor was sick of talking about the controversy, they laid off. At last, in early June, the issue of *The Mountain Journal* came in the mail. Victor slid off the wrapper with a sense of pleasure and sat down to read the interview.

The heading came as a shock: "Pterophorus Mystery Deepens. Gaps and Discrepancies in Victor Koch's Account. First Published Interview with Koch." Stung and impatient, Victor read through the tape transcript. But for some stylistic editing, it seemed to be just what he had said. An italicized epilogue, in Winston's voice, followed:

The above interview gives some idea of the difficulties of such an approach. Throughout our session, Koch seemed to stick doggedly to the same story. In recounting an incident a second or third time, he would repeat the identical phrasing, like a man grimly hanging on to a story others may not believe, in constant fear of contradicting himself.

Personally, I found Koch to be defensive, distrustful, ill-at-ease. These qualities of course do not in themselves discredit his testimony. However, though initially skeptical of Chalmers' attack, I found myself wondering more and more whether there was any truth to it.

One of the things that discomfited me was Koch's prolonged refusal to indicate on a photo exactly where his route had gone. He did not seem sure himself (and indeed, the reader will recall that a crucial vagueness about the route forms one of Chalmers' chief claims). I presented him with a good photo. After some uneasy parrying, he said, rather pathetically, to my mind, "We might have gone here, or here, or here, I'm not sure. Briles would have known."

Koch seemed also to have an intense personal vendetta against Chalmers, implying that Chalmers had faked an injury to his wrist (is this idea of "faking" something a projection on Koch's part?), and calling him such things as a "washed-up crump" and a "psych-out."

I came away from the interview very much uncertain whom to believe. If Chalmers' party climbs the mountain (they will apparently attempt the supposed Briles-Koch route) this summer, they may cast additional light on the controversy. (Rappel anchors on the upper part of the route, for instance, would certainly add credence to Koch's version. But Koch himself says the two men down-climbed nearly every pitch above the ice-filled chimney, in order to save hardware.) Probably we will never know the truth.

Rage filled Victor's afternoon; but late that night, with more than half a bottle of bourbon inside him, held tight in Vera's arms, he cried. He wept in delirious fits, recovered long enough to direct a stream of invective against

Chalmers or Winston or nameless other "betrayers," then gave in to the weeping again. Through it all Vera held him silently, stroking his head, supplying him Kleenex. At last Victor fell asleep. Vera stayed up, holding his head in her lap, smoothing his matted hair.

He woke abruptly at 6:00 A.M. and sat up with a start. Pressing his eyelids with his thumbs, he groaned. "God, I feel awful."

"You drank a lot," Vera said. "Listen, Victor. I couldn't sleep all night, and I just sat here thinking." She paused. "I want you to be honest. You didn't get to the summit, did you?"

"What are you saying?" Victor gasped, his whole body rigid. "Are you on their side?"

"Did you?"

She stared at him with her calm, knowing eyes, and at last he lowered his gaze and wept quietly. He held a hand out blindly and said, "Vee, help me. You're the only one who knows. You won't leave me, will you? You didn't last time." He sniffed and wiped his eyes. "What in Christ am I going to do?"

After a pause Vera said, "Tell them the truth. Come out with it and try to explain why it happened."

Victor's voice was even and exhausted. "No. I can't."

"Why not? It's better than living with it all your life."

"It's too late. You don't understand."

Vera sidled up close and hugged him. "I don't see why. It doesn't matter to me whether you made the summit or not. I love you for you, not for what you've done."

Victor returned the embrace; but, dimly through the nausea of hangover, the possibility appeared that it had been a terrible mistake to confess, even to Vera. Anyone was capable of betraying him. "No," he said. "It's not a matter of love. They eat you alive out there, once you've done something good. The fucking seventeen-year-olds sit there at Devil's Lake waiting for you to take too long on a 5.9 move, or grab a sling, and then they talk all afternoon about it." Victor sighed. "Oh, God, what will I tell Richards?"

"Why do you need to tell him anything?"

"Vee, I don't want to go to Alaska. I don't want to climb this summer. Hold me again."

"Then don't go. I'll get some time off, and we'll do something together. We'll drive up to Ontario."

Victor blew his nose. "You don't understand. If I crapped out of the Spires, it would prove it to everybody. I have to go."

6

On the sunny, windless sixth day of the expedition, Victor was pushing the route with Richards. They had left base camp early that morning, cramponed up the frozen snow of the steep, long couloir, and jumared up the fixed ropes. Sixteen hundred feet off the glacier, they were standing in T-shirts on a small ledge, sorting hardware. Richards had just nailed a vertical dihedral, effortlessly and fast. He wiped the sweat off his forehead now, saying, "Bomber protection everywhere. Hard to believe we're up here in Seward's Folly, isn't it?"

Victor grunted. He was nervous about taking the lead, which would be his first on the expedition. He wondered whether Richards was watching, criticizing already, as he racked his pitons.

"Hey, Victor, before you rush off, a couple of things. What are your thoughts about the other two?"

Victor scrutinized the horizon. He half wished for storm clouds. "How do you mean?"

"I mean like they're young, and haven't done too much in the mountains. I'm worried that—"

"That they'll be too rash," Victor finished for him. "They do seem, you know, impetuous."

Richards frowned. "Actually, I was going to say the opposite. Too cautious, too conservative. Ah, never mind. Don't you love this granite?"

An hour later Victor was only sixty feet above his partner. He had dropped one piton and barely caught another. The silent impatience of the great Valley climber below him seemed to goad him not into speed so much as a fumbling inefficient haste. Some of the pitch felt as if it ought to go free, but each time he got more than a few feet above his last piece of protection, the stab of terror returned, and he had to climb back down and go on aid. Now he was close to weeping with futility. Why had he come at all on this expedition? It wasn't right, he wasn't ready, he was making a fool of himself. In front of Richards. Temporizing, he yelled down a question about their supply of pitons while he fussed with a balky étrier.

That night, mercifully, the storm came, in the middle of Richards' disquisition on the need to place a camp around the 1800-foot level and to use all four men simultaneously to make real progress. For the first time Victor had heard annoyance in the man's voice, and now, as their ears picked up the sound of the first flakes on the walls of the group tent, Richards cursed uncharacteristically. The two of them had added only four new pitches during the long day, and on the last Victor had surrendered the lead partway up.

He retired early to his solitary tent. As he pulled loose the string in the sleeve door, Victor thought it seemed to have been tied in a slip knot different from his own. Alarmed, he looked carefully at the battered day pack inside. Had one of the others been prowling around inside his tent? He listened for a moment for footsteps. Methodically, he undressed and arranged himself in his sleeping bag. Then he opened the pack, rummaged under the sweaters, took out the nearest quart water bottle, and held it up to the gray light. The dark liquid level was down to less than a third. And he had been so frugal so far! He recalculated: if the first bottle lasted only eight days, and the trip were a month long . . . . He poured a small tot into his plastic cup and sniffed the warm, pungent aroma, then licked the mouth of the bottle. Hearing a sound, he thrust the bottle hurriedly back into his day pack. Was one of the others spying on him? Had they smelled it on his breath? He was careful to drink only at night, only when he would not be in the others' company again for hours. But probably he should have brought vodka.

The storm lasted for ten days, with only two short letups. During each of them Richards irritably started getting gear and food ready for what he kept calling "a big four-day push." Victor counseled waiting and seeing, and then when in fact the weather closed back in, he sat in the group tent and soliloquized smugly about long-range cycles and the significance of storms from the southeast. He was developing a cough. More than once he said, "I sure hope it isn't bronchitis." The others kept a glum silence. In the group tent there was little recreation. There were binges of hearts, and poker for matches; but one of the men was plodding through *The Brothers Karamazov* at a rate of about forty pages a day and it was hard to talk him into playing. Richards went for long walks by himself, despite Victor's warnings about crevasses.

By the time the storm broke, Richards had decided on an all-out push, two men occupying the bivvy tent at the 2000-foot level while the other two fixed as many pitches above them as they could. Then the two in the tent would go for the summit. It was obvious that Richards would be one of them, but the other slot was open. Now the skies were gloriously clear, and at five A.M. Richards was bustling around getting ropes and hardware together. Victor came out of his tent and stood appraising the mountain. At last he said, "I think we should give it a day."

"What?" Richards stopped in his tracks. "Look at the weather."

"Look at that rime ice up high. It's going to be coming off when the sun hits it."

Richards walked over. "Man, we've just waited out ten frigging days of storm. We can't waste one like this."

Victor coughed. "It's probably a major break in the cycle. In which case a day or two either way—"

"Hey. I was thinking of you and me for the summit."

Victor looked away, touching his throat. "I don't know. I don't like this cough of mine. If it's bronchitis, I just don't know."

Richards gave him a hard look. "Maybe you should stay in camp then."

"Maybe I should. We could wait a day."

"Fuck it. We gotta move. I don't know how with three, though."

The first day alone seemed a blessing to Victor. When the sun hit camp, he put his sleeping pad on the snow and sunbathed. He watched the others through binoculars until four P.M. when, on new ground, they rounded a corner and went out of sight. Until then he had been able to hear their belay signals. Now the sun went behind the peaks to the west, and the sudden chill, mixed with the silence, enfolded him in depression. He got out a new plastic bottle and started drinking. At last the fog of unhappiness lifted. He congratulated himself for not chancing complications with what were surely the first stages of bronchitis, and he felt that for the first time in months he was beginning truly to relax.

He woke suddenly in the middle of the night, cold sober. He had been dreaming about Chalmers. He stuck his head outside the tent; the morning sun was dazzling on the upper reaches of the mountain. Now the weather seemed doubly threatening, for, eighty miles to the south, Chalmers might well be taking advantage of the fine spell to push high on Pterophorus, up to the ice-filled chimney, beyond. He thought about Vera, and berated himself for confessing to her; for secrets never stayed kept, and she was bound to tell someone else, who would in turn . . . . He prayed to a private shade, the imp of his lost luckiness, against both Chalmers and his wife.

That day he held off drinking until two P.M. He scanned the mountain with the binoculars every hour and found himself listening for the stray sound; he would have liked at least to walk up the glacier to get a better look at the route, but alone, through the crevasses, it would have been foolhardy. At dinner he finished the bottle he had started the day before and opened another, the next-to-last. What a fool he had been not to bring more, for that spring he had come to know that nothing else could bring him calm quite so effectively, and now, in the potentially disastrous situation, he needed calm more than ever. The others had dashed up on the mountain all too impetuously; why, just this day he had seen a huge summit cornice break off on one of the other peaks and sweep its east face with avalanche.

A high layer of scud moved in during the night, and the following day was dull and steely, the classic harbinger of a big storm from the southeast. Victor waited anxiously, scouring the mountain with binoculars. The level in the water bottle crept imperceptibly down. By mid-afternoon he recognized that he was indeed in an emergency situation. He was by now fairly sure that he was the only one of the four left alive. They had no radio, and the pilot was not due for another two weeks. But there had been occasional planes in the sky, mail flights to Farewell, perhaps, or McGrath down on the Kuskokwim. He ought to make a signal. What was big enough? There was Richards' black tarp, the one they had futilely tried to concoct a sun still with; he could cut it into long strips and make a huge "X" on the glacier.

The project was complete by early evening. There was no way for Victor to judge how visible the distress signal was from the air, but it was all he could manage with the materials at hand. It was not only the likelihood of tragedy on the mountain, it was the near certainty of his own bronchitis. He found that the whiskey eased the soreness in his throat. Sitting inside the group tent, he caught himself listening as before, not for belay signals now, but for the blessed whine of a plane engine.

He was wakened in the wee hours by voices. They were nearby, and they were shouting for help. No, they were hooting and laughing and cheering. He jerked his clothes on and hurried out of the tent, knowing by his clumsiness that he was drunk. There in the ghostly light the three men were, arm in arm, stumbling across the last several hundred feet of glacier. Richards saw him and let out a loud whoop. Victor closed the distance, reminding himself not to breathe in the others' faces.

Richards blurted out, "Oh, man, what a climb, what a gas. You should have been with us. You can't believe it up there."

"You're all right, then?" Victor said, carefully forming the words.

"Happier'n a clam. Hey, what's with all this plastic all over the glacier?"

Victor turned to look at his "X" as if he had never before seen it. "It was, well, it was going to be a signal."

The mirth had momentarily dissolved. The others looked at him, and then at each other.

7

As he had the year before, Victor called Vera from Talkeetna. She seemed inordinately glad to hear from him. "I was really worried about you, dear. This time was the worst."

"I was fine," Victor said gruffly.

"Did you mind not climbing the peak yourself?"

"Hell, no. It wasn't that great a climb. The younger guys didn't really know what they were in for. I didn't trust them in a pinch."

"I'm just glad you're OK. I was having dreams—"

"Chalmers didn't make it, you know. He didn't even get to our bivouac ledge below the chimney."

"That's too bad."

"What do you mean?"

"I mean, I guess that's good."

"Are you distracted, or something?"

"It's the connection, I think. Your voice is faint. Victor, when will you be here? We need to have a talk."

"About what?"

"About us. About this coming year."

"Go ahead."

"Not on the phone. Hurry back here. I missed you."

A week later, after dinner, Vera turned down the light and sat beside Victor on the sofa. "Do you want another one?" she asked. He had been drinking only beer, a switch she seemed to support. Now, however, the odd mood she was in, as before a special occasion, made him uneasy. Through the ceiling he heard the muffled bass of a Kingston Trio record. They had been playing it up there for three years. Vera took his hand.

"I guess this is our talk," Victor said, forcing a laugh.

"Well, I think we should." He heard an equal nervousness in her voice. "You start."

She squeezed his hand. In the Brooks Range, that had become a ritual for them, the hand squeeze every morning, for good luck against the bears. It had seemed silly to him then. "I have to decide about my professional future," she began stiffly. "My, um, the department has offered me a post-doctoral year."

"Do you get paid?"

"Yes. Not much, of course. It's more of an honor."

"Good. So take it."

She looked at his eyes. He glanced quickly at her; there seemed to be pain in her face. "Do you really want me to?" she asked.

"Of course. What's the alternative?"

"Looking for a job. Which might, which probably would mean moving away."

"It sounds like the best—"

"Oh, Victor," she broke in, "I can't hide it. I'm having an affair."

Victor let go of the hand in his. Nothing could have prepared him for this. "With who?"

"Keith."

"Who the fuck is Keith?"

Vera looked on the verge of crying; but her voice was controlled. "Keith, my professor. Dear, I hated you not knowing."

He got up, went to the refrigerator, found a beer and levered the bottle cap violently off. "How long has it been going on?"

"Since May." Her voice was strangely flat. "I didn't think it meant anything at first—"

"But now it does, is that it?"

"Yes, it does. I thought, if only you don't go to Alaska this summer, if we could go away together, we could work it out. But it's like we haven't communicated in years." A deep sigh escaped her.

Victor paced, guzzling his beer. "Did you tell him about me?"

"What about you?"

"You know, damn it. Quit pretending."

"He knows about our marriage."

"God damn it, cut it out. About the fucking mountain."

Vera's eyes widened. "Of course not. Why would I—?"

"You could betray me just like anybody." The anger in him was gathering to a storm.

"Victor, come and hold me."

"No."

She ran her fingers through her hair. "Oh, Victor, I just gave up when you insisted on Alaska. And then I was sure you'd get hurt, just to punish me."

"You, you, you. What about me?" He found another beer. "So you want to keep seeing this bastard."

"I don't know. He means a lot. He's somebody to talk to."

"And I'm not," Victor said with intensity. "And he's somebody to screw, and I'm not." He stared with contempt at the cringing woman on the sofa, whose arms were hugging herself. "You bitch! You fucking slut!" He ran out of the apartment, slamming the door.

A certain clarity of mind stayed with him through the evening, so that he had the foresight to visit a liquor store before ten, against the inevitability of the bars closing. Now it was one A.M. and he was walking through the streets. It was a crisp, clean evening, the kind when he and Ed would have stayed up talking and gone out to the pizza place. Ed was the only one, it was clear now, who had really been loyal to him. All the rest were betrayers. With Ed he could have done anything. They would have gone to the Andes, to the Karakoram, Patagonia. He shouted to the night, in what he thought was a French accent, "Louis! Lionel!"

His steps were taking him to the bridges where he and Ed had used to boulder. He was not very drunk; if a policeman stopped him, he could walk a straight line with ease. When he got to the bridges he sat down in the darkness and opened the bottle of Old Grand-dad. The warm, familiar stinging soothed his throat, and within seconds he felt the glow bathing him with calmness. It was a good thing he had bought the bourbon. Whiskey had the power to make the truth stand out all the more clearly, to tame the rage that was snarling inside him. Without it, he might have gone home and done something really violent. Something they could arrest you for.

A car went by; no one in it saw him. Victor placed the bottle carefully on the pavement and approached the nearest bridge pillar. His fingers itched with the familiar sequences hidden in the quarried stone. He looked down at his feet: tennis shoes—but when they were in shape they had climbed this route in sandals.

He was only six feet up when he fell off, but the slip was so unforeseen that he landed hard, bruising his tailbone. A memory of playground spills surged with the pain through his body; for a moment he wanted to cry like a child. Instead he spoke softly. "Right on my ass. Right on my fucking ass." He rolled on his side and rubbed his hip, kneading away the pain. Then the anger surged back, and he screamed, "Ed! You bastard!"

He sat listening to his own voice as it seemed to echo through the streets. Would it bring the cops? But there was no one about; the world was empty. He crawled back to his bottle, the decisions suddenly clear in his head.

There was no one any more that he could trust. Fine. So he would go it alone. He had before; he could do it now. And he would quit climbing, quit it for good. That would show the bastards. None of it mattered, none of the Alaskan business, none of the fierce ego-building. He was beyond all that shit.

And tonight he would finish his bottle, and go to sleep right there, under the bridge. Bivouac. He giggled, and heard his own voice wail.

PART II: SEPTEMBER 1978

1

That Tuesday it was raining, which meant handball rather than tennis. After work Victor went home to his apartment, called his partner to confirm the time, called the "Y" to recheck his court reservation, washed the breakfast dishes, took some meat out of the freezer to thaw, and changed into his athletic clothes. He was just leaving the apartment when the phone rang. It was one of those vexing choices, a question of minimizing disorder: the likelihood of being a few minutes late for handball against the uncertainty of not knowing who had made the call. It was an unusual hour for his phone to ring. He answered it. The voice was unfamiliar.

"This is he."

"Victor? It's been a long time. This is Arthur Bowen."

It took Victor a few seconds to place the name. When he had, the first reaction was dismay: now he would certainly be late for the handball. He said evenly, "How are you?"

"Fine. How are you, Victor?"

"I'm fine. You sound long-distance."

"I'm in White Plains. I'm in business for myself here. Things are going really well."

There was an awkward silence. "How did you get my phone number?"

Arthur laughed uneasily. "It wasn't simple, my friend. You're not, you know, still climbing, are you?"

"No." Victor looked at his watch. Three minutes had already gone by. "Are you?"

"Yes. Not like we used to. I go to the Gunks every weekend, though. I have a whole different attitude about it now. Listen." The expectant edge in Arthur's voice was unmistakable. "Since you're only about eighty miles from here, why don't we get together? I'm taking a trip to Boston next week, and it would be easy to stop in Hartford, either coming or going."

One of the rules he had made years ago would have dictated a gentle "no" at this point. But he was getting later and later for handball—the court cost $7.00 an hour—and besides, an old memory of Arthur's loyalty made the rule seem breakable. Brusquely he set a date and gave directions to his apartment.

His partner won three out of five games—the first time ever that Victor had dropped a match to that particular opponent. He went home blaming a new underspin slice that he had not yet mastered for the defeat; but that night he woke up at 4:00 A.M. and could not get back to sleep until 7:00. By the day Arthur was due to arrive, Victor had resolved on a brief, friendly exchange of information, with no suggestion that they repeat the occasion.

Arthur's face was instantly recognizable, but his graying hair and genial wrinkles brought home to Victor the ages that had passed since they had climbed together. "You're looking good," he said, as he took Arthur's leather briefcase and put it in the front closet. "Come in and see the apartment."

"So are you," Arthur said cheerfully, patting Victor's flat stomach with the knuckles of one hand. "You must keep in shape."

"I play a lot of handball, and I have a workout routine at the 'Y.' Make yourself comfortable. Can I get you a drink?"

Arthur was still standing, perusing the flower photographs on the walls. "Whatever you're having."

"I usually have tea this time of day. There's a bottle of scotch somewhere, though." Victor smiled. "I don't entertain much."

"Tea's fine."

The uneasiness persisted through the first cup. Victor fled to the kitchen and returned with crackers and cheese. Arthur kept looking around the neat apartment, as if in search of some misplaced object. "So what does your business produce?" Victor asked.

"Oh, it's terribly boring to the layman. We supply the little doodads that make cable TV possible. That's the simplest explanation. This is good tea."

"I'm trying a new Ceylonese brand. Another cup?"

Arthur held out his mug. Victor began to wonder how soon he could terminate the awkward visit. It was too bad Arthur had driven so far. What could he possibly want? "How about you," Arthur was saying. "What exactly is SANOL?"

"It's a drug rehabilitation program."

"Interesting. I wouldn't have thought—"

"I got involved because of my own addiction." There was the usual startled look on Arthur's face. "To the oldest drug of all. Alcohol. It's all right, I'm comfortable talking about it. If my life has any purpose these days, it's to get other people out of the gutter. Let's talk about you, though. You keep saying 'we,' so I assume you're married."

Arthur smiled sheepishly. "Yes. Very happily. Fran climbs with me a lot. We have two kids, Jonathan, seven, and Ruth, four. I'm very happy. Are you still—"

"Married? No."

"I'm sorry."

"There's no reason to be. I broke things off."

"Are you still in touch with Vera?"

Victor was surprised that Arthur remembered his wife's name; the man had never met her. "No. Not since the divorce was final, years ago. I think she's teaching somewhere on the West Coast."

"Is there anyone, then?"

"Not at the moment." Victor scratched a mosquito bite on his forearm. "Another cup?"

"No thanks. Too much caffeine, you know." The awkwardness would not go away. Victor had the hunch that Arthur was looking for some cue. "So you really don't climb at all?"

Victor shook his head. Arthur waited. "I found in therapy that it wasn't right for me."

"Do you want to explain?"

It was a little speech he had ready. "I found that climbing was all tied up with this deep anger I had against the world. Which in turn derived ultimately from some bad early childhood experiences. I won't bore you with them. I'm happier now, without climbing. Sometimes the anger creeps back." Victor smiled. "Just the other day, in a handball game. But now I know how to govern it."

Arthur stared into his empty mug while he fiddled with the handle. "I wish I could drag you out to the Gunks, though, Victor. I've got a whole new attitude towards climbing that makes *me* much happier." He looked up. "I think we all used to be too serious about it. It shouldn't be a life-or-death sort of thing, and we shouldn't get our egos so involved. To me there's great pleasure in just climbing old classic routes, even 5.5's or 'sixes, at my own pace, my own way. And climbing with Fran is the best experience I've ever had. She can follow anything I can lead." Arthur wiped his palms on his thighs. "So couldn't I talk you into a weekend? Just for old times' sake? And to show you what I mean about climbing this new way?"

Victor smiled tolerantly. "Thanks, Arthur, but no. I know my needs by now."

"How old are you?"

"Thirty-eight."

"I'm forty myself."

"It's nothing to do with age." Victor decided to force the awkwardness out in the open. "Frankly, Arthur, why did you go to all this trouble to look me up?"

Arthur frowned, the way, Victor remembered, he always had when embarrassed. "I guess it's that I always thought you got a raw deal. That Chalmers was at the root of it all."

Victor sighed deeply. "I've come to terms with even that. If I met the man on the street today, I could bring myself to speak civilly to him."

"You hadn't heard then?"

"What?"

"Chalmers was killed on Manaslu. In an avalanche, along with three Sherpas. In 1972, I think."

"Poor fellow." Victor stared at the carpet. "I don't think he was ever happy climbing. It must have really galled him that he didn't get up the route Ed and I had done."

"Lord, it all comes back, doesn't it?"

"It does." Victor closed his eyes. "I can remember as if it were yesterday every step of the way above our bivouac ledge. I remember our conversation on the summit." It was true; now, in his mind's eye, he saw Ed skillfully bridging his way up the atrocious chimney, saw himself take the lead on the mixed terrain above, saw the faint white outline of the summit against the blowing snow, saw himself turn in his joy to Ed. He opened his eyes. "Sorry. I got carried away." With the images had come an old pain in the throat, associated with his desperate thirst on the descent. Victor poured himself more tea.

"Before I go, I want to show you something. Where did you put my briefcase?"

"The front closet."

Arthur returned with a magazine called *Climb*. "Page thirty-four," he said as he handed it over.

Victor looked at the impossible overhang being tackled on the cover. "They didn't have this journal in our day, did they?" He turned to page thirty-four and was shocked by the title: "The Legacy of Victor Koch." "Who's Tom Kinney?" he asked.

"He's a young climber who's done some very hard things in Alaska. Read it."

Victor read:

Fourteen years have passed since the famous controversy over Pterophorus. The consensus of climbing opinion today is that Ed Briles and Victor Koch did not make the summit, and that Koch tried to fake the ascent on his return to base camp after Briles had been killed when a fixed rope broke. The consensus is based, of course, originally on Chalmers' article in *Piton* laying out the reasons why he thought Koch had faked it; secondarily, the interview with Koch in *The Mountain Journal* made his own case weaker, and the rumors of Koch's behavior on Richards' expedition to the Kichatna Spires hurt his image all the more, along with his subsequent disappearing act from the climbing scene. Additional weight against the ascent came from Richards' two failures on the southeast face, and Chalmers' three failures, the last two on the north face (including, that is, the Koch-Briles expedition).

In an absolute sense the truth will never be known. What interests me is that climbers have turned their backs so completely on Pterophorus and the unnamed peaks near it. The explosion of big-wall routes on the fine granite of the Spires and the peaks south of McKinley, along with Richards' and Chalmers' tales of the horrible decomposing rock on Pterophorus, have led to the neglect. But a very difficult mountain remains today with at most one, more likely no, ascent.

If we can set aside the problem of whether Koch was telling the truth, it is worth noticing in how many ways his and Briles' attempt was years ahead of its time, In 1964 all hard climbs in Alaska were fixed to a point near the summit, with elaborate build-up of tent camps and supplies. In contrast, Koch and Briles "went for it" from a bivouac tent only 2000 feet up; they were prepared to climb the last 2500 feet with only four days' food, no fixed ropes, and a bivvy sack. Today this would be regarded as admirable style. Second: climbers who knew Koch said that he was incomparable on the kind of dangerous mixed ground that mountains like Pterophorus are made of. He was supposed to have been very fast and very nervy on bad rock, loose and hollow snow, even on blue ice (taking into account the old step-chopping style). Technical and gear improvements have revolutionized big-wall routes of the kind found in the Spires. But there have been almost no improvements (except for bivouac gear) that would make a significant difference on a mountain like Pterophorus.

Koch's legacy, then, is a call to all of us to turn our sights somewhat away from Yosemite-style routes on perfect granite in expeditionary ranges, in favor of a return to total mountaineering, to the acceptance of bad rock and devious routefinding and inaccessibility by airplane . . .

There followed a discussion of climbing possibilities in the unexplored parts of Alaska. Victor closed the magazine. The tight feeling in his throat had grown worse. "Can I keep this?"

"Of course."

"Thank you, Arthur."

"How do you feel about it?"

It would, Victor knew, be a matter of days before he could sort out and subdue the feelings the article had provoked. But he said to Arthur, "It's very nice. Do you suppose it will have any effect on the younger climbers?"

When Arthur left, the two men shook hands in the doorway. "If you change your mind about an afternoon of climbing, let me know. And keep in touch, old man."

During the next week Victor went about his business, and even his leisure, with an even more fastidious attention to routine than usual. He put the copy of *Climb* in a bottom drawer and refused to look at it again. On the days when his partners were occupied, he did a double workout at the "Y." One day he was walking past a downtown climbing store; for the first time in a decade he felt the urge to go in, and only avoided doing so with an effort of will. He concentrated on the reports and referrals he had to read at work, but the print kept blurring into phrases like, "incomparable on dangerous mixed ground" and "very fast and very nervy." Several nights he woke in the small hours and lay in the darkness, feeling old, his life without purpose or promise. In the last few years, he would have said, he had not once been lonely; now he discovered a hunger for a confidant, someone to talk with the way he had done only with Vera.

At last he called Arthur. He had decided to go climbing once only, to prove to himself that he could do without it, in the same way that, if he really had to, he could drink a single glass of bourbon and yet never need a second. Obviously pleased, Arthur invited him for a weekend to meet his family. Victor pleaded a shortage of time, and arranged to meet Arthur at the Gunks.

It was a crisp, sunny Saturday when the two men met at the Uberfall. His initial excitement at the breathtaking sweep of the cliffs seemed dampened for Victor by the hordes assembled on the Carriage Road. "This is incredible," he said. "I suppose we'll have to wait in line."

"Not if we go down a ways. Glad you could make it. Shall we start with something 5.4-ish?"

As they walked down the road, Victor eyed Arthur's rack with suspicion. "You don't even carry a hammer?"

"The resident pins are mostly solid. You'd get shamed out of the Gunks if somebody caught you pounding away."

"But do you you really trust those things?"

"You get used to them."

Through Victor's head a number of thoughts were swarming. The cliffs looked alarmingly steep; he was afraid he might feel fear, even on an easy climb. He had only pretended to be interested in Arthur's notion of "mellow" climbing; what he wanted was to see just how hard a 5.8 pitch seemed after all the years. Ideally, he would sense that, with practice, he could be at least as good as he had once been. Then, tested by temptation, he could go back to his normal life.

The first fifty feet were fine. Victor was beginning to feel smug about how easy the ladder-like steps in the rock were, when he found himself at grips with a small overhang. Arthur had hauled himself easily over the bulge, but Victor paused, hung on his arms, and tried to crane outward to look for the holds above. He felt his fingers cramping, and, shamefully, his calves were beginning to quiver. An angry burst of strength got him over, but he nearly slipped. Then he was seized with the idea that his tie-in knot was coming undone. The sense of open space about him was disturbing. He checked his knot and tried to breathe deeply. And that was only 5.4, he thought. I've lost it all; I never should have come.

On the belay ledge Arthur was beaming. "What a day. How did it feel?"

Victor tried to catch his breath. "I had a little trouble with that overhang. Wasted a lot of strength."

"It takes getting back into. Want the next lead?"

"I don't think so." There were scrapes on the backs of his hands already.

"It's only about 5.2."

"You go ahead. I don't feel comfortable with those nuts yet."

The whole day was upsetting. After another easy climb Victor felt tired and shaky. Arthur kept apologizing for him, repeating too earnestly that it took time to get the head for it again. In mid-afternoon he asked, "Something a little harder?"

Victor wanted only to go home. But the test was incomplete. "Sure," he said. "As long as you lead it."

"5.7-ish?"

"Why not?" In his good years 5.7 had been child's play. Surely he could follow a climb of that rating now without making a fool of himself. Arthur led the way across the highway to an area he called the Near Trapps. Here the rock seemed even steeper, more angular, festooned with awesome ceilings. "The crux is on the second pitch. Use your feet on the nubbins and it's not bad."

But it was very bad. Some of the moves below gave Victor trouble, and by the time he had reached the crux he was feeling psyched out. The long step was across an empty void. Arthur, out of sight around a corner above and well to the right, had left a nut beyond the hard move. But, Victor thought, what if I fall and that nut comes out? I'll pendulum way out into space, maybe even be left hanging in the air. He tried to dry his palms on his pants. His throat was sticky, as if full of wax. At last he forced himself to go at the move. With one foot starting to shake itself off a nubbin, he yelled for tension. The pull came; Victor lunged for the sling dangling from the guardian nut and heard himself whimper with fear.

He had begun to recompose himself by the time he reached Arthur. The top of the cliff was only forty easy feet above.

"What do you think?" Arthur said, his voice that of a man whose party has not come off.

"I've had enough for today. It's, well, discouraging."

"No reason for it to be. You haven't been out in years."

"I thought I was in shape."

"Gym shape's different. Look." He pointed.

Across a featureless slab to their right, Victor saw a person climbing a dead-vertical layback. The head shook long blond hair out of the eyes, and he could see the face. It was a woman's. Victor looked below for a partner, and realized with a shock that there was no rope trailing. His breath caught in his throat. The woman moved, walking her feet up the opposing wall to just below her fingers, then making a quick, jerky series of hand-over-hand reaches to gain height. She paused, let go with one hand and dipped it hurriedly into a small bag of chalk hanging from her waist. There was a ten-foot section above her where the crack seemed to narrow almost to a seam. As the face turned again, Victor realized that he had seldom seen a woman so beautiful anywhere. It was excruciating to watch her, imagining the fall should she slip.

"Who is she?"

"Diana Volk."

Victor had forgotten himself completely in the drama of watching. The woman's hesitation unnerved him; he wondered if she were in trouble. Then, with deliberation, but no false effort, she reached for and found the only places in the crack where her fingers would fit. Within seconds she had moved in her rough, efficient way up to the safety of a large ledge. She stood and shook out her arms, then, looking around, caught sight of the two of them. She waved and yelled exuberantly, "Hello, Arthur."

"You're looking great, Diana!"

"See you at Rudi's a little later?"

"Probably."

The woman turned and climbed easily out of sight. Victor was still dumbfounded. "How hard is that climb?"

"That's Head Trip. Hard 5.8." Arthur laughed. "I can't get up it."

"Does she solo a lot?"

"That was routine for her. She's easily the best woman climber in the East."

"She's beautiful."

Arthur frowned. "Too many men think so."

"What do you mean?"

"I'll explain later. Let's go on up."

At the top of the cliff Victor stared out over the farms and trees while Arthur coiled the rope. His forearms were pumped up with blood, the muscles knotted, and his hands were covered with raw scrapes. He felt that he had let Arthur down. "It's an amazing place," he said, to fill the silence.

"You can see why some of the guys move to New Paltz. Sometime we should walk down to Mohonk, too. Even the hike there is lovely." Arthur also sensed the letdown. "How about stopping at Rudi's?"

"Somebody's house?" Victor asked, remembering Mr. Siffler's.

"No, it's a tavern just down the road. A climbers' hangout."

"I'd rather not."

"The drinking?"

"It's not that. It's, well, the old business about—"

"Nobody will know about that." Arthur cinched up the coil. "It's all on a first-name basis. Come on, one beer for old times' sake."

The feeling of paranoia that had struck Victor when they had walked into Rudi's—Arthur having been greeted with salvos of hellos—was ebbing now, as the two men sat in a corner and talked. Victor was nursing a Coke. "That first beer after climbing," Arthur said. "I don't know anything better. Do you miss it at all?"

"No," Victor lied. The smell of rock on his hands was bringing back all the old associations; he thought of that very first six-pack with Ed at Mr. Siffler's. His Coke was sweet and insipid. "I'm surprised by something," he went on.

"What?"

"You seem completely accepted here. I thought climbing had gotten really competitive."

Arthur's eyes wrinkled. "Oh, it's desperate. If I were a young prodigy trying to get Stanton or Welsch to recognize me, I'd be miserable. But everybody knows where I'm coming from. My friendships here mean a lot to me. And you know, when Fran comes up, she's included, too. It's not like the old 'oh,-that's-so-and-so's-chick' thing."

Victor's eye wandered to the door, where he saw Diana Volk enter with a group of men. Arthur saw too. He continued, "Diana's as much the reason as anything. People know they have to take women seriously as climbers now." Arthur waved.

Victor looked at his watch. "I should be getting back."

"One more beer," Arthur protested. "I still want to check out how you feel about it all."

"All right. A quick one."

As Arthur was trying to catch the waitress's eye, Diana yelled across, "Hey, Arthur. Let me buy you a beer. I owe you one." The men around her had envious looks on their faces.

Arthur glanced at Victor. "What do you say?"

Victor was torn. He hesitated, then said, "Well, as long as you don't—"

"I know. Don't worry. Come on."

The introductions were rapid and perfunctory. Arthur presented him, however, as "Vic." Through the first minutes of chat Victor sat burning with a private humiliation. He told himself, as he had countless times over the years, that the problem was all with the others—he could hold up his head out of simple pride in what he had done. If he had never actually climbed Pterophorus, that would be another matter. Slowly the preoccupation with himself wore away, and he drifted into the talk. A second Coke had arrived.

He watched the assembled faces, gradually discerning that all the power in the group lay centered in Diana. The seemingly nonchalant name-dropping and route-chatter was all aimed at winning her attention; and right now the frustration around the table was mounting, for she was showing interest only in Arthur. Behind his anonymity, he allowed himself to look at her. There was a tiny scar beside one very blue eye. She had a habit of wetting and licking her lips, and when she laughed her whole face was given over to it. The backs of her dirty hands were covered with tiny scabs. With alarm Victor realized that he was in the grip of a feeling he had not had, it seemed, for years and years.

It was hard for him to answer, then, when she suddenly turned the spotlight on him. "How about you, Vic? Just started climbing?"

"No, I used to do it, years ago," he managed.

"Around here?"

"In the Midwest."

"Oh." Her tongue teased at her lips. "How did you like Slow Joe?"

"Is that what we were on?" Victor temporized. Arthur nodded. "I had trouble with it. I'm pretty out of shape." To divert the attention away from himself, he said, "I was really impressed with your soloing that climb."

"Did you do Head Trip, Diana?" one of the others intruded. She ignored him.

"That move across is hard," Diana went on. "It used to be done as aid."

"Well, that's some comfort." Abruptly Victor's defenses came to his rescue. Really, he told himself, this is banal, this empty chat. It was time he got on the road. The woman was being polite. He turned to Arthur. "I should be going. Long drive."

"Of course." Arthur stood up. "See you all next weekend?"

Victor allowed himself one last glance at Diana. In his infatuation he imagined a look of faint disappointment on her face.

In the car during the short drive back to the Uberfall, Victor asked Arthur, "What did you mean before? About too many men—"

Arthur seemed deep in thought. "Sometimes I think I'm too hard on her. She's in a tough position. All those guys are in love with her, as you could see. I suppose I'd act the same."

"How does she act?"

"She lets them hang around, like puppy dogs. Then she'll turn all her charm on someone like me, because I'm safe, not after her. I get the feeling she does it just to torment them."

"But you get along with her."

"I love climbing with her. Here's your car. How about another weekend, sometime soon?"

"We'll see," said Victor, reaching for the door handle. "I'll call you." He hesitated. "So none of those guys was her—"

"Who knows? She goes through them the way other women go through boxes of Kleenex. That's I guess what bothers me. That, and the thing about Andy."

"Who's Andy?"

"Was. One of the best young climbers here. Only eighteen. He was hopelessly in love with her. They were lovers for a month or two, then she dropped him. For someone who used to climb with Andy."

"Go on."

"He was found at the bottom of Birdline."

"He was soloing?"

"Nobody was there to see. But everybody knows he must have jumped off."

"Why?"

"Andy could have soloed Birdline in the dark. Also, they had a thing about it. It was 'their' climb."

Victor sucked air through his teeth. "Can you really blame her for it, though?"

"I don't know. I suppose not."

"She really is beautiful."

"Oh, yes."

2

During the next two weeks Victor fell back on his methodical daily routines with a sober dedication. His handball game improved—simply, he thought, because he put a little more effort into winning each point. On his days alone at the "Y" he kept up at first the double workout; but one afternoon in the middle of his third set of forearm curls the absurdity of the exercise came home to him. After that he found it onerous to complete a single workout, despite the habit of years' standing. At work, in the middle of precounseling interviews or over memos, he found his mind wandering as it had never used to.

The insomnia persisted. He would wake predictably around 5:00 A.M. and see in the neat, familiar furniture of his bedroom the accoutrements of a prison cell. Over the recent years he had convinced himself that saving others was noble and important work: he was careful not to sound Messianic about it, but the rare cases of true rehabilitation filled him with satisfaction. Now, however, at that predawn hour, the absence of any true quest of his own, for himself, glared him in the face. The rest of his life would be the same as it was now. Twenty years from now he would be coming home from the "Y" to broil the thawing drumsticks.

For years he had dreamed very rarely, and remembered the odd exception only hazily. Now his short nights seemed to teem with exotic and disturbing visions. Several times he dreamed about Diana Volk, waking to find himself sexually aroused.

He reread Tom Kinney's article. It was disappointing that the man had not gone the small step further and asserted his faith in Victor's achievement: all the reasons for doing so were there, in his own argument. As he thought back over the day at the Gunks, the embarrassment and the fear tended to dwindle in memory. He began again to look at doorsills and building buttresses in terms of holds and routes. At last he called Arthur and arranged another weekend.

They made six climbs during a long Saturday, the weather as splendid as it had been before. Victor got up a pair of 5.7 routes without too much trouble, climbing in rock shoes Arthur had borrowed for him. He led a number of pitches, up to 5.5. "It's coming back," he told Arthur happily, as they stood on top of the cliff.

"See? It doesn't have to be all guts-and-glory. It's a different thing, just climbing for the fun of it."

On Sunday morning they were reading the bulletin board at the Uberfall when a young climber belaying his girlfriend up Horseman shouted down: "Hey, Arthur, how you doing?"

"Good, Bernie. And you?"

"Hey, I hear Victor Koch is around here this weekend."

Arthur turned a stunned face toward Victor, then answered, "I don't know about that."

"He'll probably wander in and tell everybody he's soloed Foops."

Arthur shouted up, "You just keep your mouth closed, Bernie, all right?"

Arthur caught up with him down on the highway, as Victor was getting into the front seat of his car. "Wait a minute, Victor. It doesn't mean anything. He's just a young fool."

Victor was beginning to control his emotions. After all the years, he knew how to do so deliberately. But the words that came out were bitter. "See? I told you I couldn't be anonymous here. How did he know?"

"I don't have the faintest. I didn't tell anyone. Climbing gossip is incredible."

Victor put the keys into the ignition. "Thanks, Arthur. But it was stupid from the beginning. I should have known better." Yet the sense of having been cheated prickled in his blood: he had just begun to climb well again.

Arthur said, "Don't rush off. It doesn't matter what Bernie and the like—"

Anger broke through the control. "Don't give me that bullshit, Arthur." He was alarmed; it was the first time he had used a swear word in years. "I'm going." In the rearview mirror he saw Diana Volk approaching, a rope and a rack slung from her shoulders.

Arthur turned. "Not, now, Diana. We're having a talk."

She ignored him and poked her head close to the window. "Hey, man, I just want to say I'm sorry. Bernie's a fucking asshole."

The urge to flee was upon him. He started to turn the key. "How did you—?"

"Oh, everybody's buzzing away about it up there. Listen." She moved her head closer. Despite his anger and humiliation, the spell of her beauty kept him momentarily paralyzed. "I don't give a shit what happened on some mountain way off somewhere back in the last ice age. You seem like an OK guy to me, and anybody Arthur hangs out with is stamped and certified. Let's go do a climb, the three of us."

Arthur looked hopeful. "No," said Victor.

"I guess not, Diana."

Clearly she was used to having her way. "Nothing hard. A good long mellow climb."

"No," Victor repeated. "Can't you see—?"

"It'll die down. Listen, we'll go way off to Millbrook. Nobody climbs there. Maybe we can put up something new."

His own ambivalence kept him off balance, and the spell of her will and beauty, mingling with the traces of the dreams about her, pushed him over. "All right," he said. "Just one climb."

Diana and Arthur swung leads on the long meandering route she chose. While Victor belayed her he admired her economy of movement; during Arthur's leads, she forced an awkward trivial conversation on him. There was in fact no one else nearby; but Victor's thoughts were fixed on an image of a horde of detractors at the Uberfall. The afternoon sun on the yellowing treetops was achingly beautiful, a glimpse of a country from which he had been exiled. At the top he thanked Diana formally, his mind already dwelling on the drab but comfortable certainties of his future back in Hartford. She wormed his phone number out of him before he left.

The next evening she called. On Saturday, she said, she was going to be at a cliff called West Peak, not so far from Hartford. It was an undeveloped crag similar to Ragged. Nobody would be around. She wanted him to join her.

"But I can't climb at your level," Victor said, feeling the flattery of her attention weaken him.

"There's just one hard thing I want to try, and it's only one pitch." Victor supposed that Diana had planned to visit West Peak anyway. The alternative seemed unimaginable. "You can clean it on jumars, or I'll rappel it. The rest of the day we can do moderate stuff. What do you say?"

Her spell was potent even over the telephone. Against the firm resolves of his dogged drive home from the Gunks, he heard himself say yes.

Every weekend for the next two months Victor climbed with Diana for at least one day. He could never fathom why she was eager to spend so much time with him, but he did not want to spoil anything by asking. With her leading above him, effortlessly dismissing the apparent difficulties, he began to feel the kind of confidence he had associated with Ed and with no one else. His own skill developed rapidly; soon he could follow most 5.9's and lead a well-protected 5.8. When Diana went off with someone else to try a really hard climb, he felt a vexation strangely like jealousy. When she soloed, he could not bring himself to watch, but waited anxiously for her to return.

His first time back at the Gunks—she had insisted on going there—Victor had an attack of nerves. After their first route she deliberately lingered at the Uberfall, hailing friends, trading gossip; initially irked with her, Victor slowly realized that to be seen with Diana was to be legitimized in the other climbers' eyes. That afternoon they drank at Rudi's, and the celebrants crowding around the table included Victor in their questions and their laughter.

He climbed with Arthur a few times. On a high belay ledge, his friend complimented him. "You're getting awfully good."

"It's Diana. She's lucky for me."

"Victor, it's none of my business, but—"

"But what?"

"Be careful."

The relationship developed with its own odd logic. On any subject besides climbing, Diana seemed bored, her conversation automatic. She never asked him about Pterophorus, or his past, and he did not offer information about either. The weekends included Saturday nights drinking in New Paltz, after which she would throw down her sleeping bag next to his on the Carriage Road; yet he had never touched or kissed her, and so theirs did not seem like a real intimacy. It was in that very possibility, Victor knew, that the danger lay: the events of his past, Ed's death and Vera's betrayal, above all, had had the power to hurt him only because he had allowed himself intimacy. Yet his five-day week now dragged its way out against the anticipated weekend; each Saturday morning as he drove the highways toward his rendezvous, Victor fought down the dread that she might have forgotten, might not show up.

One night in October they were in a rowdy bar in New Paltz. The overzealous band prohibited conversation. Diana had been downing drafts steadily, and in fact everyone at the table seemed drunk except Victor. She had asked him to dance, but he had held up his palms, pleading incapability; instead she danced with a series of other partners, flinging herself expertly around the floor, tossing her blond hair, while Victor watched everyone in the bar watch her. The band took a break, but the juke box was almost as loud. A climber Victor vaguely recognized came up to Diana and shouted in her ear. She waved him away, but he kept yelling; Victor saw by the muscles in the face that the man was furious. Finally he heard Diana shout, "Hey, fuck off!"

Victor started to get to his feet, as the climber was clutching a beer bottle with dangerous intensity. But instead of violence, abruptly the man spun away, choosing retreat.

After the bar closed, Victor drove Diana back to the cliffs. There was a gibbous moon, and the trees were swaying in a warm wind. Sleeping bag in hand, Victor started up to the Carriage Road. Diana clasped his arm, saying, "Let's go up on top. Across the road. It's such a night." The touch of her hand on his arm—the first such contact—sent Victor's blood racing.

They found a clearing at cliff-edge, with barely enough room for their bags on a bed of pine needles. The sense of a drop just beyond reminded Victor of mountain bivouacs. He got into his sleeping bag. Diana paused halfway inside her own, her hands starting to unbutton her shirt. "Victor, can I ask you something?"

"Certainly." He sat up to look at her. Her hair was gleaming with the moonlight behind her.

"Do you find me unattractive, or something?"

Victor's pulse quickened. Was she drunk, after all those beers? But no one held her liquor better than Diana. He said, "Of course not."

"Well, what is it, then? You haven't showed, you know, the slightest interest."

Impulsively, Victor blurted out the truth. "I don't want to ruin anything. I'm half in love with you, and it scares me."

Diana laughed gaily. "Well, for Christ's sake. Let's make love, then." She undid the rest of her buttons and threw off her shirt; she wore nothing underneath. "I'll get in your bag. Unzip it all the way."

Long after the sex was over and Diana lay on her back, asleep, Victor leaned on one elbow, feasting his eyes on her. His rapture had a streak of pure greed in it. This is all mine, he said to himself, mine to have and touch and hold. The years of sterile caution stretched like a wasteland behind him.

The working week began to seem to Victor nothing more than an ordeal of patience. About the rest of Diana's life, which she was so bored when describing, he remained largely ignorant. She lived for climbing, as she put it. He was not really sure what her occupation was—something to do with a dance company in New York City. She never invited him to her apartment in Manhattan; instead, it was assumed that they would meet every weekend at the Gunks. Through Diana he gradually joined the circle of top climbers at the tables in Rudi's and the diner in New Paltz; gradually they seemed to accept him, or at least to cease regarding him as a curiosity of nature.

On a Thursday in early November Victor stared at the newspaper in dismay. The forecast was unequivocally for freezing rain all weekend. He had never phoned Diana before, so that now it took a long while to get up the nerve. She did not answer all that afternoon or evening. He finally reached her Friday morning.

"Did I wake you up?"

"No," she said sluggishly. "Yes, I guess you did. Ugh. Wait a minute while I put the coffee water on."

When she had returned, he said, "Diana, it's supposed to rain all weekend."

"I know."

"I thought maybe I could come see you in New York. We could spend the weekend there."

There was a long silence. Thursday's premonition of trouble seemed to Victor to be assuming material form. "Diana?" he asked.

"I'm thinking. There must be someplace in the East where it won't rain. What about Seneca?"

"It's awfully far for a weekend."

"Take Monday off."

"I can't. Wait. The paper says even West Virginia." He paused. "Would you like me to come down?"

"Damn it. I want to climb. I'll tell you what. I'll come up there."

"Great. Friday night?"

"Saturday. There's this performance Friday. What will we do?"

"I'll think of things."

As it turned out, they spent most of the weekend in Victor's apartment. Diana seemed restless, pacing the floor as she peered at the flower photographs or examined the spartan furniture; but when Victor suggested entertainments—a movie, a flute recital—she seemed uninterested. They spent much of the time making love. As always, Victor's sense of luxury and privilege manifested itself in his urge to pore over every square centimeter of her body. Diana accepted the homage as if it were naturally her due; in sex she drove confidently toward her own orgasm, reaching it often before he had his.

On Sunday afternoon the subject of Pterophorus at last came up. Uncharacteristically shy, she asked him if he wanted to tell her about it, adding, "If it's too painful, forget it."

"Not at all. I haven't talked about it in years. Did you see Tom Kinney's article in *Climb*?"

"No. Some of the guys were talking about it, though."

Victor resisted the vanity of ferreting the copy from his bureau drawer. He launched into a long resumé of the expedition. When he spoke of Chalmers, it was not in heat, but with philosophical pity. He described the summit dash with an abundance of detail.

Diana seemed contemplative. She tossed her hair out of her eyes and said, "So you really did it. I didn't tell you this before, but the guys talking about it . . . well, all but one or two of them were positive you hadn't."

"I know."

"Damn it, there must be some way even now you could prove you did it. Did you leave anything on the summit?"

"No. We were too tired." Victor had a dim memory of suggesting to Ed that they deposit some object there, in the snow; but he could not be sure it hadn't been Ed's idea. "I don't care about proving it any more. I've come to terms with the whole thing."

Later, in bed again, Diana asked, "Do you really love me?"

"Of course." He wanted to ask if she loved him. But he said, "Why do you like me?"

She kissed his ear teasingly. "I don't know. You're so different from the others. You've been through a lot, that makes you interesting. Maybe it's just that you didn't go after me. I'm not used to that."

Victor puzzled over his disappointment. Diana yawned, stretching, while he gazed at her breasts. "Why did you get divorced?" she asked.

"We were on different tracks. She was headed for her history career, and I was a college dropout. But the thing I couldn't forgive, the thing I'm still angry about, is that she sided with the others, the ones who claimed we hadn't made it."

"That's incredible."

"I know. I was pretty mixed up by then. I was drinking a lot. I had these rages."

"You're so, you know, even-tempered now." She rubbed her hand across his chest. "Want to make love again? Can you?"

"Let's try." As he took her in his arms, the sense of wealth flooded through him again.

Afterwards she resumed the discussion. "So you really went off the deep end with the booze? I suppose I could myself. What's it like?"

"The scary thing is that you're not really aware what's happening. There are so many defenses, so many rationalizations for having a drink. Even when I was having serious memory blankouts, waking up and not knowing where I was, I didn't know what trouble I was in."

"What did you do all those years? Stanton says nobody in climbing knew what had happened to you."

The only person Victor had ever told about the bad years was his therapist, when he had finally gotten to SANOL and begun to want to save his life. Now he started to brush aside Diana's curiosity, as he had Arthur's. But the prospect of a lifetime of secrecy struck him all at once as empty and depressing. And she lay right there beside him, her warm skin against his, the hand circling on his chest.

"If I tell you this, will you promise you'll never tell anyone else?"

"I promise," she said easily.

He closed his eyes, as he always had with his therapist. "When I left Vera in, let's see, 1966, I was at loose ends. I got a job painting houses that spring. It was what my father had done, and it was the only thing besides climbing I knew how to do. My god, it was boring, though. I fell in with a card shark who taught me poker scams. We went to Reno and cruised for tourists looking for what they thought was a friendly game upstairs in somebody's room. He'd use me to bump the pots in seven-card hi-lo, or vice versa."

"What's that?"

"It doesn't matter. We made some big killings, but I blew a few pots, too. I was drinking all the time, and it got hard to keep track of the signals."

He opened his eyes briefly to look at Diana. Her gaze was calm but attentive. He went on, "A guy caught on to my partner dealing seconds and nearly beat the life out of him. I got out of town. I went to Las Vegas, got a job taking the change out of slot machines. I tried out for blackjack dealer, but my hands weren't good by then. I got into a strange line instead. It was a male escort service. Getting paid by lonely ladies to accompany them to parties and things. Diana, there are more lonely women in Las Vegas than anywhere on earth. Sometimes they wanted sex, too, and it would mean extra money. But they weren't young. I would drink so I could go through with it, but then I'd have trouble. I think I lost all interest in sex for a few years because of it. And when you're drinking as much as I was, you lose interest anyway." He opened his eyes again. "Does this shock you?"

"Not at all," she said, kissing the back of his hand. "I'm fascinated."

Victor pressed his fingers against her mouth. "I got into drugs—not taking them, just dealing. It was 1969, and there was a big demand for mescaline and LSD and peyote. I got into a really bad thing in Mexico." Should he tell her everything? Something about her nonchalance bothered him. He chose to summarize. "The upshot was that I had to get as far away from there as possible. Which is why I ended up in New England.

"I spent two years really scraping along. I'd get bartending jobs but always lose them for drinking. I sort of let myself go about then, not changing clothes for weeks at a time, living in the cheapest rooming houses and not paying rent, getting evicted or just clearing out. I don't even remember large parts of those years. The one thing I learned really well from that time is what it's like to be alone. Finally I passed out drunk on a bad cold night in New Haven. The police got me to a hospital, but I came close to dying even so." Victor surveyed his fingers. "I don't know why I didn't get frostbite. Especially since I'd had some on Pterophorus." He closed his eyes once more. "I was in and out of hospitals. I tried A.A. but it didn't stick. I know now that I just wanted t die, to get down under and forget how everybody I cared about had betrayed me." Victor paused. The angry feeling was coming back. His habitual cautionary mechanism went into play. "To make a long story short, I finally happened upon a rehabilitation program that worked. And I've been with SANOL since."

"Why are they so good?" Diana asked, stretching.

"It's too long to tell. They remake you from scratch, essentially. For instance, I didn't used to talk this way."

"You mean sort of formal?"

Victor smiled. "SANOL believes that language embodies one's pathology. When I was down and out, all I talked was slang and profanity. I've learned to speak all over again. I learned to read, to like good music, to think for myself. The most important thing I learned was how to be alone and feel OK about it. And how to govern the anger. It's the key to all the rest. My father beat me when I was a child—" The uneasiness bloomed in Victor's brain. Something to do with Diana's languid acceptance of everything that he was saying. If nothing could shock her, nothing could be that important, either. "I'll go into it all some time. I don't want to bore you." He turned and nuzzled her bare shoulder. "Does this change how you feel about me?"

"Silly, of course not. I'm glad you told me. It makes us closer." She smiled her all-embracing smile.

"It felt good to tell somebody. To tell you." But that was not exactly true; the disturbance lingered. "I love you, Diana."

She kissed him for answer. "Hey, what'll we do next weekend?"

It was almost December. The crowds at the Gunks had dwindled; the gatherings at Rudi's had become cozier but less animated. One afternoon the talk wandered to Alaska. Brewer and Stanton were discussing the unclimbed walls in the Ruth Gorge. Brewer seemed half-serious about going there. Stanton was dubious because of rumors of lousy rock. Victor felt the stirrings of the old infectious expedition urge. The wind was gusting bitterly outside. Stanton abruptly asked Victor, "You've been up there. Ever see the Ruth Gorge?"

Caught off balance, Victor cleared his throat. "Actually I have. On the flight in to Foraker. It's impressive."

"I didn't know you'd done Foraker."

"We didn't do it. It was a fiasco. We only got to ten-five. We were too slow."

The change in atmosphere around the table was unmistakable. There was a tension waiting to be discharged, and the faces fixed on his were hungry with curiosity. Victor pressed his knee against Diana's under the table. Stanton, sensing the discomfort, said, "Well, summer's a long way off, anyway."

When they parted that Sunday afternoon, Diana said, "Let's give it one more weekend. Did that bother you, in the bar?"

"No," Victor said. "Let's make it Friday night, too."

"I don't know. I hate these cold nights. I wish our bags zipped together."

"Let's stay in a motel."

The moment at Rudi's, however, stuck with Victor through the week like a speck of dust in the eye. His apartment became claustrophobic, and even the pattern which the fall had begun to assume—the work week as a rite of preparation for Diana—left him edgy now and morose. They had not discussed how—or even whether—to see each other after the climbing was done for the year. December, January, and February seemed to represent a gulf that gaped before him, a reminder of the absence of any quest in his future. He had followed a few 5.10's, and was solid now on 5.9: among the Gunks regulars, only Jacobs was climbing so well at his age. But what would the climbing with Diana ever become, but more of itself? And would she eventually grow tired of it?

He had an upsetting dream involving both Ed and Vera. He tried in the morning to banish the lingering overtones with coffee and the paper. As he stared at the meaningless newsprint, all at once there came creeping among the alien letters the micro-organism of an idea.

He spent Friday night with Diana in a motel near the Thruway. They took a bubble bath together and Diana drank champagne, and they made love all through the night. In the morning she rose, naked, and pulled open the curtains. "It's snowing," she said. "Damn it."

"Let's go on up for a walk, anyway. Around by the Outback Slabs. I want to talk about something."

Well bundled, they strolled hand-in-hand down the Carriage Road. There had been not even another parked car on the highway. Diana said, "What is this thing you want to talk about?"

Victor held out a palm and caught a snowflake. "This may sound crazy, but listen. I want to go back. With you." He squeezed her hand.

"Back where?"

"To Alaska. To Pterophorus."

She stopped walking. "Are you serious?"

"Yes. I've been thinking hard about it. If I climb it again, nobody can ever doubt me. It's the answer. And with you—well, I know we could do it together."

"I haven't done any mountaineering to speak of."

"We'll train. We'll go ice climbing all winter. We can train in June in the Wind Rivers, say."

"I was planning on the Valley in June."

"It doesn't matter. You'll pick up things really fast. It would be us, Diana, against everybody. We'll keep it a secret until July."

"I can't afford to go to both the Valley and Alaska."

"I'll pay your way."

She took a long deep breath, then shook the snow out of her hair. "Let's go get a cup of coffee somewhere and talk this over."

3

Victor taught himself modern ice climbing by consulting Chavois' book, which had just been published. To have showed up at Chapel Pond and begged a lesson from Stanton or Brewer would have been too obsequious, and might have dropped the hint that something was up for Alaska. Diana had trouble getting away from the city and did not take to ice climbing very well: she hated the cold, especially when they camped out, and seemed unsure of herself on ice the way she never had on rock. Distrustful as ever of the complexities of gear, Victor at first made hesitant progress with the various tools he swung at the gullies and slabs. Everything was simplified, he found, if one soloed; and Diana's absence dictated that choice often enough anyway. As the ice he assaulted on his solitary weekends grew steeper and longer, the phrase "very nervy and very fast" rang in his head, a talisman of success.

At home Victor spent the evening hours making lists, poring over the maps, jotting down from memory notes about the route. After weeks of pondering approaches, he decided on a flight in to Desolation Creek. Ferrying loads for thirty miles to base camp would be slow and discouraging, but it was surer and cheaper than an airdrop—and in better style, too, as Tom Kinney would appreciate. Under the glare of his desk lamp, he slaved over poundage and hardware and food, the kind of obsessive fussing Ed had once been far fonder of than he. When he talked to Diana over the phone about details, she seemed bored, parrying his questions with the formula, "Whatever you think's best."

For the first time in ages his life seemed to concentrate on a meaningful, specific event in the future. More than once he caught himself marveling, "This is why it was always so good, why we used to do it year after year; this is what gave the twelve months shape and sense." He dug out the few letters he had received from Ed and reread them, sniffing for the elixir of their former quest. Two qualms only troubled him during the early winter: the problem of precisely when and how to announce his plan to the world, and the possibility, ineradicable no matter how he scribbled and charted into the night, of failure on Pterophorus.

In March he resumed meeting Diana at the Gunks. Brewer invited them to sleep on the floor of his apartment in New Paltz, which solved the cold-camping problem. In the snug silence of the living room, however, Diana seemed squeamish about making love, for fear Brewer would overhear. Except for that aspect, their weekends together seemed at first to afford Victor all the gratification the fall had. Diana was climbing well, having no trouble with 5.8's even when there was still snow on the ledges.

He invited her to share his week off at spring vacation with a trip to Seneca. Work in the city, however, prevented her. He spent half the week in Boston shopping for gear and half the week at the Gunks. Diana joined him on Thursday but had to leave Saturday afternoon, a pattern, she told him, that the dance group would force upon her for the rest of the spring. Thus in April Victor had to resign himself each weekend to only one day of climbing with her, one night of drinking in New Paltz and sleeping together. To keep up his shape, he climbed Sundays with Stanton and Jacobs, and occasionally with Arthur. He seemed stuck at a level of difficulty, however, unable to lead the harder 5.9's, or to follow more than a few 5.10's that happened to be "made" for him. After a particularly galling back-off, Jacobs joked, "What the hell do you want? We're old men, Victor." He throttled a petulant response.

One afternoon in April he was sitting on the Grand Traverse Ledge with Diana. Only an easy pitch remained above. She said, "Before you dash off, I want to talk about something."

Victor fiddled with a sticky carabiner gate. "What is it?"

"I was talking with Brewer the other day, and I asked him how many people you ought to have for a big route in Canada or Alaska."

"Diana, you didn't—"

"Relax. I didn't breathe a word about our plans. It was purely, you know, theoretical." Victor sat down beside her. She was wearing knickers and a bright blue tank top that emphasized her breasts. Despite his irritation he felt the tug of desire. "Anyway," she went on, "he thought two was iffy. Three or even four would be better."

"What does Brewer know?"

"He knows a lot. He did all those—"

"I know what he's done," Victor snapped. In the silence that followed they could hear the clanking of hardware on a nearby route.

Diana persisted. "He said the problem with two is you've got too much weight per person. He said the two girls who did the Nose almost couldn't haul their own gear." She looked at him coolly. "And we're talking about ferrying loads thirty miles in?"

"You don't understand. I wanted this to be just us, just you and me. We have this destiny together, Diana." He hated himself for saying the word out loud.

"Yeah, but."

Victor sighed. For weeks he had been going over weights, juggling the figures to come up with manageable loads. Diana had never carried a heavy pack, and she weighed only 120 pounds. "Brewer's right," he said at last.

"Who, then?"

"I don't know." He had been thinking long and hard about Arthur; but that was the wrong choice, even if the man could be persuaded to go.

"Let's keep our eyes out."

Everything seemed so simple to her. "But not a word about—"

She waved an impatient hand. "I know, I know."

In May began a pattern of quarrels, the first they had had. They occurred regularly on Friday night, after an evening of drinking and dancing. Diana would pick the quarrel, teasing or nagging at Victor until he was goaded to respond. Sometimes she would simply leave him at the table drinking his Coke while she danced all night with others, or traded gossip promiscuously. Late in the night, after he had sulked for hours, he would turn to her with words of apology. "That's OK," she would say. "I got pretty loaded." It disturbed him that she could not bring herself to apologize, not once, but he attributed her inability to do so to her youth. She would give him her body instead, and always Victor would slip back into the dark pool of his incredulity at having her, and he would lie awake for hours after she was asleep, running his fingertips over her thighs and stomach and breasts.

He got through the weekends on the strength of the four or five climbs they would do each Saturday. Diana was climbing brilliantly, leading 5.10's with confidence. He never tired of watching her move with that strange nervous efficiency up the thinnest of sequences, or pass an overhang that was already making his palms sweat as he sat below. But back in Hartford the disturbances in their relationship nudged him out of the comfort of his charts; his eyes would leave the figures and maps to stare at the walls of his study while he tried to pin down what was wrong. His thoughts traversed the years back to the planning months with Ed: how mutual the obsession had been in those days! In a bad moment he let himself wonder if the main reason Diana was willing to go to Alaska was that he was paying for it.

One night in May, as they were lying in their sleeping bags on the Carriage Road, Victor kissed Diana and said, "There's something I want to tell you that I've never told anybody."

"Go ahead."

It was not something he could deliver over as easily as she seemed to think. He wavered. All through his adolescence and early adulthood he had been sure that to share his secret would be to lose his luck. But a few nights before, lying sleepless in his apartment, he had decided that the malaise between them needed some counter-magic, a charm to reinforce the climbing bond that was stronger than luck. Hesitantly he started, "After my mother died, there was no one who knew about this." The telling became easier, as soon as he had spoken the plain fact about his kidney. He told her about his playground prowess, about starting climbing, then about his fall on Hungabee, and how close he had come to telling Ed. In the dark with his arms around her shoulders, he felt very close to crying; but it was a warm, purgative feeling. At last he was done. "So now you know, too."

She hugged him. "But why was it a secret?"

"Don't you see? I thought I explained it all." The malaise perched on his shoulder. The scarecrow of his tale had failed to chase it away.

"It's nothing to be ashamed of, having one kidney."

"It's not that. It's the whole thing."

"Do you really believe it caused your luck?"

"I don't know," Victor said, dispirited. "Maybe I don't have the luck any more. Maybe it went away when they started listening to Chalmers." He turned over. To himself he said, And maybe it left tonight, when you blabbed it away to her. He struggled against tears, until the habit of control regained its power.

In mid-May Diana announced that she had found a likely third. His name was Derek Hudson. "You've seen him at Rudi's," she said. "I know you have."

"His name's familiar."

"He's real strong. He's pushing Stanton these days. I've been climbing a lot with him on Fridays."

"Does he have any mountaineering experience?"

"Yeah. He's ice climbed in the Palisades, and I know he's done stuff in the Cascades."

"He's pretty young, isn't he?"

"He's my age. For Christ's sake, Victor, time's getting short."

Diana arranged a sequestered meeting in a New Paltz cafe. Derek's tall, wiry, dark good looks were indeed familiar to Victor. A competitive instinct put him on guard, but as they talked, Derek's shy politeness won him over. At last Victor unfolded the plan. The young man did not seem as surprised as Victor might have expected. Nor did he have any difficulty deciding. He seemed flattered to be invited to Alaska, glad for a chance to go on an expedition—as simple as that. The three of them climbed together that afternoon and the next Saturday. Derek was a powerful leader, not so much graceful as immensely strong, with a prodigious reach. Victor warmed to the man's quiet poise, and August took on in his mind the promise of success.

In late June Diana and Derek drove out to Yosemite. A postcard informed Victor that they had done the Salathé in three days, despite intense heat. In Hartford he threw himself feverishly into the last weeks of planning, exhausting himself to the point where even his work at SANOL began to suffer—something he had never previously allowed to happen. He ran five miles a day to get in shape, but found less and less time for climbing. His last act before leaving was to mail a long letter to Arthur, explaining the expedition and asking him to spread the news of it through the climbing world.

He took a bus to Edmonton, where he waited a day for Derek and Diana. With minor breakdowns they continued up the gravel highway to Anchorage in Derek's old Volvo, taking four days for the passage. Exhausted, Victor slept most of the hours he wasn't driving. There was only desultory conversation, mostly about the month in the Valley. They arrived at midnight on a clear day. Victor pointed jubilantly to the hulking outlines of the three great volcanoes across Cook Inlet to the west. "It's back there a ways, behind Gerdine. We'll be there in no time."

But it took two days of frantic shopping in Anchorage, and another two days of waiting in Talkeetna, before their pilot was able to deposit them on the gravel bar where Desolation Creek exited westward from the mountains. Neither Diana nor Derek was much help with the last-minute logistics. On the flight in the pilot told Victor that the summer had been the driest in years. As they flew past the numberless unclimbed peaks, Victor saw that the snow cover was down to a minimum: blue ice gleamed everywhere. Then came the first glimpse of Pterophorus. Victor grabbed Derek's arm and pointed, shouting over the engine noise. Derek gave voice to a whoop. Diana, in the back seat, smiled.

The first stages of the hike in, however, had a demoralizing effect. The loads were heavier than Victor had calculated, and for the first two days they were reduced to triple-packing, until, at Diana's insistence, they cached ten days' food and some of the hardware and went ahead with double loads. A drizzly overcast set in on the third day, and the debris of the lower moraines gave only the most illusory relief to their treadmill progress. The marches were exhausting, six miles' effort yielding a gain of only two miles in their advance. They took lunch breaks in a glum silence, batting away the mosquitoes. The two small tents made for unsociable camping, with dinner passed from one door to the other.

Diana's mood grew progressively more irritable. She was developing blisters, and neither she nor Derek was in the kind of hiking shape to keep up the pace Victor set. Every afternoon it was Diana who pleaded for the halt. In the tent she fell asleep early, too tired to make love. Derek was willing to talk for hours, however, and several evenings Victor kept up long dialogues with him, their voices raised to pass from tent to tent over the patter of rain on the fly. He began to appreciate the younger man's deference and politeness. Always during the planning months his private image had been of Diana and himself going for the summit. Now he began to wonder whether, should they fail to go as a rope of three, Derek was not the more likely companion.

After six days they had covered only nineteen miles. That evening, as they sat crowded into Derek's tent for dinner, Diana demanded a rest day.

"But we've only got fourteen days' food left," Victor protested.

"I don't care. My blisters are killing me. Besides, listen to the rain."

"You've got to move in bad weather up here. You can't pamper yourself. What do you think, Derek?"

The dark eyes met his own, then glanced away. "I'd like to get there, but I'm pretty beat myself."

"We're only five miles from the junction. You can see the mountain from there."

Diana spoke. "Look, I need a rest day, OK? You're driving us like a goddamned slave master." In a softer voice she added, "I didn't think it was all going to be like this."

He kneaded the muscles in her neck. "All right, Diana. I'm sorry. I'm just so hyped for getting there." Derek looked relieved. "What do you want to do with the day?"

"We can play poker," Diana said. "I brought a deck."

"Not for money," said Derek, exchanging a look with Diana.

Hours later, when they were alone in their tent, Victor confronted Diana.

"What was that about?"

"What?" She yawned as she got into her sleeping bag.

"That remark about the poker. 'Not for money,' he said."

"How do I know?"

"Diana, have you told him about everything? About what I did during those years?"

"Goddamn it, leave me alone."

"Keep your voice down."

"Fuck you."

Victor brooded. He could feel the magnetic pull of the mountain, as if it were right outside the door of the tent. And now they had to waste the whole next day on account of blisters. Perhaps he could gain something by ferrying loads all day by himself. Had he been reading too much into Derek's remark? But the glance between the two had seemed full of irony. He could not leave it alone. "Why would Derek say 'not for money' unless he knew I'd been a card player?"

"Fuck it all," said Diana. Suddenly she was getting out of her sleeping bag and putting on her clothes.

"What are you doing?" Victor asked in alarm.

"Victor, you schmuck. You're so nearsighted. Yeah, Derek knows all about you. I told him. So he let it slip." She was throwing her belongings into a stuff sack. "I'm going to sleep in his tent the rest of this trip. I've been fucking him for months. I don't want to sleep with you any more. You're so goddamn demanding. And I'm not sure I want to go on with this expedition. I think I want to go back and wait for the plane."

Through the ringing in his ears Victor managed to say, "Diana. Please. Wait."

"You're so pathetic, Victor. I can't believe you didn't catch on. Why do you think I started coming to the Gunks on Thursdays? And all last fall, I used the dancing stuff just to keep you away from the city. There was even a guy back there I was getting it on with. I suppose it was good for a while, you and me, but I'm sorry now we ever got started. And I don't know why I let myself get talked into this trip." Her eyes blazed. "You think you can own me. Nobody owns me." Then she was gone.

Victor sat unmoving in his tent for an hour, listening to his heart pound. It was almost beyond the power of his long-practiced control to quell the impulses that were coursing through his veins. At last he heard a succession of noises, all too familiar. Unbelievably, Diana was making love with Derek, was broadcasting to him the sounds of her own orgasm.

He put on his cagoule and went out into the drizzly night. When he had walked a mile up the glacier, he sat down on a moraine boulder. It was almost dark, and the drizzle had a nasty chill to it. He looked at his hands. They were shaking. But the dim outlines of a course of action were forming in his mind.

4

As he hoped, the other two were sound asleep when he returned to camp. With care to make no noise, Victor packed up in the heavy drizzle. The note he left in the now-empty tent read:

You're right. There's no point going on with the trip, given what's happened. I have been very upset and so I am starting the hike-out alone. Take your time returning to the Creek, as the plane, you remember, isn't due for the aerial check for another nine days. I've taken the hardware as it's the heaviest and most valuable. Leaving my tent—will camp light, using bivvy sack. Throw away all expendables and you can make it in one heavy load. If you get to the gravel bar and I'm not there, it's because I've decided to hike on out to Lime Village to get word out we want to be picked up. Don't worry about me—faster if one man goes, and I'm in shape. Just wait at Desolation Creek for the plane.

The note had neither salutation nor signature. At the last minute Victor pondered adding a few regretful words to Diana, but his rage vetoed the impulse.

With the heavy pack on his back, he hiked down-glacier until the pair of tents was out of sight. Then he made a sharp turn, headed for the edge of the glacier, turned again and, having effectively circled camp, settled into a steady upward trudge. His legs were sore from the previous day's effort, but he seemed to float along. The gray gloom of 5:00 A.M. combined with the rain to shrink his sphere of being around him.

The realization was growing on him that he had always misunderstood his own luck, the thing that he called his destiny. The kidney had nothing to do with it: the worm in the apple was trust. He had always been too trusting, had given himself over whole to others. For with trust came the opportunity for betrayal. It was clear now, as he strode along the mottled ice, that all the difficulties in his life had been occasioned by betrayal—first by Chalmers, then by Vera, now by Diana. Only Ed, among those he had deeply trusted, had justified the loyalty.

So the answer was the simple one he had resolved on now—the same choice, really, that he had made that night under the bridge in Minneapolis so long ago: to go it alone. When they woke and found the note, Diana and Derek might be puzzled, but it would never cross their minds that he was in fact still heading for the mountain. And even if they did think, days from now, to search up-glacier, they had shown so little interest in the maps that he doubted whether they would even recognize the junction with the stagnant glacial arm when they stumbled upon it. He was alone in the universe.

As for the climb itself, Victor had to recognize the odds against him. And there was, he admitted, a significant chance of getting killed. But did it matter? Did anything in the world matter more than Pterophorus? How fast he would be able to travel, unencumbered with Diana's blisters, with the fears or hesitations of weaklings. He was pretty sure that he could do the climbing solo, if he self-belayed the harder spots. In his notes back in Hartford, he had indicated that he thought no single pitch had been more difficult than 5.9. There was so little aid, too, and the pitons they had left in 1964 should still be in. The specter that gave him pause was his memory of the vertical ice-filled chimney a thousand feet below the top. His recollection of Ed's lead had him bridging strenuously near the rounded lips of the chimney, using ice screws for protection. Perhaps this time he could attack the ice directly. All that ice work that he had done alone last winter was vital now. True, no single pitch in Vermont or New Hampshire had been quite vertical. But he would see when he would see.

The plan was brilliantly simple. As long as he had the energy, he would force the march right to the base of the mountain. He felt capable of twelve miles in a single push—already he must have covered two. He would find a spot to bivouac below the route, try to get a good night's sleep, then go for it the next morning. Three days' food on the climb—soloing, he was bound to be fast. He could wear a pack on the mixed ground, haul it on the steeper pitches. In leaving his tent behind, he had eschewed the single most conspicuous sign of his presence. No airplane, even, would be able to spot him on the mountain. This time he would be sure to take photos all the way, and to leave some piece of gear on the summit. He would return to civilization, seemingly from the grave, and at last there would be no skeptics and belittlers.

The plodding effort lulled him gradually into a numbness, almost a euphoria. He had been forcing himself not to think about Diana, not to remember the sounds from the other tent. Something—adrenalin, he supposed—seemed to be doing the work of movement for him. But he knew that he would need rest and food, to be ready for the climb the next day. He forced himself to make a lunch stop at 8: 00 A.M.

Halfway through his second candy bar, his feelings crashed in upon him. A wild pang of loss surged through his limbs as he pictured Diana. With her image came a throng of memories from the fall, when he had been so vain as to believe that she could love him. She was right: he had been a nearsighted fool; for now a dozen details that had puzzled him in May—absences, discrepancies, looks of preoccupation on her face—made perfect sense in terms of her taking up with Derek. He remembered Arthur's prescient warning way back in October, and the story about the climber found dead at the bottom of Birdline, which, out of consideration, he had never quizzed her about.

He did not think he was angry with Derek. The man would discover in his turn what Diana was like. Only Derek's extreme passivity rankled, as in the fact that they had exchanged not a word after Diana's outrageous flaunting of her sex with him. Victor was sad about the destruction of what had begun to seem like a good friendship. But he had placed no blind hopes in Derek, had invested no love.

Shortly after lunch he came to the junction. The mist had been rising from the bottom all morning, and now as he stared up the stagnant arm, he could see gray rock far in the distance that might well be the lower reaches of the north face of Pterophorus. Only seven more miles, he told himself, as he made the tricky traverse through the seracs and left the main ice flow for good. He thought he recognized a particular serac: was it possible it had stood for fourteen years? He picked his way through the ubiquitous rock debris, around dank potholes in the ice, slipping on rubbly slopes, clawing here and there with his axe for purchase. The going was much slower than on the main glacier, but he was animated now by the wall at the head of the gloomy canyon that gradually took on detail as he approached.

His tiredness was catching up with him. He took another rest stop, and resolved to go only two more hours. The drizzle had not let up, despite the rising clouds; the temperature seemed to have dropped a few degrees. He was soaked with sweat inside his cagoule.

At last he made a camp, pitching the nylon fly like a lean-to from a large rock, scraping a level site for his bivvy sack on the ice underneath. He guessed he was only two miles from the base of the mountain. He crawled into his jacket and half bag and fell asleep.

Within the hour he awoke, shivering. Everything was too wet for comfortable sleep. A wind had come up, and the rain seemed half snow. He needed sleep desperately. He thought about taking a sleeping pill, but decided against it on the grounds that he needed alertness as much as sleep. After turning over a dozen times, he sat up and cooked himself a cup of tomato soup. It was five P.M. The soup restored his confidence. He decided to go on up and begin the climb. By the time it grew dark he might be five hundred feet off the glacier. There were good bivouac sites down low, he remembered. It might actually be warmer and drier on the mountain.

As he trudged toward the head of the glacier, Diana's betrayal weighed on his spirit like extra pounds in his pack. The damnable thing, he made himself acknowledge, was that he was still in love with her. It would take days, weeks—the climb itself—to cure him of the folly of caring about her. Now he hated her, too, as he had hated no one since Chalmers.

At last he came to the névé line. It was a good mile further up-glacier than it had been in 1964. The summer had indeed been incredibly dry. Above the Dorsal Fins, especially, there would be an abundance of bare ice. The gray-black wall ahead of him was taking on hints of familiar features; he could not be sure, but he thought he recognized the dihedrals that marked the start of the route. Snow was falling lightly, and the wind was up. He turned at one point and saw with satisfaction that his shallow footprints were starting to drift full only moments after he had passed. There would not be even that ephemeral trace of his passage.

The sky seemed all at once to grow brighter. He looked up. The mist was beginning to coalesce into distinct clouds; he could follow their movement as the strong south wind blew them down the glacier. Suddenly a patch of summit ridge flashed into view through a hole in the clouds. Amber sunlight fell on half a dozen castellated promontories, which were gleaming with fresh rime. The sight filled Victor with fear and joy. The mountain belonged to him.

The glacier was sloping upwards toward its termination in abrupt slabs of granite. Victor appraised the features before him and decided he was too far to the right for the beginning dihedrals. If only he had paid better attention to such things in the old years. He began traversing to his left, kicking four-inch-deep steps in the hard snow.

There were clean-cut pieces of rock scattered along his path, the relatively recent debris from collapsing fins and towers above. A series of crevasses narrowed his route to a transverse lane. He had been going for about ten minutes when an odd detail caught the corner of his eye and slowed him. The apparent piece of rock fifty yards up the slope seemed to have a faded orange hue. He stared at it for a moment. There was a crevasse between him and the object. He retraced his steps to make an end run of the crevasse.

As he approached the vaguely colored thing, he saw that it was some kind of gear. A small melange of gear, in fact: a pack, the torn remnants of some garment, and, remarkably, a boot, sole up. He bent over and grasped the boot; it was half frozen into the snow. He dug around the boot with his axe. The axe uncovered something sticking out from the snow. It was a bone. Victor recoiled in horror.

"It's Ed," he said softly, out loud. He recognized the Löwa boot. The details of debris took on a sudden gestalt: he could see the position of the body. "The dry summer," Victor murmured. "He's come out of the glacier, after all these years." He knelt and tugged at the orange cagoule. The rotten fabric tore easily in his fingers, uncovering sodden wool and more bone—the back of the skull, Victor saw. Again he recoiled. There was a nylon loop of hardware still associated with the body: he could see a broken carabiner and a rusty soft-iron piton. He put his hand out and touched the skull, then sniffed at his fingertips.

Standing up again, he looked from the debris upwards along the line of clean granite that had been Ed's fall. The clouds were blowing off the summit ridge, and there were sparkles of light in the ice crystals up high. Victor thought he could see the ledge below which the fixed rope had broken. With the clarity of a revelation their last days together sprang into his mind: the horrible storm, the forty hours of waiting, the anguish of the decision to go down. A chill settled behind his shoulders, at the top of his neck. He said out loud, "We didn't climb it, then."

He looked around. It was as if someone had been there, just behind him. Were those dots down the glacier Diana and Derek? No, they were just rocks. A rage seized him. He screamed into the wind, "Yes I did! I did climb it! I did!"

He looked down again. The pieces of Ed's body seemed to say, "No, we didn't. Don't you remember?" Once more Victor was possessed by the conviction that there were people coming up the glacier. He whirled around and stared at the distant rocks sitting on the ice. He was sure one of them had just moved. Perhaps they knew he was looking, and had frozen in place, imitating inanimate objects. He held his breath, listening, but heard only the whistle of the wind.

In a frenzy he seized the boot and yanked on it. The leg bone came loose with it. He scuttled downhill fifty feet to the middle of the crevasse, approached the edge, and threw boot and bone in. A dull thud of impact was succeeded by a fainter one. Hurriedly he returned to the body. When he grasped the cagoule, it ripped into shreds in his hands. He gathered up all the loose gear and clothing that was not frozen into the ice and made a second trip to the crevasse. On his third effort he started excavating with his axe around the back of the skull and the other bone—a hip apparently—that protruded from the glacier. When he had got enough of the hip exposed to get a good hold, he yanked furiously on it. The bones broke and an asymmetrical piece of pelvis was left in his hands. He hacked at the ice around the skull. Down a few inches, muddy in the ice, there seemed to be something like flesh—the front of Ed's face? He got the pick of his axe under it and pried. The skull came loose, minus the jawbone. He returned to the crevasse. The pelvis was clotted with a heavy mass of ice and wool. Victor lugged his burden to the lip of the crevasse and pushed it in. Again the inconclusive thudding sounds. On his hands and knees he leaned over the edge to look in. It was very dark inside.

He leaned a little further, and heard a sudden soughing sound, deep but close. The world gave way beneath him. He was falling. In a flash of awareness he knew that the overhanging lip of snow must have broken beneath his weight. He seemed to be upside down. His head hit something hard.

When he came back to consciousness, he had no idea how much later it was. He felt his forehead and looked at his hand in the murky darkness. His fingers were wet. He tasted the wetness, but could not tell if the flavor were blood. There was pain all through his body, and he was cold. He looked up at the tiny gap in the ceiling through which he had fallen. On the Lacuna Glacier below Foraker he had fallen twenty feet into a crevasse. This time, he guessed, he was about forty feet in. His eyes seemed relatively accustomed to the darkness. He looked around.

The first hope, of walking out one end of the crevasse, was dashed: he had come to rest on a jammed platform of ice, beyond which on either end the gulf opened as the crevasse widened and deepened. So he would have to climb up one wall and tunnel through the overhanging lip. He still had his pack on, with the crampons attached. But where was his axe?

With a sting of dismay he pictured the axe left in place beside his excavation site. Well, he said to himself, you've got an ice hammer. It should be tough, but not impossible. He rolled up on one knee and screamed with pain.

Pulling his pants leg up, he looked at the damage. There was a bone protruding through the skin, shattered splinters of it covered with blood. He reached down and felt a greasy smear of blood. Whimpering, he felt his head go black again. He came back in a matter of moments.

Somewhere in the pack, he thought grimly, is the first-aid kit. With an enormous effort he got the pack off and rummaged through it. But when he came to the small box of pills and tape and band-aids, the full hopelessness of his situation came home to him. He groaned out loud. The pain was getting worse. He fished a couple of codeine tablets out of the bottle and chewed them down.

Next to him on the platform were pieces of Ed's cagoule, along with the partial skull and the boot and bone. The pelvis seemed to have vanished further down the crevasse. He tore loose a strip of cagoule and tied a tourniquet around his lower thigh. But he was too weak to tighten it sufficiently to make the blood stop spreading. There was a dank, putrid odor in the air.

I can't make it myself, Victor thought. The only hope in the world is if Diana and Derek come up the glacier. Then he remembered the careful strategem of his note, the twelve miles between him and them, the wind drifting full his footsteps. He groaned again. He was starting to shiver. He managed to find his dacron jacket and fit it over his shoulders.

The sense of despair lightened. It was clear what he could do. He opened the medical kit and shook out all the codeine. There were about fifteen tablets. One by one he chewed them. Then he found the sleeping pills and managed to swallow all of them.

Within moments the pain had been reduced to an ache so remote it seemed to be happening to someone else. His brain was fogging over. He reached out and grasped Ed's skull, then propped it up beside himself, the empty eye sockets facing towards him.

"So this is what it all comes to, Louis," he said out loud. "This is all we ever did, is go and get ourselves killed. This is that wonderful destiny I thought we had. But at least we ended up in it together, and at least we managed to vanish. They'll never find us down here, those bastards, so they'll never know what happened to us." He yawned mightily. The skull stared back at him. "All for a mountain. All just to be able to say we were first. But what else would have been any better? Not a person, not a job—we knew that. It's as good a way to die as any—you must have known that, just in the second that the rope broke." It was hard to keep his eyes open. His lips felt fuzzy. "Louis, goddamn it, we were good on a rope together. They didn't come any better than we were. I'm sorry, old man, I wanted to end up on the summit, I wouldn't have minded dying there. But this is OK, too. It's quiet and cozy, and we don't have to go out in the cold ever again . . . ."

SLOUCHING TOWARD EVEREST
A CRITIQUE OF EXPEDITION NARRATIVES

David Roberts

There is no genre in mountaineering literature more formulaic than that of the expedition book. In its classic form (British and Himalayan), its specimens can be counted on to observe most of the following conventions:

- A team of immensely gifted and selfless climbers will be assembled by the author; averaging in age well over thirty, they will have in common, whatever their technical ability, deep funds of judgment and experience.
- There will be hideous delays in customs, solved by the leader's dogged penetration into the mysteries of Asian bureaucracy.
- On the approach march, a porter strike that threatens to wreck the whole expedition will be averted by the liaison officer's brilliant harangue, exhorting the hill men not to disgrace their people's proud tradition of service.
- Base camp will not be reached before page 100.
- Dangerous conditions in the icefall will result in a shortage of supplies for the upper camps, and the expedition will find itself seriously behind schedule.
- Two stalwarts will be incapacitated, one because he never recovers from dysentery acquired by foolishly sampling the native cuisine, the other due to an inexplicable inability to acclimatize.
- The young technical whiz will solve the crux pitches on the route, but will be passed over in choosing the summit team.
- One Sherpa, who as a boy had carried loads for the German attempt on the mountain thirty-one years earlier, will distinguish himself by hauling twice as many loads to Camp VII as anyone else.
- The leader will marvel over the utter self-sacrifice and team spirit of each and every member, nowhere revealed more strikingly than in the stoic acceptance by all of the leader's choice for the summit pair.
- The radio will report the monsoon due in three days.
- On the summit day, the pair at Camp IX will: a) spend a fitful night listening to the tent flap in the stiff wind; b) have trouble with the oxygen apparatus; c) manage a tepid cup of tea at dawn; d) spend an hour getting on each boot; e) pass the whole day recurrently taking two steps, then leaning on their axes to rest; f) find their strength just adequate to the summit, where they take out-of-focus snapshots of each other; g) regain camp with a desperate effort well after dark; h) accept the inevitable frostbite as the price one pays for a great triumph.
- On the descent, one climber will die a pointless death when a serac collapses, or else several Sherpas will be lost in an avalanche.

There is nothing duller than a dull expedition book. In recent years climbers seem disaffected not only from narratives of large expeditions, but from those expeditions themselves. Shipton and Tilman, with their four-man treks, have become retroactive heroes of the avant-garde. The iconoclasm of

Overleaf: Dhaulagiri from the southeast. *Allen Steck.*

Viewed from Paiyu Peak, the debris-covered Baltoro Glacier flows sinuously down from the foot of Gasherbrum IV. Broad Peak lies to the left. *Allen Steck*.

Joe Brown, who described Kangchenjunga as "a long slog," has credibility far beyond the earnest chroniclings of Norman Dyhrenfurth.

Curiously, large expensive expeditions continue to flourish, and "good climbers" swallow their scruples and go on them. And the books that get written, even by authors who profess themselves bored to tears by most previous examples of the genre, continue to follow the old formula.

It is not simply a question of realism. Any story can be told in a myriad of different ways. I suspect there is something deeply satisfying about the formula itself, however tedious or hackneyed. For me, at age ten or twelve, mountaineering expedition books were a favorite form of escape literature, long before there was any inkling of being able to do that sort of thing myself.

The long approach march, far from defeating attention, served the necessary role of lulling the senses away from the familiar, into an alien world of rock and ice and wind. The unquestioning loyalty of true comrades seemed to demonstrate how important the mountain was, and promised a magical adult alternative to the internecine squabbles of playground gangs. The tiny margin of success was wholly believable; and death proved beyond doubt that the game was more serious than the one the Yankees and Dodgers were playing.

My interest in a formulaic literature lies not in seeking radical departures from the norms—nobody wants the crime to go unsolved in a detective novel—but rather in the variations and nuances possible within the formula. The purpose of this essay is to consider the genre itself, and to offer my list, admittedly subjective and biased among other ways by a disproportionate familiarity with English-language books, of the best expedition narratives of the last 150 years.

The mountaineering expedition book did not spring, in the last half of the nineteenth century, full-grown from the brows of the first great trekkers in the remote ranges. It evolved as a species of a genus that had already reached maturity—that of the exploration narrative in the broadest sense. Because of its similar glacial terrain, the climbing narrative seems to today's reader to bear the closest affinities with the great Arctic and Antarctic narratives of the period 1815-1915. Characteristically, those accounts appeared in lavish folio volumes, handsomely illustrated with engravings, maps, and photographs, and festooned with appendices; it was not uncommon for the prose to occupy five or six hundred pages. Impatient modernists find such books slow going. But at their best those volumes matched the experience with the form in which it was presented: the leisurely pace and obsession with detail imitated the very progress of explorers on trips that lasted as long as five years; the booty brought home, in a century that had begun to outgrow gold-seeking and soul-saving, could be appendicized as "Science"; magnificent and accurate landscapes bespoke the care of observation that went into them. In general, the sense of being "out there," beyond the hope of rescue, self-sufficient in an utterly alien place, was communicated by the monumentality of the books themselves. The two pinnacles of that literature are perhaps Fridtjof Nansen's *Farthest North* and Apsley Cherry-Garrard's *The Worst Journey in the World*.

At its feeblest the nineteenth-century mountaineering book is an overblown parody of the above, all the lavishness of production going to glorify a two-month stroll in a quaint foreign country. But there were magnificent Himalayan and Andean reconnaissances, even some ascents; and in rare cases the quality of the book matched the quality of the achievement.

In 1848 Sir Joseph Hooker, a botanist who had been on Sir James Ross's pioneering Antarctic expedition, undertook an equally extraordinary walk through parts of Sikkim, Bengal, and Nepal, in many places realizing he was the first Western visitor. His *Himalayan Journals* is a symphony of loving yet precise description of everything cultural and botanical. He was fascinated with the tribes he met and had a kind of proto-anthropological curiosity,

Overleaf: Mount Everest with its typical snow plume. Nuptse rises on the right. *Allen Steck*.

though the chauvinism of his day limited his receptivity: "The Lepcha is in morals far superior to his Tibet and Bhotan neighbors, polyandry being unknown, and polygamy rare." The account is not very personal. But for rapturously specific word-paintings of plants and insects, Hooker has few peers.

Half a century later Douglas Freshfield made a nearly complete circle tour around Kangchenjunga with photographer Vittorio Sella. *Round Kangchenjunga* is a certifiable masterpiece. Freshfield weds an eye for detail almost as sharp as Hooker's to a poet's sensibility, converting what could be hackneyed Romantic landscapes into epiphanies of the alien—as in this description of a jungle waterfall: "a superb cataract rushing down a cloven ravine over which pale hydrangeas dripped, while the grey lichens on the nodding trees were shaken by the perpetual blast." His zest for the incongruous graces every page, and the book is bejeweled with parenthetical musings and asides. When the sun comes out blindingly on a glacier near Kangchenjunga, "the coolies put on the dark spectacles with which we had provided them, and tied rags under their chins; the Bhotias smeared their faces with more soot and tallow; the Lepchas undid their pigtails and tied their long black locks as a screen before their eyes." In another memorable passage, the party stands beneath an apparently unclimbable mountain.

> Siniolchum is, for the climber, the ideal snow mountain; the throne where
> > "Power dwells apart in its tranquillity,
> > Remote, serene, and inaccessible."
> Inaccessible! For my own generation I am not afraid to use the word. But others will come, and, standing on our shoulders, will boast, as men did in Homer's day, that they are much better than their fathers.

The most striking contrast with Freshfield is afforded by Oscar Eckenstein's *The Karakorams and Kashmir,* which details, among other adventures, the second penetration of the Baltoro Glacier to a point near K2. Eckenstein, with his friend Mattias Zurbriggen, had joined up with Sir Martin Conway's British expedition in 1892; but he found himself disenchanted and left the party. With characteristic bluntness he records:

> We had a sort of general meeting, at which it was arranged that I should leave the expedition. There had been a great deal of friction from time to time, and, as we had now been some two and a half months in the mountains without making a single ascent of importance, having only crossed two previously known passes, I was not anxious to go on.

(Conway's own account has it differently: "Eckenstein had never been well since reaching Gilgit. It was evidently useless for him to come further with us, so I decided that he had better return to England.")

On his own, Eckenstein came into his element. He spent his first day bouldering on the giant rocks near the Baltoro, and set up a local competition, "the object being to see how these natives compare with Swiss guides." The best man, he concluded, would outclimb the best Swiss guide on any kind of rock. Eckenstein was perhaps the first Westerner to give Himalayan peoples their due (his book is dedicated "To my friend, the Heathen"), even when suffering embarrassments like his attempt to buy the dress a native woman is wearing, which results in the shock of discovering he has bought the woman, not the dress.

The best early Alaskan narrative is Belmore Browne's *The Conquest of Mount McKinley.* Browne combined three talents—as overland explorer, painter, and writer—in a superb chronicle of his three determined attacks (in 1906, 1910, and 1912) on the continent's highest peak, the last failing in a blizzard so near the summit that he estimated the remainder as "five minutes' walk in clear weather." The 1906 account casts light on the enigma of Frederick Cook's faked ascent. Having been Browne's ally on the summer's bold penetration up the Ruth Glacier, Cook hurried back in September with one companion for a dash at the summit. Browne doubted Cook's claim from the moment he heard it and was the first to identify the insignificant lump on which Cook shot his "summit photo."

Two Andean chronicles tower above the rest. One is Edward Whymper's classic *Travels amongst the Great Andes of the Equator,* which records the brilliant mountaineer's first ascents of Chimborazo, Antisana, Cayamba, and other peaks, as well as his bivouac on the summit of Cotopaxi. Hounded out of England by the controversy surrounding the deaths on the Matterhorn, Whymper headed off to the great ranges. In South America much of his climbing was done with Jean-Antoine Carrel, his chief rival on the Matterhorn, down upon whom he had rolled rocks from the summit to gloat over his victory.

Less well known is Edward FitzGerald's *The Highest Andes,* his account of the first ascent of Aconcagua in 1897. FitzGerald, a strong traveler, was the master of a laconic, tongue-in-cheek style, as evidenced in the following passage. While fording a river on a mule, his companion, Mattias Zurbriggen, has been swept out of control, only to fetch up underwater, pinned to a rock by the frantic animal. The native driver is worried only about the mule, but FitzGerald manages to dislodge the beast and rescue Zurbriggen.

I laid him down on the grass, and with the help of a little brandy succeeded in restoring him to life . . . Zurbriggen has a fixed idea in his head that he is to die by drowning, so that little episodes of this character have a most distressing and demoralizing effect on him.

FitzGerald finally talks his friend back into riding a mule.

He said to me, "I know I do get killed today," and as luck would have it, we had not gone more than a mile when he and his mule quietly rolled over the edge of a rock precipice. . . . When I ran and picked him up, he turned to me, and said slowly, "You see, I do get killed today." I did my best to encourage him by pointing out that he was still alive. . . . About sunset we reached the next and last ford. This time Zurbriggen remarked, "It is all over, I do die now."

The four summits of
Nevado Huandoy in the
Cordillera Blanca of Peru.
Chacraraju lies at the far left.
Leigh Ortenburger.

Chimborazo, one of the great volcanoes of the equatorial Andes. *Allen Steck.*

Sure enough, his mule tips over and he takes another long swim. Zurbriggen survived to be the only member of the party to reach Aconcagua's summit.

Though short in duration in comparison with contemporary polar expeditions, these early ventures were longer than what we call a mountaineering expedition today (four to six months were perhaps average), and involved logistical and navigational problems far more immense than we are used to dealing with. As Eckenstein complained, the trips tended to be short on actual climbing; but they were masterworks of exploratory travel. Thanks to aerial photography, we can never again have as part of the mountaineering experience the erasing of a blank on the map; we will never know what an expedition is like in which half the battle is simply finding one's way to the mountain. That tradition persisted as late as 1950, when the French climbed Annapurna. It is often overlooked by readers of Herzog's book—still the most famous, and still one of the best, of expedition narratives—that the effort nearly failed even to get to the mountain. The triumph was brilliant, especially given the few pre-monsoon days remaining before the party actually started climbing.

In making a survey like this one, a maddening source of frustration creeps in. There have always been wonderful expeditions the accounts of which are not particularly distinguished. It is not so much that the books are *bad,* as that the prose is merely competent: these books lack the flair that sets Freshfield or FitzGerald apart. In one's enthusiasm for the style of the adventure, one is tempted to ignore the ordinariness of the writing. Of course one can read such books with much profit and inspiration. But a discriminating list must, alas, exclude them. The Duke of the Abruzzi's magnificent ascent of

St. Elias and his attempt on K2 come to mind: the climbing style, Sella's photography, the boldness of the plan—all were wholly admirable. Yet Filippo de Filippi's writing is not up to the the standard of Whymper or Browne. Sir Martin Conway made three fine voyages—the Karakoram journey with Eckenstein, the first crossing of Spitsbergen, and the third ascent of Aconcagua combined with a visit to Tierra del Fuego—but his long chronicles of those trips remain workmanlike. The same can be said of Sir Francis Younghusband, one of the great early Himalayan adventurers; and, more recently, of Fosco Maraini, whose *Karakoram* chronicles the daring ascent of Gasherbrum IV.

There are rare cases of "bad" expeditions resulting in good books, as discussed farther on. In even rarer cases the defects of the writing make it difficult to judge the achievement. It is hard, for instance, to separate Annie Smith Peck's whining, paranoid style from the controversy over whether she was carried by guides to the summit of Huascaran. Sometimes the smoothest of successes make the dullest of reading. Sir John Hunt's *The Ascent of Everest* simply fails to bring character and drama to life; but even Wilfrid Noyce's immensely more engaging *South Col* succumbs in part to the apparent clockwork operation of the first ascent of the world's highest mountain. The official 1924 Everest book is, for its prose, no more lively than Hunt's narrative; yet Odell's account of his last glimpse of Mallory and Irvine stands like a sacred text in mountain literature.

There was no more tragic arena of expedition failure than Nanga Parbat in the 1930s; but not one of the books to emerge from that struggle is really topnotch. Perhaps hardest of all to bring to life is the big international expedition. Its plot seems inherently unreadable, with no obvious climax, a plethora of subplots, loose ends everywhere—and too many *people*. The best piece of writing to come out of Dyhrenfurth's 1971 Everest fiasco was Murray Sayle's piece in *Life,* which focused on the dissension. Probably the best of these books is Malcolm Slesser's *Red Peak,* which handles the deaths of Noyce and Robin Smith in the Pamirs with dignity; but it is not a great book.

All too infrequently the "perfect" expedition finds a first-rate literary expression. The 1932 American Minya Konka expedition was a prodigy of exploratory mountaineering—1500 miles by boat up the Yangtze, by bus through Szechwan, 150 miles by porters, yaks, horses and even a cow to base camp, culminating in the first ascent of a mountain rumored to be higher than Everest. And in *Men Against the Clouds* Richard Burdsall and Arthur Emmons put together an unpretentious, exciting book, ranging in tone from the grim account of Emmons's loss of all his toes and miserable recovery from gangrene to the whimsy of Katrina Moore's poem on the yak:

> Behold the ever-patient Yak,
> With four explorers on his back.
> He treks for miles across the snows,
> Wearing a bracelet in his nose;
> And when they stop to have a snack,
> It's slices of the useful Yak!

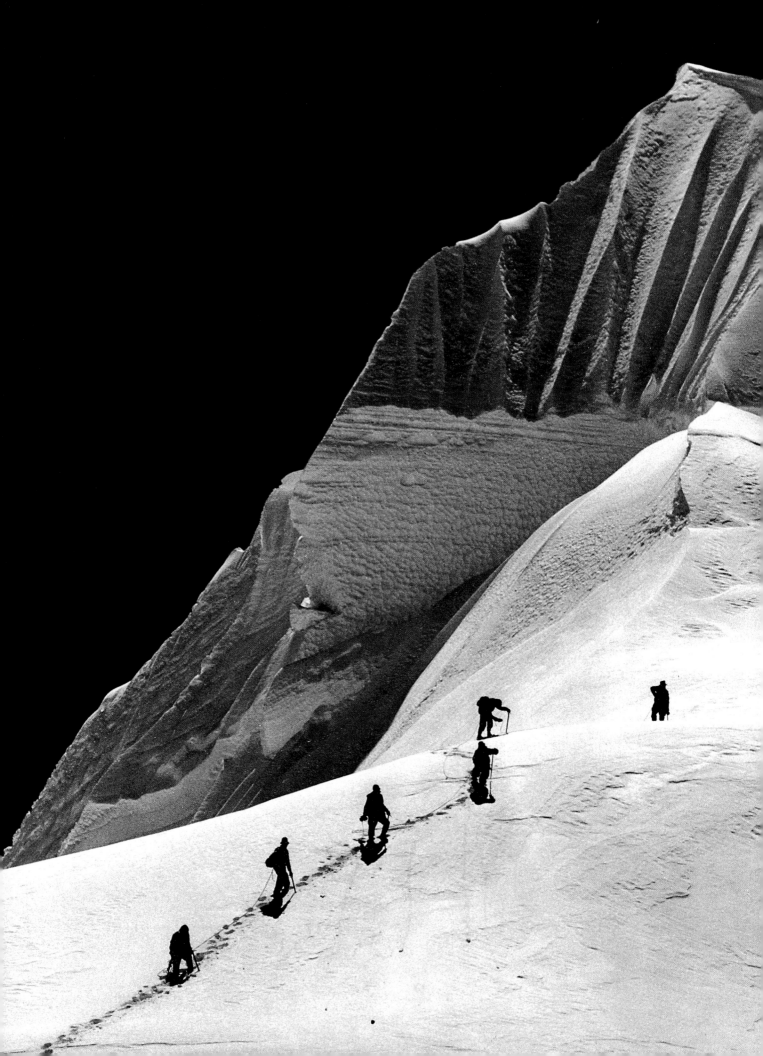

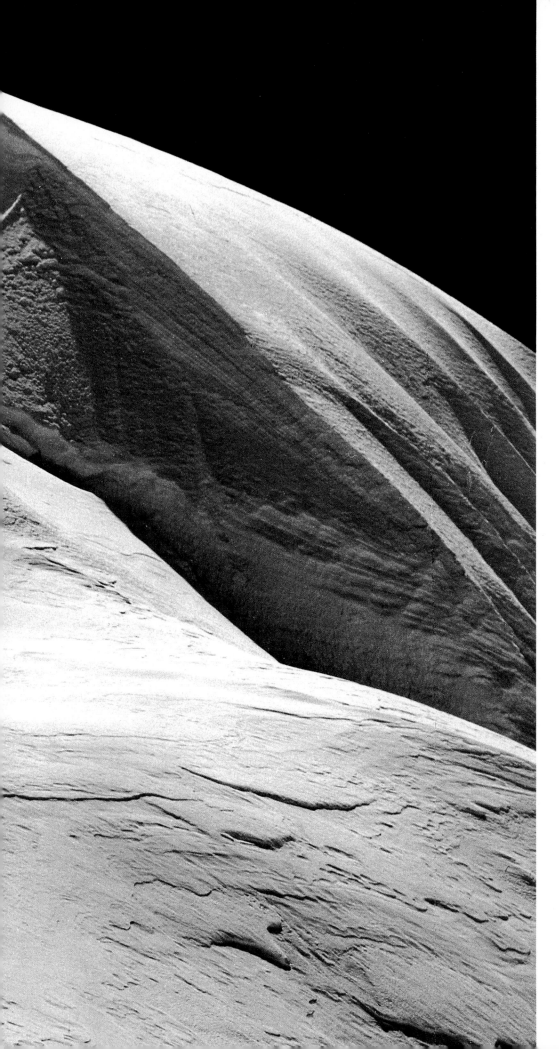

Wind-carved flutings grace the summit of Chopicalqui in the Cordillera Blanca of Peru. *Leigh Ortenburger.*

No Picnic on Mount Kenya, by Felice Benuzzi, records an achievement unique in mountaineering history: the 1943 ascent of Mount Kenya by three Italians who had escaped from a nearby British POW camp. This amazing feat finds an able chronicler in Benuzzi, who describes such incidents as manufacturing their own crampons and ice axes out of the materials available in the compound in a vivid, personal, unaffected style.

The early chapters of M. A. Azéma's *The Conquest of FitzRoy* are not impressive; in particular, the absurd death of Jacques Poincenot in a botched river crossing comes across with virtually no evidence of its emotional repercussions. But in losing himself for the latter part of the book in an almost novelistic firsthand report of Terray's and Magnone's brilliant summit push, Azéma accomplishes perhaps the finest vicarious climb in the literature—and records for posterity one of the immortal exclamations: "Guido, the sardine tin!" (A responsible reviewer would explain the allusion, but I will refrain in the interest of driving readers to the source.)

Running through our century and a half of mountaineering literature is a special current, stretching from Freshfield to Tom Patey, that accounts for a large part of its best writing. The voice we hear in that writing—almost invariably British—is a conversational one, which however polished, gives the effect of casual speech. At its best the voice cultivates qualities the slight exaggeration of which leads to all that is worst about British wit. It remains urbane without being pompous; ironic without straining for effect; cozy without being cute; ingenuously enthusiastic rather than back-thumping hearty. Not coincidentally, those qualities carry over into the climbing, so that the expeditioneers who speak in its accents tend also to prefer light, mobile,

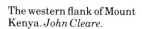

The western flank of Mount Kenya. *John Cleare.*

imaginative journeys, and to avoid the blare of publicity. The Noyce of *Climbing the Fish's Tail* (Machapuchare) finds easy articulation in this vein, having reined in the metaphysical urges that mar his *The Gods Are Angry* and *The Springs of Adventure*. Tom Longstaff's wonderful memoir, *This My Journey,* is one of the classic pillars of the style; it is a pity that he never wrote a full-length expedition book. W. H. Murray combines extreme clarity of prose with a doctor's lively curiosity about everything to do with native peoples in his sparkling account of a modest 1950 expedition to the Garhwal Himalaya, *The Scottish Himalayan Expedition*. He can be whimsical: "The Bhotia husband never calls his wife by her first name, or indeed by any name at all. Often he does not know her name, because he has forgotten it." Or, in the same breath, laconically chilling, as in a note about Bhotia women gathering firewood in bear country:

They always carry a sickle in one hand and a forked stick in the other. They try to jam the stick into the bear's open mouth. As the head goes back they step sideways and slash the exposed throat with the sickle. The bear may sometimes be killed, but more usually the woman gets mauled, and perhaps half her face is torn away.

The quintessence of that understated British voice is found in the two friends who remain England's most splendid traveler-mountaineers, Eric Shipton and H. W. Tilman. A list of the best expedition books that included all the *opera* of both men would not be stretching their due by much. Each of them wrote a book about Nanda Devi, and both are worth reading—not only Tilman's classic about the 1936 ascent, but Shipton's account of the reconnaissance two years earlier, with its rapturous tale of the first penetration up the Rishi Gorge into the Inner Sanctuary:

My most blissful dream as a child was to be in some such valley, free to wander where I liked, and discover for myself some hitherto unrevealed glory of Nature. Now the reality was no less wonderful than that half-forgotten dream; and of how many childish fancies can that be said, in this age of disillusionment?

Both men turned, in their middle years, toward a hybrid expedition style combining sailing with climbing. Tilman, in fact, was lost at sea in November 1977. All his *Mischief* books are delightful, none more so than the first, *Mischief in Patagonia,* in which Tilman explains the reasons for turning his back on the Himalayas.

By 1956 not only had [Everest] been climbed again but the six next highest peaks had been, in the classic phrase, 'knocked off,' and there were some forty expeditions afoot, eleven of them, employing 5,000 porters, in Nepal.

The Himalaya are extensive, no less than 1,500 miles in length, but a quiet man might well shrink from going, say, to Katmandu, the starting place for the Nepal Himalaya, if he thought he was likely to meet there eleven other parties with their 5,000 porters. Moreover, if he had the misfortune to find himself traveling in the wake of one of these parties he would find food hard to come by, and local transport either unobtainable or at a premium. Such inhabitants as did remain would all be wearing

Aconcagua's summit rises
above the arid terrain of
west-central Argentina. This
view shows the infrequently
visited northeast side of the
peak. *Allen Steck.*

climbing boots and wrist-watches and would drive uncommonly hard bargains. Added to these considerations is the undoubted fact that the Himalaya are high, too high for those who are not 'in the vaward of youth', and though the ageing mountaineer will assuredly find rich solace in its valleys and upon its glaciers, he is not likely to resort to them when he knows there are peaks in other parts of the world still within his feeble grasp. So I began thinking of those two white blanks on the map, of penguins and humming birds, of the pampas and the gauchos, in short, of Patagonia, a place where, one was told, the natives' heads steam when they eat marmalade.

Ridge climbing in Alaska.
Alan Kearney.

How masterfully, and how inconspicuously, those sentences shift from the general proposition to the personal testament! And that is the clue to what might generically be labeled the Shipton-Tilman style: the discovery of a voice in which to speak about one's own adventures with neither false modesty nor braggadocio.

A short step, but a crucial one, separates that ironic style from the satire of true self-mockery. The latter vein can be appropriate to mountain writing, but is full of pitfalls for the unwary. Patey mastered his own macabre-hilarious version of it; but his imitators, like Ian McNaught Davis, lapse too easily into buffoonery, and raucous American variants such as Warren Harding's have the self-conscious machismo of beer-chugging contests. For handling an expedition of "bunglers," the satirical style may do. It has at least one minor masterpiece in Eric Newby's *A Short Walk in the Hindu Kush*. By portraying his partner Hugh Carless as a kind of a mad scientist of climbing, Newby produces an endless stream of funny scenes. High on a peak in Nuristan, the two men see distant lightning.

"North India," Hugh said, with the tremendous authority that I had learned to mistrust. "Pakistan. Electric storm, possibly monsoon. Must be a hundred miles away. Lucky; if it reached here we'd be in a nasty spot."
"This is a nasty spot."

Or (Hugh is assailing some reluctant porters):

"... that you would not come with us to Nuristan because the way is hard and because you are faint-hearted I can perhaps forgive, but that you should call the Nuristanis who are your brothers 'idolatrous unbelievers,' they who have only recently been converted to Islam and need your prayers—Sunnites like yourselves and probably better ones—*that is another matter.*"
Here Hugh paused, glaring frightfully. After allowing his words to sink in he resumed: "When I return *from Nuristan* (masterly stroke) I shall demand audience of General Ubaiddullah Khan and tell him what you said about 'idolatrous unbelievers.' General Ubaiddullah Khan is a man of importance and," Hugh added with the final touch of genius, "he is also a Nuristani."
The effect of this was remarkable. At once all opposition ceased. Before we finally fell asleep long after midnight I asked Hugh who General Ubaiddullah Khan was.
"So far as I know," he said, "he doesn't exist. I just invented him; but I think he's going to be a very useful man to know."

There are at least two interesting versions of the "Bunglers Abroad" approach. Woodrow Wilson Sayre's *Four Against Everest* has been widely hailed as a good book; but it is simply too dishonest (about "borrowing" the helicopter intended for the evacuation of Willi Unsoeld, for instance) and too vainglorious (evaluating their push to 25,400 feet—a height lower than that reached by the first attempt in 1922—by saying, "We struck a blow . . . for the tradition of the small expedition.") to leave a very good taste in the mouth. On the other hand Robert Dunn's little-known *The Shameless Diary of an Explor-*

Seen from Concordia, at the upper end of the Baltoro Glacier, K2 looms over the Godwin-Austen Glacier. The right skyline is the Abruzzi Ridge, route of the first and second ascents. *Jack Turner*.

The east face of Cerro Fitzroy, the highest peak of the Fitzroy group. The sharper and lower summit to the left is the Aiguille Poincenot. *Chris Jones.*

er may be the most outrageous of climbing books—to the point sometimes of downright savagery. An unexpurgated account of Frederick Cook's 1903 attempt on Mount McKinley, it refers to the party only by pseudonyms (Cook is called "the Professor"); Dunn uses this transparent veil mercilessly to expose the idiocies and incompetence of his teammates. The book makes the reader feel like a Peeping Tom. Yet *Diary* stands as the single expedition narrative most candid about interpersonal frictions, as well as the chronicle that best captures the day-by-day details of overland travel. A sample:

> Here in camp, we've been holding a post mortem of the day. Fred baited Simon unmercifully, and Jack observed that he'd seen the fifth wheel washing gravel out of hair. Simon was burning in a frying-pan his indigestible biscuits insides—the old trick—when King drawled, "What yer carryin' around that smudge with yer for?" Even the Professor added his mite by issuing the fiat that no more pancakes, on which Simon lives, are to be cooked, because they use too much sugar. Those two seem tuckered out, and now are asleep with their mouths open; not beautiful sights, with Alaskan crops of whiskers. I've said good-bye to my toes. For days they've been sticking through my boots, so I've capped them with leather from one of the two Abercrombie saddles, and Belgian nails. Our legs are badly chafed. We smear them with vaseline. Jack is riveting a flour sack to his overalls. Miller can't find any currants. . . .

If one of the cardinal failures of expedition books is the boyish fiction that all the team members were paragons of selflessness who got along with each other like Brothers of the Cross, there are a few books (besides Dunn's) that attempt to get beneath the surface of personality. Noyce's *South Col* and Tom Hornbein's *Everest: The West Ridge* make lively use of dialogue, internal monologue, and character portrait in an effort to transform huge and drudgerous expeditions into human enterprises. If the men and movements end up still blurred in most readers' minds, the fault lies more with the plots of the stories than with those able authors. Chris Bonington's *Annapurna: South Face* may have been the first book deliberately to puncture the myth that a successful climb carried out by topnotch alpinists was not all peaches and cream, interpersonally, that in fact it was played out with large doses of selfishness and route-politicking. To his credit, Bonington uses taped radio messages and remembered dialogue to be frank about the tensions, without undercutting our sense of the excellence of the achievement.

Otherwise praiseworthy books, like Azéma's, often have extreme difficulty in dealing honestly with accidents; and of course the hardest event of all to handle judiciously is death. A tone of almost blasé fatalism—one kind of authorial embarrassment—creeps in at such junctures with a frequency matched only by its twin, the tone of solemn-but-trite eulogy. Perhaps because he was a professional writer and not present on the 1957 Oxford expedition to Haramosh, Ralph Barker avoids those traps in *The Last Blue Mountain*. He slips partway into another one—the temptation to moralize and second-guess from an armchair about the errors that led to the deaths of Bernard Jillott and Rae Culbert. But his telling of this grim expedition story maintains an impressive detachment as it winds its way with gothic inevitability toward the tragedies.

Among firsthand accounts of disastrous expeditions, none is more moving than Bob Bates's and Charles Houston's *K2: The Savage Mountain*. The story of Art Gilkey's thrombophlebitis, the desperate attempt to evacuate him from the mountain, the intertangled falls of roped pairs held by Pete Schoening's miracle belay, Gilkey's loss in an avalanche, and the crippled retreat of the demoralized and injured climbers is virtually canonic in mountaineering memory. But it is not the mere fact of the accidents—as it is the mere fact of Mallory and Irvine's disappearance—that has made those events so well known. Much of the credit must go to Bates's and Houston's unexaggerated telling of the tale. Few disasters have been handled with comparable honesty—as exemplified by the authors' admission that Gilkey's death brought a certain relief with it, for at the rate the team was moving his litter, the whole party might well have perished.

Stepping back from the individual works, one notices a few broad patterns. The best expedition books do follow the age-old formula, complete with narrow escapes and victories; but they convince us of their authenticity by transcending some of the formula's limitations—like the reticence about human fallibility, in the case of the K2 book, or the taboo against "dirty laundry," in Robert Dunn's case. No single narrative stands head and shoulders above its companions; yet, despite the feeling that expedition accounts are almost intrinsically dull, this essay argues that there is a surprisingly large number of good books in the genre.

Overleaf: The north face of Annapurna in the Nepal Himalaya. *Allen Steck.*

The best of them all? Despite its condescension toward Himalayan natives, despite subscribing to the Brothers-of-the-Cross myth, despite the geographical dizziness of its early chapters—despite, above all, its fame—Herzog's *Annapurna* seems to this reader to be—well, maybe—the best expedition book. But the best expedition writer? Tilman, just as he was arguably the century's best explorer-mountaineer, whittling his whole life to a sunny vagabondage that held him in its thrall even as he sailed off into the Antarctic Ocean in his eightieth year.

My list of the best expedition books follows. The date in parentheses indicates the date of publication; the dates in brackets are the dates of the expedition.

Asia
Barker, Ralph. *The Last Blue Mountain.* (1959), [1957].
Bonington, Chris. *Annapurna: South Face.* (1971), [1970].
Burdsall, Richard L. and Arthur B. Emmons. *Men against the Clouds: The Conquest of Minya Konka.* (1935), [1932].
Eckenstein, Oscar. *The Karakorams and Kashmir: An Account of a Journey.* (1896), [1892].
Freshfield, Douglas W. *Round Kangchenjunga: A Narrative of Mountain Travel and Exploration.* (1903), [1899].
Herzog, Maurice. *Annapurna.* (1951), [1950].
Hooker, Sir Joseph. *Himalayan Journals: Notes of a Naturalist in Bengal, the Sikkim and Nepal Himalayas, the Khasia Mountains, etc.* (1855), [1848-51].
Hornbein, Thomas F. *Everest: The West Ridge.* (1966), [1963].
Houston, Charles S. and Robert H. Bates. *K2: The Savage Mountain.* (1954), [1953].
Murray, W. H. *The Scottish Himalayan Expedition.* (1951), [1950].
Newby, Eric. *A Short Walk in the Hindu Kush.* (1958), [1956].
Noyce, Wilfrid. *Climbing the Fish's Tail.* (1958), [1957].
————. *South Col.* (1954), [1953].
Shipton, Eric. *Nanda Devi.* (1936), [1934].
Tilman, H. W. *The Ascent of Nanda Devi.* (1937), [1936].

South America
Azéma, M. A. *The Conquest of FitzRoy.* (1957), [1952].
FitzGerald, Edward A. *The Highest Andes: A Record of the First Ascent of Aconcagua and Tupungato in Argentina, and the Exploration of the Surrounding Valleys.* (1899), [1897].
Tilman, H. W. *Mischief in Patagonia.* (1957), [1956].
Whymper, Edward. *Travels amongst the Great Andes of the Equator.* (1892), [1880].

Alaska
Browne, Belmore. *The Conquest of Mount McKinley.* (1913), [1906, 1910, 1912].
Dunn, Robert. *The Shameless Diary of an Explorer.* (1907), [1903].

Africa
Benuzzi, Felice. *No Picnic on Mount Kenya.* (1952), [1943].

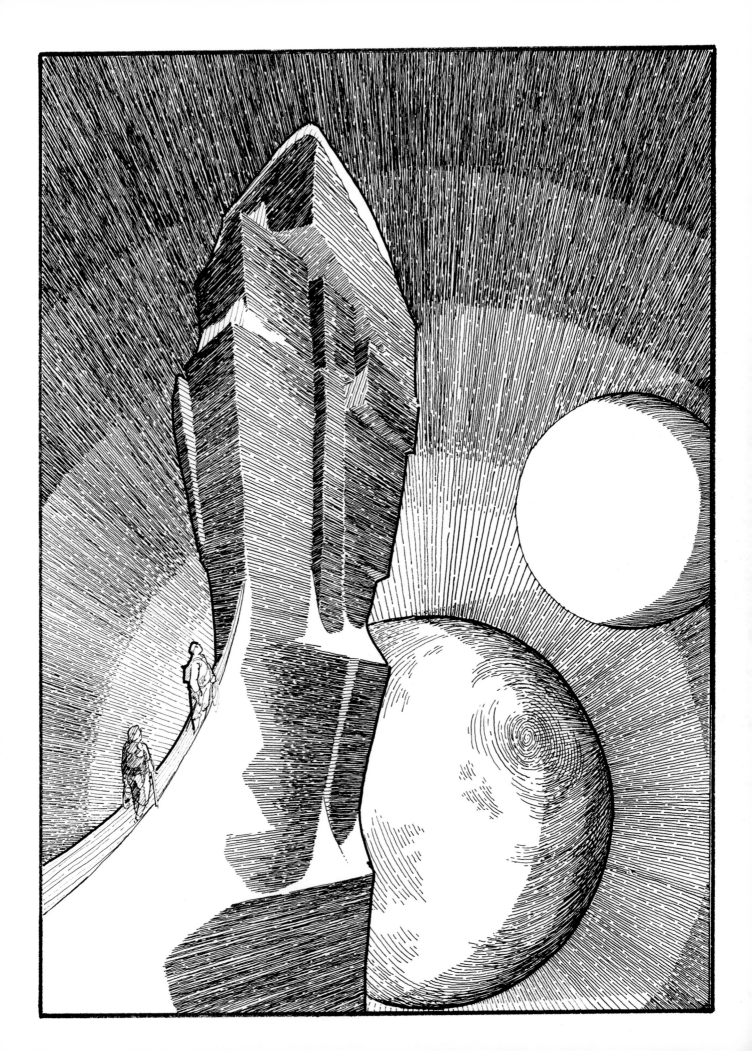

ANTI-CLIMBING AT PINNACLES

Tom Higgins

I n the long, low shafts of late afternoon light, a ridge of gnarled rock stumps appears below me. This is the Pinnacles, a place where lava squirted up and punished the ground, where the mangling motion of earth plates scraped along a fault.

Our single-engine airplane hums deeply as we circle, like explorers looking for prehistoric creatures in a strange land. During our slow circling, I understand why the complex jumble of canyons and protuberances were once a sanctuary for bandits. I imagine them crashing their whiskey bottles down over hot sagebrush fires, while lizards dart back. Perched on the shattered rock knobs, a turkey vulture flaps once, caws until the walls caw, then glides off on its homeward mile.

"Captain George Vancouver, do you read me? This is Tom Higgins. We are flying in a minuscule contrivance over territory now known as Pinnacles National Monument, California. You were the first to explore the area, as you were mapping the west coast of North America in 1792. What did you think of the volcanic rock? The surrounding peaks rising to nearly 3000 feet? The views of arid hills and long valleys? Imagine these valleys teeming with vineyards, roads, towns, and industry. Captain? Come in, sir . . . your Grace?"

I want to talk with Vancouver on the plane's radio, leap across the requisite time span and find out what he thought as he kicked his mule toward, in his words, "the most extraordinary mountain I have ever beheld." I imagine bumping into him in his explorer's garb, reincarnated with his mule. Would he understand the climbing motive or care about our progress? Would I exchange my days for his, for his perspectives on the fresh, untrammeled land? Perhaps we would begin talking about food, as I offered him something from my pack. Then we might go on to farming, technology, autos, flight, moon travel, power, electricity, energy, government, nations, states, democracy, war, bombs, atoms, science, geology, and Pinnacles. Would he believe that a mountain 8000 feet high once stood here, then exploded in outpourings of lava and rubble heaved into the air? All this sixty million years ago?

A crackle of static fills the airwaves. "This is Captain Vancouver. If you would care to read my diary, you will find I traveled by horse, not by mule, and the purpose of my journey to your "Pinnacles" was in part exploratory, but equally a brief diversion from the endless task of mapping the west coast of the continent, assessing the nature and extent of Spanish settlements, and negotiating certain matters with the Spaniards. Our ships, *Discovery* and *Chatham,* were in need of caulking and sail repair in November, 1792. We anchored at the Port of Monterey for this work and, after visiting the Mission of San Carlos, I joined a party traveling to the valley through which the Monterey River flows. I was there gratified, as my diary records, by the sight of the most extraordinary mountain I had ever beheld:

On one side it presented the appearance of a sumptuous edifice fallen into decay; the columns which looked as if they had been raised with much labor and industry, were of great magnitude, seemed to be of an elegant form, and to be composed of the

Facing page: Chris Vandiver moves up a black streak on Shake and Bake. *Tom Higgins.*

same cream-colored stone, of which I have before made mention. Between these magnificent columns were deep excavations, resembling different passages into the interior parts of the supposed building, whose roof being the summit of the mountain appeared to be wholly supported by these columns rising perpendicularly with the most minute mathematical exactness. The whole had a most beautiful appearance of human ingenuity and labor; but since it is not possible, from the rude and very humble race of beings that are found to be the native inhabitants of this country, to suppose they could have been capable of raising such a structure, its being the production of nature, cannot be questioned. . . .

My arms are glistening with sweat in the ninety-degree air. Directly overhead, one blistered hand is turning a rubber-handled drill. The other is swinging a hammer into the mushroomed end of the holder. Fine dust puffs from around the drill tip. My chalky hand pinches an egg-shaped knob. I move one foot from its hold, shake it, and make the return. Suddenly my eye is pulled beyond the knobs to the sweeping gulf below. I feel an upwelling wave and reeling sensation at the prospect of toppling over backwards. Overhead, the black indentation we are climbing curves up and outward. From a distance, this shallow, water-worn groove, darkened by eons of slow seepage from the grassy terraces above, gives the appearance of a deep excavation between columns—perhaps this cliff, now called the Balconies, is the "sumptuous edifice" described by Vancouver. Below, the indentation sticks straight down like a black tongue. A few of the twelve protection bolts below sparkle against the black. Several of these bolts had to be started without looking at the drill overhead for fear that any backward leaning might instigate a somersaulting cascade down the knobby tongue.

The prospect of climbing the bulge above makes my moves tight and flat to the rock, like those of a beginning climber. No bolts will be possible on the overhang, and a fall will mean I could smash into my partner, Chris Vandiver. Chris says he hates this climb, for there is too much tension, too much reiterating calculus. The rock at Pinnacles is noted for its undependability, and we must test each hold and gingerly distribute weight over them on the assumption each might pop off. To Chris, it seems perverse to endure such mental strain. But we do continue the strain, we do finish the route we name Shake and Bake. We do look back on the dark 350-foot rock curtain called the Balconies and feel a foolish pride at having been up there with birds shooting by like meteors, with patient vultures circling, with the bursts of hot, high breezes, with every pore electrified by the job at hand. And we do, if only to ourselves, blur the climb and the wall and come to think that the path of holds is ours, first touched, first assembled into a sequence of thinking and reaching by our brains and hands, and punctuated with just the right number of bolts to hold the thought and action together.

"My efforts," says Captain Vancouver, "were always directed toward more practical affairs than climbing, as you describe it. My concerns were with commerce, conflict, and compromise. My main purpose in the journey was to settle a dispute with Spain regarding fur trade and territory on the

Bruce Cooke on Shake and Bake. *Tom Higgins.*

coast. Of course, I also mapped and recorded the bays, harbors, and useful resources of other places on the same expedition, including Australia, Tahiti, and Hawaii. My explorations were purposeful, but what propels you toward such great effort, if not for profit or Country?"

"I know the climb I just did seems ludicrous, Captain, but not *all* climbing is like this. Some of it is pure gymnastic delight in pristine places, such as certain routes over knobby granite in the high mountains of California. However, there is other climbing which, as with any strenuous adventure, makes you buzz with why, what, and where you are. You mapped the coast of California. The climber of a new route weaves like a vessel, watching, heading, hoping for better rock sometimes keyed by color, white and pink being the most dangerous. As explorer, the climber is astonished and fascinated by a big mossy patch, a pocket of clicking, whirring bats, or a strong scent of foreign urines. And as climber, there is some kind of sensational ricochet in feeling fearful and stupid, then elated and accomplished at having navigated through yet another vertical assemblage of strange and untouched stones.

"Perhaps," I continue, "such climbing is a pleasure reserved for those a little jaded by the deluxe routes of great centers for the sport. Is it possible that the very grandeur of the best walls and consequent chain of ascents can cause one to turn away? Imagine, Vancouver, a long and lovely flake of rock shaped like your boot there, seemingly glued high on a shimmering, 3000-foot granite cliff. And great roofs and towers, all eventually connected by a marvelous climbing route. Do you see how even this might become dull from the doing? Where the elation, once so private, becomes so common, so implanted in a growing collective that the heart becomes a little tired and sad from it all? It is then that we turn to darker jewels—elusive, out of fashion, even fragile—as if in search of anti-climbs."

Resurrection Wall was Ruprecht's dark jewel. Ruprecht Von Kammerlander schemed and teamed with several different partners, until in 1978 he completed a route on this magnificent wall. Mossy on its lower reaches, then building to a dangerous pink higher and finally streaked in black over several intervals, the entire vertical mass suggests an ominous megalith. Ruprecht's friends will peer into this shadowy face, celebrate his climbing courage, remember his fatal motorcycle accident, and perhaps feel something like a haunting about the great wall.

I fall again into the void, dangling below the bulge on Resurrection's second pitch. My partner, Frank Sarnquist, looks on impatiently. Above, I can see Ruprecht's fifteen aid bolts dotting the bulging wall. These are the only aid points on the three-pitch climb, and we are trying to pass them free. Surprisingly, the rock here turns solid after the fantastic mounds of fuzzy moss and fragile holds on the first pitch. I try again to surmount the bulge, this time finding a sequence of holds leading right of the bolt ladder to a small pocket. Here I can rest without using my arms. Ten more bolts remain on a slightly overhanging wall. As I begin this section, I find that the moves are consistently 5.9 and 5.10. Clipping into the bolts is a desperate struggle. Five bolts up, I lose all strength and float once again into space. Frank lowers me to the pocket, and I begin again, now more efficiently. At the last bolt I face the final move to the belay ledge, and I see exactly what to do. I know such a move by heart. It is 5.8, but it might as well be 5.30. My arms are spent. I rush the move, make it, then fling a hand onto the belay ledge, a melon-sized stone embedded in the wall. A hold breaks under my foot. I can't keep a grip on the massive stone and am off again into space! Frank lowers me to a poor resting point. One arm can dangle, then the other, but not both at once. I repeat all the sequences as fast as possible up to the last bolt. A little less tired this try than last, I grab the belay stone. I don't trust any of the knobs this time and instead friction my feet flat on the face as I mantle. I'm up!

The next pitch is a surprisingly moderate piece, something of an optical illusion. From below it appears awful, but once on it, large holds lead the way. The bolts turn out to be more illusory than the climbing. Frank leads way out, looks and looks, then spies a couple. Near the top, the wall scoops in below us, making the exposure incredible for a mere three-pitch climb.

On the summit we see a family of foxes shoot through a brushy gully. The sun is low and drenches us in amber light. In the canyon below, lost in deep purples, a host of frogs starts up. The misty air envelops us. I feel utterly remote and safe among the oaks and wispy, gray-green pines. Lower on our walk down, I see Resurrection shooting upward steeply, hazy, as if rubbed in charcoal, and now echoing onto us all the evening sounds.

"Sport never interested me much," Vancouver observes, "but in the realm of sports, this is indeed an odd one."

"Why do you think so?"

"There is so much useless searching, it seems to me. First you exploit the most exquisite walls in well-known places, then grow tired of it all and turn to inferior, obscure rock for your pleasure. Where does the anti-climber go next—underwater? Is this what modern civilization brings, so much useless leisure?

"It is not so much that Pinnacles climbers scorn all else," I reply. "Rather, this place provides welcome relief from the climbing bustle elsewhere. And it is uniquely beautiful. I am not alone in liking the Pinnacles—just in a comfortable minority. Since the 1930s, small, select groups of climbers have practiced their sport here, particularly in the winter months, when the high mountains are covered with snow. The result has been a set of pleasing miniatures such as the Hand, the Monolith, Freedom Dome, Tuff Dome, the Machete Ridge, and Mechanic's Delight. Yes, these climbs are totally useless except to our 'leisure,' yet they stand in one's mind like gallery prints or Chinese vases on a display shelf. As for the inferior rock, it's strange how quickly one forgets about it when relishing the colors and forms."

"Perhaps the explorer and climber," Vancouver speculates, "share a similar propensity for discounting the past. The horrors of the last adventure dim as the open seas or far-flung peaks call on familiar yearnings. The beauty of the world is indeed to be appreciated, but the climber seems far too preoccu-

A typical Pinnacles climb: vertical, knobby rock. *Tom Gerughty*.

pied with internal reactions and sentiments. Are these not the province of poets, not of explorers and adventurous men?"

The miniature is Mechanic's Delight. Barry Bates said only four words to me about his first free ascent—"a very hard mantle." With Jim Crooks one late afternoon, I search out the overhanging start and find the embedded rock on which Barry must have done his mantle. It is a downsloping snout the size of my palm, with no decent footing below and no decent holds above. After attempting it once, I immediately give up. I mutter something about Barry being too strong, and how I'll have to find a trick. The plan unravels itself slowly. I pull up on the snout, make a flurry of foot changes, one extremely hard right-hand pull, then fall off. The rock is so much more complex than granite, first requiring extensive searching for a hold, then testing it, then comparing options. Jim and I stand at the bottom talking over the foot-and-hand options and risks, like stockbrokers comparing companies. "If you do this, you'll have no margin for error; if you do that, you'll have no reserves left by the time...."

A few minutes later I'm trying the identical foot maneuver and right-hand pull, our labored calculus having arrived at the same place as my initial intuition. This time I make the move correctly, reach far left to clip into an ancient bolt, then pull left, stepping on a tiny knob which shakes as I test it with a foot tap. More calculus—how much weight do I dare put there? Get the hands doing the main job ... gently now ... gently. Soon I'm back on the main line of bolts and discover sharp flakes, excellent if I pull and step straight down on them.

On top, I wave to our friend Tom Gerughty, on the nearby trail. He takes our picture. I like the clean, quick snap of his Hasselblad. Now Jim and I are forever interlocked with this lovely miniature. Later, Tom snaps another of us on Freedom Dome. I am content to be positioned in time on the perfection of these bumpy rocks, thrust up like whales' snouts to heaven, bursting from ancient and mysterious origins.

Repulsion is again welling up in Chris Vandiver. He squints through cigarette smoke, peers upward at a dripping, leaning dihedral and says what he always says at Pinnacles: "I hate it." We are standing at the base of another route on the Balconies, this one created by Frank Sacherer and Steve Roper in 1961. It is a horror of horrors. The dihedral is seeping black ooze. Whines, buzzes, bleats, and chirps emanate from it, sounds we cannot associate with any familiar life form.

"Bats and birds," Chris mumbles to assure himself we are still on planet Earth. He reluctantly begins to free climb the initial bolt ladder. The route has about thirty aid bolts, perhaps half of them placed on this first pitch, and wisely placed on the wall slightly left of the terrifying dihedral. Thank God we won't have to insert any limb into its dark, humming recesses. We hope to free climb past each and every old aid bolt, some of which poke out far from the rock, droop, or wiggle. To our knowledge, no one previously has mustered the

Contemplating a difficult
step, Tom Higgins moves up a
route on Discovery Wall.
Tom Gerughty.

slightest ambition to free climb this wizened classic; this surprises us very little.

After free climbing past the first few bolts, Chris glides back to the ground. He is not certain the bolts are good. I take over, following the ladder, finding sustained 5.9 and 5.10 climbing and occasionally a good bolt, even a new one. The rock is amazingly sound. But gradually the bolts lead closer and closer to the dihedral. Finally, I'm obliged to stick a hand into the crack, lie back a bit, and otherwise become far too intimate with damp, dark places.

Whirr . . . bip . . . bip . . . bip . . . eeeooo . . . all the fearful sounds begin, and as I peer into the crack I see tucked-up limbs and fuzzy ears. God, I've got to get out of here! The dihedral bends left at this point, forcing me onto the face. A very hard stem to the left brings me to easier ground and eventually to the belay spot. Here I clip into two anchor bolts, three higher aid bolts, and a nut, but I still feel insecure. Chris climbs smoothly and quickly up to the stem, then falls off trying to move across. There's no way to traverse back to try it again, so he just continues.

"5.11," Chris says tersely.

"Can't be," I say. I always say that, thinking 5.11 must be equivalent to the worst boulder moves I've ever done. The mood turns more and more glum as we hop on little holds, trying to find a comfortable stance, suspecting that the whole patch of rock and bolts might burst off with a pop, like a faulty door of an airplane at high altitude.

The next pitch takes off on a steep wall above and beyond the dihedral. Black, brown, pocketed, and knobby, the rock sweeps upward. The aid bolts stop and an aid crack begins, meaning that the bolts we are accustomed to for protection become farther and farther apart. Chris refuses to lead the second pitch, again concerned about the doubtful bolts. I start out, reach the crack and find it takes nuts only grudgingly. No move is over 5.9, and most are 5.8, but I'm exerting tremendous energy, moving as if each hold might snap off. My moves become more and more rigid. I start to think like Chris, unable to blank out the vision of the line of bolts plucked out of their roost, clinking and tingling down the rope to meet me as I ram to a halt.

At the end of this pitch I hang out on a sling belay from two fairly good-looking bolts. Above, the wall bends outward, showing another bolt ladder. As Chris comes up, unclipping from bolt after bolt and about to leave us both on just my two, I panic at the thought of popping the anchor bolts. I ask him to stop, then clip us both through the next higher bolt. I inform Chris I'm just too rattled to take the next lead.

He glowers upward, calculates, broods, then attacks the headwall. He's careful and more fluid than I've been, testing holds, obviously desperate but still in control. He's hating it again, but smells the relief of the summit and pushes on. Soon he disappears around a corner and gains a belay tree. Another short pitch ending on clunking hunks of rock, and we're on top.

We are in a hilarious mood, stomping up and down in the dry weeds, enormously relieved, proud and mystified at how and why we free climbed through this minefield of wobbly rock and shaky bolts. Our socks are full of

stickers. Chris gurgles a little, squeezes up a laugh, then bursts forth with whooping hollers. Laughs echo off the grotesque boulders which surround us like monsters, then vanish into the darkening air. We feel like children who have just touched a tarantula and gotten away without a bite—that slow, devilish black rambler, so beautiful and frightening all at once.

Facing page: Pinnacles is not known for its dihedrals; this one on Discovery Wall is one of the most dramatic. *Tom Gerughty.*

"Your thoughts and actions," Vancouver remarks, "are much akin to those of the childlike Indians I observed. As I wrote in my diary, most had not bettered themselves, had not made habitations more comfortable than those of their predecessors. I would wager this is still true."

"Must we judge a people by their shelter? Did you not ever discover something of yourself on those long journeys? Yes, we gratefully lost all care for anything beyond the crackling weeds underfoot, the purple and brown of evening, and the straggling path down. What occupied us was a little howl of glee as we flipped prudence on its back. We were emptied of care and filled with nothing more than . . . a rolling giggle. So whole did we feel that no man, woman, vocation, promise, or problem could hold a moment's thought. And when we looked back to our horrible shroud of rock, still oozing, it was no longer with the wicked terror we had first known. Our wonder had transformed it into a magnificent, hulking friend, and in that moment, somehow always with us, all else in nature became comprehensible, including our brief lives so tiny on the spinning globe.

"Can we go on to something else?" asks Vancouver.

"Such as?"

"Well, anything but climbing. Tell me more about electricity, as you call it, or the flying contraptions."

Our small plane straightens out from its circling over Pinnacles, and we head north. After a minute or two, the view back reveals little of consequence in the smooth, rolling ranchlands and cultivated valleys. Above, caught deep in cobalt blue, are the first stars. I doze to the drone of the engine and remember the echo of frogs below Resurrection, the smooth, slender foxes, and the view to the dusky Balconies. I realize that I love most of all the moments at the ends of climbs, when the earth smokes in its beauty and innocence. Vancouver, do you read me? You, the mapmaker, negotiator, loyal subject of the Crown, are the outward explorer; I am the inner. I would not trade my days or perspectives for yours, and I know again that all of consequence for me lies in fleeting wonder near the towers and foxes, thoughts emptied of human exploits, technologies, and history.

IMAGES
OF THE
SOUTHWEST

by Ed Webster and others

Below: Mark Rolofson follows an off-width jamcrack on the first ascent of "Cactus Flower," a 400-foot route near Canyonlands National Park, Utah. *Ed Webster.*

Facing page: Bryan Becker stems a dihedral in Escalante Canyon, Colorado. *Ed Webster.*

Preceding page: Moses Tower at sunset, Canyonlands National Park, Utah. *Ed Webster.*

Facing page: On the fourth pitch of the "Primrose Dihedrals Route" on Moses Tower, Canyonlands National Park, Utah. *Steve Hong.*

Top left: Steve Hong muscling up steep face climbing on the "Primrose Dihedrals Route" on Moses Tower. *Ed Webster.*

Bottom left: The perfect desert rack: chocks and the newly developed camming devices known as "Friends." *Ed Webster.*

Right: On the first ascent of the "Lightning Bolt Cracks" on North Sixshooter Peak, a climber ponders a 5.10 move. *Ed Webster.*

Below: The leader struggles up the crux moves of the Kor-Ingalls Route on Castleton Tower. *Ed Webster.*

Facing page: After completing the ascent of the Mace, near Sedona, Arizona, a climber returns to a nearby mesa via a tyrolean traverse. *Ed Webster.*

Overleaf: On the first ascent of the Supercrack, near Canyonlands National Park, Utah. *Mike Gardner.*

THE CONQUEST OF THE RIFFELBERG

Mark Twain

Although Mark Twain is best known for his Mississippi River tales and his parodies of American life, he wrote several books dealing with his travels in Europe. One of these, A Tramp Abroad, *describes an 1878 journey which began in the new nation called Germany, passed through the marvelous Alps of Switzerland, and ended in art-filled Italy. Twain decided before this trip to travel in an unorthodox manner: "One day it occurred to me that it had been many years since the world had been afforded the spectacle of a man adventurous enough to undertake a journey through Europe on foot. After much thought, I decided that I was a person fitted to furnish mankind this spectacle."*

Hiring an agent known to us only as Mr. Harris, Twain moved slowly south from Hamburg, his port of call. He observed at firsthand the German educational system ("idle students are not the rule"); fidgeted in a Munich opera house ("the tenor's voice is not a voice at all, but only a shriek—the shriek of a hyena!"); and tried to master the German language, finding the rules concerning gender perplexing indeed ("A fish is a he, *his scales are* she, *but a fishwife is neither. A young lady has no sex, but a turnip does.").*

Twain and Harris, walking short distances but using the railway for the long hauls, next visited Baden-Baden. Calling the noted spa "an inane town filled with sham," the sarcastic author continued: "I fully believe I left my rheumatism in Baden-Baden. . . . I would have preferred leaving something that was catching, but it was not within my power."

Later, Twain wandered through the enchanted Black Forest, finally discovering something to his liking: "The diffused light . . . pervades the place like a faint, green-tinged mist, the theatrical fire of fairyland."

Farther south, at the end of an interminable day of walking, Twain's pedometer indicated that the two men had hiked 146 miles. With tongue in cheek, Twain noted that "the guidebook and the Imperial Ordnance maps make it only ten and a quarter—a surprising blunder, for these two authorities are usually singularly accurate in the matter of distances."

Upon his arrival in the Swiss Alps, Twain and Harris were at first enthralled by the famous yodelers of the region. But after generously tipping the first few yodelers, the author grew weary of the "Tyrolese warblers." At the end of the day he was offering one franc to every yodeler who promised to remain silent. "There is somewhat too much of this yodeling in the Alps."

The first ascent of the Matterhorn had taken place only thirteen years earlier, and Twain was fascinated by Edward Whymper's account of the success and subsequent tragedy on the descent. Now, seeing the glorious Alps at close range, the forty-three-year-old writer desired a firsthand mountaineering experience. Getting into decent physical shape was an obvious prerequisite, so Twain and Harris decided to ascend a mountain path which led to a hotel atop a minor peak. After passing over dozens of false summits, the two men were trapped by darkness and dense fog at the base of an insurmountable wall. The shivering, quarreling neophytes spent a miserable hour until the mist parted, revealing the south face of . . . yes, the hotel itself! "Our first emotion," wrote Twain, "was deep, unutterable gratitude; our next was foolish rage."

When the two adventurers arrived in the famous mountain village of Zermatt, they found themselves in the heartland of mountaineering. Although the Matterhorn loomed in the background, the men had no illusions about making such a dangerous ascent. Instead, Twain perused the guidebook for an easier outing. Soon he came to a courageous decision.

Our slightly condensed excerpt from A Tramp Abroad *(the title and part-titles are ours) begins as Twain shares his plan with his companion; it ends with a notable scientific discovery atop the mighty Riffelberg.* THE EDITORS

After I had finished my readings, I was no longer myself; I was tranced, uplifted, intoxicated by the almost incredible perils and adventures I had been following my authors through, and the triumphs I had been sharing with them. I sat silent some time, then turned to Harris and said:

"My mind is made up."

Something in my tone struck him, and when he glanced at my eye and read what was written there, his face paled perceptibly. He hesitated a moment, then said:

"Speak."

I answered, with perfect calmness:

"I WILL ASCEND THE RIFFELBERG."

If I had shot my poor friend, he could not have fallen from his chair more suddenly. If I had been his father, he could not have pleaded harder to get me to give up my purpose. But I turned a deaf ear to all he said. When he perceived at last that nothing could alter my determination, he ceased to urge, and for a while the deep silence was broken only by his sobs. I sat in marble resolution, with my eyes fixed upon vacancy, for in spirit I was already wrestling with the perils of the mountains, and my friend sat gazing at me in adoring admiration through his tears. At last he threw himself upon me in a loving embrace and exclaimed in broken tones:

"Your Harris will never desert you. We will die together!"

I cheered the noble fellow with praises, and soon his fears were forgotten and he was eager for the adventure. He wanted to summon the guides at once and leave at two in the morning, as he supposed the custom was; but I explained that nobody was looking at that hour and that the start in the dark was not usually made from the village but from the first night's resting place on the mountainside. I said we would leave the village at 3 or 4 P.M. on the morrow; meantime he could notify the guides and also let the public know of the attempt which we proposed to make.

I went to bed, but not to sleep. No man can sleep when he is about to undertake one of those Alpine exploits. I tossed feverishly all night long and was glad enough when I heard the clock strike half past eleven and knew it was time to get up for dinner. I rose, jaded and rusty, and went to the noon meal, where I found myself the center of interest and curiosity, for the news was already abroad. It is not easy to eat calmly when you are a lion, but it is very pleasant nevertheless.

As usual, at Zermatt, when a great ascent is about to be undertaken, everybody, native and foreign, laid aside his own projects and took up a good position to observe the start. The expedition consisted of 198 persons, including the mules; or 205; including the cows. As follows:

Chiefs of Service
    Myself
    Mr. Harris
  17 Guides
   4 Surgeons
   1 Geologist
   1 Botanist
   3 Chaplains
   2 Draftsmen
  15 Barkeepers
   1 Latinist

Subordinates
   1 Veterinary Surgeon
   1 Butler
  12 Waiters
   1 Footman
   1 Barber
   1 Head Cook
   9 Assistants
   4 Pastry Cooks
   1 Confectionery Artist

Transportation, Etc.
  27 Porters
  44 Mules
  44 Muleteers
   3 Coarse Washers and Ironers
   1 Fine ditto
   7 Cows
   2 Milkers

Rations, Etc.
  16 Cases Hams
   2 Barrels Flour
  22 Barrels Whisky
   1 Barrel Sugar
   1 Keg Lemons
2000 Cigars
   1 Barrel Pies
   1 Ton of Pemmican
143 Pair of Crutches
   2 Barrels Arnica
   1 Bale of Lint
  27 Kegs Paregoric

Apparatus
  25 Spring Mattresses
   2 Hair Mattresses
      Bedding for same
   2 Mosquito Nets
  29 Tents
      Scientific Instruments
  97 Ice Axes
   5 Cases Dynamite
   7 Cans Nitroglycerine
  22 40-foot Ladders
   2 Miles of Rope
154 Umbrellas

The Expedition Leaves Zermatt

It was full four o'clock in the afternoon before my cavalcade was entirely ready. At that hour it began to move. In point of numbers and spectacular effect, it was the most imposing expedition that had ever marched from Zermatt.

I commanded the chief guide to arrange the men and animals in single file, twelve feet apart, and lash them all together on a strong rope. He objected that the first two miles was dead level, with plenty of room, and that the rope was never used except in very dangerous places. But I would not listen to that. My reading had taught me that many serious accidents had happened in the Alps simply from not having people tied up soon enough; I was not going to add one to the list. The guide then obeyed my order.

When the procession stood at ease, roped together and ready to move, I never saw a finer sight. It was 3122 feet long—over half a mile. Every man but Harris and me was on foot and had on his green veil and his blue goggles, and his white rag around his hat, and his coil of rope over one shoulder and under the other, and his ice axe in his belt, and carried his alpenstock in his left hand, his umbrella (closed) in his right, and his crutches slung at his back. The burdens of the pack mules and the horns of the cows were decked with the Edelweiss and the Alpine rose.

I and my agent were the only persons mounted. We were in the post of danger in the extreme rear, and tied securely to five guides apiece. Our armor-bearers carried our ice axes, alpenstocks, and other implements for us. We were mounted upon very small donkeys as a measure of safety; in time of peril we could straighten our legs and stand up, and let the donkey walk from under. Still, I cannot recommend this sort of animal—at least for excursions of mere pleasure—because his ears interrupt the view. I and my agent possessed the regulation mountaineering costumes, but concluded to leave them behind. Out of respect for the great numbers of tourists of both sexes who would be assembled in front of the hotels to see us pass, and also out of respect for the many tourists whom we expected to encounter on our expedition, we decided to make the ascent in evening dress.

At fifteen minutes past four I gave the command to move, and my subordinates passed it along the line. The great crowd in front of the Monte Rosa Hotel parted in twain, with a cheer, as the procession approached; and as the head of it was filing by, I gave the order: "Unlimber, make ready, HOIST!" And with one impulse up went my half mile of umbrellas. It was a beautiful sight and a total surprise to the spectators. Nothing like that had ever been seen in the Alps before. The applause it brought forth was deeply gratifying to me, and I rode by with my plug hat in my hand to testify my appreciation of it. It was the only testimony I could offer, for I was too full to speak.

We watered the caravan at the cold stream which rushes down a trough near the end of the village and soon afterward left the haunts of civilization behind us. About half past five o'clock we arrived at a bridge which spans the Visp, and after throwing over a detachment to see if it was safe, the caravan crossed without accident. The way now led, by a gentle ascent carpeted with fresh green grass, to the church at Winkelmatten. Without stopping to examine this edifice, I executed a flank movement to the right and crossed the bridge over the Findelenbach, after first testing its strength. Here I deployed to the right again and presently entered an inviting stretch of meadowland which was unoccupied save by a couple of deserted huts toward its furthest extremity. These meadows offered an excellent camping place. We pitched our tents, supped, established a proper guard, recorded the events of the day, and then went to bed.

Panic and Paregoric

We rose at two in the morning and dressed by candlelight. It was a dismal and chilly business. A few stars were shining, but the general heavens were overcast; the great shaft of the Matterhorn was draped in a sable pall of clouds. The chief guide advised a delay; he said he feared it was going to rain. We waited until nine o'clock and then got away in tolerably clear weather.

Our course led up some terrific steeps, densely wooded with larches and cedars, and traversed by paths which the rains had guttered and which were obstructed by loose stones. To add to the danger and inconvenience, we were constantly meeting returning tourists on foot or horseback, and as constantly being crowded and battered by ascending tourists who were in a hurry and wanted to get by.

Our troubles thickened. About the middle of the afternoon the seventeen guides called a halt and held a consultation. After consulting an hour they said their first suspicion remained intact—that is to say, they believed they were lost. I asked if they did not *know* it? No, they said, they *couldn't* absolutely know whether they were lost or not, because none of them had ever been in that part of the country before. They had a strong instinct that they were lost, but they had no proofs—except that they did not know where they were. They had met no tourists for some time, and they considered that a suspicious sign.

Plainly we were in an ugly fix. The guides were naturally unwilling to go alone and seek a way out of the difficulty; so we all went together. For better security we moved slowly and cautiously, for the forest was very dense. We did not move up the mountain, but around it, hoping to strike across the old trail. Toward nightfall, when we were about tired out, we came up against a rock as big as a cottage. This barrier took all the remaining spirit out of the men, and a panic of fear and despair ensued. They moaned and wept, and said they should never see their homes and their dear ones again. Then they began to upbraid me for bringing them upon this fatal expedition. Some even muttered threats against me.

Clearly it was no time to show weakness. So I made a speech in which I said that other Alp-climbers had been in as perilous a position as this, and yet by courage and perseverance had escaped. I promised to stand by them; I promised to rescue them. I closed by saying we had plenty of provisions to maintain us for quite a siege—and did they suppose Zermatt would allow half a mile of men and mules to mysteriously disappear during any considerable time, right above their noses, and make no inquiries? No, Zermatt would send out searching expeditions and we would be saved.

This speech had a great effect. The men pitched the tents with some little show of cheerfulness, and we were snugly under cover when the night shut down. I now reaped the reward of my wisdom in providing one article which is not mentioned in any book of Alpine adventure but this. I refer to the paregoric. But for the beneficent drug, not one of those men would have slept a moment during that fearful night. But for that gentle persuader, they might have tossed, unsoothed, the night through; for the whisky was for me. Yes, they would have risen in the morning unfitted for their heavy task. As it was, everybody slept but my agent and me—only we two and the barkeepers. I would not permit myself to sleep at such a time. I considered myself responsible for all those lives. I meant to be on hand and ready, in case of avalanches. I am aware now that there were no avalanches up there, but I did not know it then.

We watched the weather all through that awful night and kept an eye on the barometer to be prepared for the least change. There was not the slightest change recorded by the instrument during the whole time. Words cannot describe the comfort which that friendly, hopeful, steadfast thing was to me in that season of trouble. It was a defective barometer and had no hand but the stationary brass pointer, but I did not know that until afterward. If I should be in such a situation again, I should not wish for any barometer but that one.

The Mule that Ate Nitroglycerine

All hands rose at two in the morning and took breakfast, and as soon as it was light we roped ourselves together and went at that rock. For some time we tried the hook-rope and other means of scaling it, but without success—that is, without perfect success. The hook caught once and Harris started up it hand over hand, but the hold broke and if there had not happened to be a chaplain sitting underneath at the time, Harris would certainly have been crippled. As it was, it was the chaplain. He took to his crutches, and I ordered the hook-rope to be laid aside. It was too dangerous an implement where so many people were standing around.

We were puzzled for a while; then somebody thought of the ladders. One of these was leaned against the rock, and the men went up it tied together in couples. Another ladder was sent up for use in descending. At the end of half an hour everybody was over and that rock was conquered. We gave our first grand shout of triumph. But the joy was short-lived, for somebody asked how we were going to get the animals over.

This was a serious difficulty; in fact, it was an impossibility. The courage of the men began to waver immediately; once more we were threatened with a panic. But when the danger was most imminent, we were saved in a mysterious way. A mule which had attracted attention from the beginning by its disposition to experiment, tried to eat a five-pound can of nitroglycerine. This happened right alongside the rock. The explosion threw us all to the ground and covered us with dirt and debris; it frightened us extremely, too, for the crash it made was deafening and the violence of the shock made the ground tremble. However, we were grateful, for the rock was gone. Its place was occupied by a new cellar, about thirty feet across and fifteen feet deep. The explosion was heard as far as Zermatt, and an hour and a half afterward many citizens of that town were knocked down and quite seriously injured by descending portions of mule meat, frozen solid. This shows, better than any estimate in figures, how high the experimenter went.

We had nothing to do now but bridge the cellar and proceed on our way. With a cheer the men went at their work. I attended to the engineering myself. I appointed a strong detail to cut down trees with ice axes and trim them for piers to support the bridge. This was slow business, for ice axes are not good to cut wood with. I caused my piers to be firmly set up in ranks in the cellar, and upon them I laid six of my forty-foot ladders, side by side, and laid six more on top of them. Upon this bridge I caused a bed of boughs to be spread, and on top of the boughs a bed of earth six inches deep. I stretched ropes upon either side to serve as railings, and then my bridge was complete. A train of elephants could have crossed it in safety and comfort. By nightfall the caravan was on the other side and the ladder taken up.

The Creeping Rope Incident

Next morning we went on in good spirits for a while, though our way was slow and difficult, by reason of the steep and rocky nature of the ground and the thickness of the forest. But at last a dull despondency crept into the men's faces and it was apparent that not only they, but even the guides, were now convinced that we were lost. The fact that we still met no tourists was a circumstance that was but too significant. Another thing seemed to suggest that we were not only lost, but very badly lost; for there must surely be search parties on the road before this time, yet we had seen no sign of them.

Demoralization was spreading; something must be done, and done quickly, too. Fortunately, I am not unfertile in expedients. I contrived one now which commended itself to all, for it promised well. I took three-quarters of a mile of rope and fastened one end of it around the waist of a guide and told him to go and find the road while the caravan waited. I instructed him to guide himself back by the rope in case of failure; in case of success he was to give the rope a series of violent jerks, whereupon the Expedition would go to him at once. He departed, and in two minutes had disappeared among the trees. I paid out the rope myself while everybody watched the crawling thing with

eager eyes. The rope crept away quite slowly at times; at other times with some briskness. Twice or thrice we seemed to get the signal, and a shout was just ready to break from the men's lips when they perceived it was a false alarm. But at last, when over half a mile of rope had slidden away, it stopped gliding and stood absolutely still—one minute, two minutes, three—while we held our breath and watched.

Was the guide resting? Was he scanning the country from some high point? Was he inquiring of a chance mountaineer? Stop—had he fainted from excess of fatigue and anxiety?

This thought gave us a shock. I was in the very act of detailing an Expedition to succor him when the cord was assailed with a series of such frantic jerks that I could hardly keep hold of it. The huzza that went up then was good to hear. "Saved! saved!" was the word that rang out all down the long rank of the caravan.

We rose up and started at once. We found the route to be good enough for a while, but it began to grow difficult, by and by, and this feature steadily increased. When we judged we had gone half a mile, we momently expected to see the guide; but no, he was not visible anywhere; neither was he waiting, for the rope was still moving: consequently he was doing the same. This argued that he had not found the road yet, but was marching to it with some peasant. There was nothing for us to do but plod along, and this we did. At the end of three hours we were still plodding. This was not only mysterious, but exasperating. And very fatiguing too; for we had tried hard, along at first, to catch up with the guide, but had only fagged ourselves in vain; for although he was traveling slowly, he was yet able to go faster than the hampered caravan over such ground.

At three in the afternoon we were nearly dead with exhaustion, and still the rope was slowly gliding. The murmurs against the guide had been growing steadily, and at last they were become loud and savage. A mutiny ensued.

The men refused to proceed. They declared that we had been traveling over and over the same ground all day, in a kind of circle. They demanded that our end of the rope be made fast to a tree, so as to halt the guide until we could overtake him and kill him. This was not an unreasonable requirement, so I gave the order.

As soon as the rope was tied, the Expedition moved forward with that alacrity which the thirst for vengeance usually inspires. But after a tiresome march of almost half a mile, we came to a hill covered thick with a crumbly rubbish of stones, and so steep that no man of us all was now in a condition to climb it. Every attempt failed and ended in crippling somebody. Within twenty minutes I had five men on crutches. Whenever a climber tried to assist himself by the rope, it yielded and let him tumble backwards. The frequency of this result suggested an idea to me. I ordered the caravan to 'bout face and form in marching order; I then made the tow-rope fast to the rear mule and gave the command:

"Mark time—by the right flank—forward march!"

The procession began to move, to the impressive strains of a battle-chant, and I said to myself, "Now, if the rope don't break, I judge *this* will fetch that guide into the camp." I watched the rope gliding down the hill and presently, when I was all fixed for triumph, I was confronted by a bitter disappointment: there was no guide tied to the rope—it was only a very indignant old black ram!

The Treacherous Guide

The fury of the baffled Expedition exceeded all bounds. They even wanted to wreak their unreasoning vengeance on this innocent dumb brute. But I stood between them and their prey, menaced by a bristling wall of ice axes and alpenstocks, and proclaimed that there was but one road to this murder and it was directly over my corpse. Even as I spoke, I saw that my doom was sealed, except a miracle supervened to divert these madmen from their fell purpose. I see that sickening wall of weapons now; I see that advancing host as I saw it then; I see the hate in those cruel eyes; I remember how I drooped my head upon my breast; I feel again the sudden earthquake shock in my rear, administered by the very ram I was sacrificing myself to save; I hear once more the typhoon of laughter that burst from the assaulting column as I clove it from van to rear like a Sepoy shot from a Rodman gun.

I was saved. Yes, I was saved, and by the merciful instinct of ingratitude which nature had planted in the breast of that treacherous beast. The grace which eloquence had failed to work in those men's hearts had been wrought by a laugh. The ram was set free and my life was spared.

We lived to find out that the guide had deserted us as soon as he had placed a half mile between himself and us. To avert suspicion, he had judged it best that the line should continue to move; so he caught the ram, and at the time that he was sitting on it making the rope fast to it, we were imagining that he was lying in a swoon, overcome by fatigue and distress. When he allowed the ram to get up, it fell to plunging around, trying to rid itself of the rope; this was the signal which we had risen up with glad shouts to obey. We had followed this ram round and round in a circle all day—a thing which was proven by the discovery that we had watered the Expedition seven times at one and the same spring in seven hours. As expert a woodsman as I am, I had somehow failed to notice this until my attention was called to it by a hog. This hog was always wallowing there, and as he was the only hog we saw, his frequent repetition, together with his unvarying similarity to himself, finally caused me to reflect that he must be the same hog, and this led me to the deduction that this must be the same spring also—which indeed it was.

To return, for an explanatory moment, to that guide, and then I shall be done with him. After leaving the ram tied to the rope, he had wandered at large for a while, and then happened to run across a cow. Judging that a cow would naturally know more than a guide, he took her by the tail, and the result justified his judgment. She nibbled her leisurely way downhill till it was near milking time, then she struck for home and towed him into Zermatt.

Some Scientific Observations

We went into camp on that wild spot to which the ram had brought us. The men were greatly fatigued. Their conviction that we were lost was forgotten in the cheer of a good supper, and before the reaction had a chance to set in, I loaded them up with paregoric and put them to bed.

Next morning I was considering in my mind our desperate situation and trying to think of a remedy, when Harris came to me with a Baedeker map which showed conclusively that the mountain we were on was still in Switzerland—yes, every part of it was in Switzerland. So we were not lost, after all. This was an immense relief; it lifted the weight of two such mountains from my breast. I immediately had the news disseminated and the map exhibited. The effect was wonderful. As soon as the men saw with their own eyes that they knew where they were, and that it was only the summit that was lost and not themselves, they cheered up instantly and said with one accord, let the summit take care of itself; they were not interested in its troubles.

Our distresses being at an end, I now determined to rest the men in camp and give the scientific department of the Expedition a chance. First, I made a barometric observation to get our altitude, but I could not perceive that there was any result. I knew, by my scientific reading, that either thermometers or barometers ought to be boiled to make them accurate; I did not know which it was, so I boiled both. There was still no result, so I examined these instruments and discovered that they possessed radical blemishes: the barometer had no hand but the brass pointer, and the ball of the thermometer was stuffed with tin foil. I might have boiled these things to rags and never found out anything.

I hunted up another barometer; it was new and perfect. I boiled it half an hour in a pot of bean soup which the cooks were making. The result was unexpected: the instrument was not affected at all, but there was such a strong barometer taste to the soup that the head cook, who was a most conscientious person, changed its name in the bill of fare. The dish was so

greatly liked by all that I ordered the cook to have barometer soup every day. It was believed that the barometer might eventually be injured, but I did not care for that. I had demonstrated to my satisfaction that it could not tell how high a mountain was; therefore I had no real use for it. Changes of the weather I could take care of without it; I did not wish to know when the weather was going to be good; what I wanted to know was when it was going to be bad, and this I could find out from Harris' corns. Harris had had his corns tested and regulated at the government observatory in Heidelberg, and one could depend upon them with confidence. So I transferred the new barometer to the cooking department to be used for the official mess. It was found that even a pretty fair article of soup could be made with the defective barometer, so I allowed that one to be transferred to the subordinate messes.

I next boiled the thermometer and got a most excellent result: the mercury went up to about 200° Fahrenheit. In the opinion of the other scientists of the Expedition, this seemed to indicate that we had attained the extraordinary altitude of 200,000 feet above sea level. Science places the line of eternal snow at about 10,000 feet above sea level. There was no snow where we were; consequently it was proven that the eternal snow line ceases somewhere above the 10,000-foot level and does not begin any more. This was an interesting fact, and one which had not been observed by any observer before. It was as valuable as interesting, too, since it would open up the deserted summits of the highest Alps to population and agriculture. It was a proud thing to be where we were, yet it caused us a pang to reflect that but for that ram we might just as well have been 200,000 feet higher.

The success of my last experiment induced me to try an experiment with my photographic apparatus. I got it out and boiled one of my cameras, but the thing was a failure: it made the wood swell up and burst, and I could not see that the lenses were any better than they were before.

I now concluded to boil a guide. It might improve him; it could not impair his usefulness. But I was not allowed to proceed. Guides have no feeling for science, and this one would not consent to be made uncomfortable in its interest.

The Latinist and the Chaleteer

In the midst of my scientific work, one of those needless accidents happened which are always occurring among the ignorant and thoughtless. A porter shot at a chamois and missed it and crippled the Latinist. This was not a serious matter to me, for a Latinist's duties are as well performed on crutches as otherwise—but the fact remained that if the Latinist had not happened to be in the way, a mule would have got that load. That would have been quite another matter, for when it comes down to a question of value, there is a palpable difference between a Latinist and a mule. I could not depend on having a Latinist in the right place every time, so, to make things safe, I ordered that in the future the chamois must not be hunted within the limits of the camp with any other weapon than the forefinger.

My nerves had hardly grown quiet after this affair when they got another shake-up, one which utterly unmanned me for a moment: a rumor swept suddenly through the camp that one of the barkeepers had fallen over a precipice!

However, it turned out that it was only a chaplain. I had laid in an extra force of chaplains, purposely to be prepared for emergencies like this, but by some unaccountable oversight had come away rather shorthanded in the matter of barkeepers.

On the following morning we moved on, well refreshed and in good spirits. I remember this day with peculiar pleasure, because it saw our road restored to us. Yes, we found our road again, and in quite an extraordinary way. We had plodded along some two hours and a half, when we came up against a solid mass of rock about twenty feet high. I did not need to be instructed by a mule this time. I was already beginning to know more than any mule in the Expedition. I at once put in a blast of dynamite and lifted that rock out of the way. But to my surprise and mortification, I found that there had been a chalet on top of it.

I picked up such members of the family as fell in my vicinity, and subordinates of my corps collected the rest. None of these poor people were

injured, happily, but they were much annoyed. I explained to the head chaleteer just how the thing happened, and that I was only searching for the road, and would certainly have given him timely notice if I had known he was up there. I said I had meant no harm, and hoped I had not lowered myself in his estimation by raising him a few rods in the air. I said many other judicious things, and finally when I offered to rebuild his chalet, pay for the breakages, and throw in the cellar, he was mollified and satisfied. He hadn't any cellar at all before; he would not have as good a view now as formerly, but what he had lost in view he had gained in cellar, by exact measurement. He said there wasn't another hole like that in the mountains, and he would have been right if the late mule had not tried to eat up the nitroglycerine.

I put a hundred and sixteen men at work, and they rebuilt the chalet from its own debris in fifteen minutes. It was a good deal more picturesque than it was before, too. The man said we were now on the Feli-Stutz, above the Schwegmatt—information which I was glad to get, since it gave us our position to a degree of particularity which we had not been accustomed to for a day or so. We also learned that we were standing at the foot of the Riffelberg proper, and that the initial chapter of our work was completed.

The mule road to the summit of the Riffelberg passed right in front of the chalet, a circumstance which we almost immediately noticed because a procession of tourists was filing along it pretty much all the time. The chaleteer's business consisted in furnishing refreshments to tourists. My blast had interrupted this trade for a few minutes, by breaking all the bottles in the place; but I gave the man a lot of whisky to sell for Alpine champagne, and a lot of vinegar which would answer for Rhine wine; consequently, trade was soon as brisk as ever.

Success at Last

I formed the caravan in marching order, presently, and after riding down the line to see that it was properly roped together, gave the command to proceed. In a little while the road carried us to open, grassy land. We were above the troublesome forest now and had an uninterrupted view, straight before us, of our summit—the summit of the Riffelberg.

We followed the mule road, a zigzag course, now to the right, now to the left, and always crowded and incommoded by going and coming files of reckless tourists who were never, in a single instance, tied together. I was obliged to exert the utmost care and caution, for in many places the road was not two yards wide, and often the lower side of it sloped away in slanting precipices eight and even nine feet deep. I had to encourage the men constantly to keep them from giving way to their unmanly fears.

We might have made the summit before night but for a delay caused by the loss of an umbrella. I was for allowing the umbrella to remain lost, but the men murmured, and with reason, for in this exposed region we stood in particular need of protection against avalanches; so I went into camp and detached a strong party to go after the missing article.

The difficulties of the next morning were severe, but our courage was high, for our goal was near. At noon we conquered the last impediment—we stood at last upon the summit, and without the loss of a single man except the mule that ate the glycerine. Our great achievement was achieved—the possibility of the impossible was demonstrated, and Harris and I walked proudly into the great dining room of the Riffelberg Hotel and stood our alpenstocks up in the corner.

Yes, I had made the grand ascent; but it was a mistake to do it in evening dress. The plug hats were battered, the swallow-tails were fluttering rags, mud added no grace; the general effect was unpleasant and even disreputable.

There were about seventy-five tourists at the hotel—mainly ladies and children—and they gave us an admiring welcome which paid us for all our privations and sufferings. The ascent had been made, and the names and dates now stand recorded on a stone monument there to prove it to all future tourists.

I boiled a thermometer and took an altitude, with a most curious result: *the summit was not as high as the point on the mountainside where I had taken the first altitude.* Suspecting that I had made an important discovery, I prepared to verify it. There happened to be a still higher summit above the hotel, and notwithstanding the fact it overlooks a glacier from a dizzy height, and that the ascent is difficult and dangerous, I resolved to venture up there and boil a thermometer. So I sent a strong party, with some borrowed hoes, in charge of two chiefs of service, to dig a stairway in the soil all the way, and this I ascended, roped to the guides. This breezy height was the summit proper, so I accomplished even more than I had originally purposed to do. This foolhardy exploit is recorded on another stone monument.

I boiled my thermometer, and sure enough, this spot, which purported to be 2000 feet higher than the locality of the hotel, turned out to be 9000 feet *lower*. Thus the fact was clearly demonstrated that, *above a certain point, the higher a point seems to be, the lower it actually is*. Our ascent itself was a great achievement, but this contribution to science was an inconceivably greater matter.

CRUISING UP THE SALATHÉ WALL

Dick Shockley

S ayings come and go, and like the seasons, they never repeat themselves exactly. In the back of my mind I can hear someone singing, "Climbing is a drug, and I neeeeed a fix. . . ." But right now asphalt is all around me as I sit in the Oldsmobile dealer's waiting room with other stranded souls, waiting to have my U-joints replaced. It could take hours. My mind reverts to the route. The city fades away. I shrink to a mere speck, a dot carrying a big sack up the base of the monolith, El Capitan.

We are well prepared, with a minimum of two quarts of water per man per day, rye-crisp crackers, a six-pack, anchovy paste, kippers, wheat-berry bread, cream cheese, canned fruit, salami, chicken-salad spread, a few illicit goods, and even toothbrushes and toothpaste. We are stoked. The late May days are so fine that I never want to go back to work; and the view of swollen waterfalls and a band of purest white around the valley rim, results of heavy snow from a recent storm, is in itself worth the trip from San Diego.

Rick is an old hand. At twenty-three he has already done several Grade V and VI routes in Yosemite, including first ascents; he has also spent two summers in the Alps. He wishes to climb the Salathé Wall on El Capitan. I am eager, because I love climbing and walls are new to me. In eight years of climbing in Southern California, I have been to Yosemite only twice.

But already there has been a tragedy. We were walking to the base early one morning, thinking about nothing and pleased by the five deer who serenely greeted us near the stream. We were planning to fix three pitches that day. We looked up and saw a climber in or near the Stoveleg Cracks on the Nose. We watched briefly and resumed walking. Then we heard a loud, tearing sound, like a falling rock, and it seemed to last forever. We backed away into a clearing in fear and looked up again. The climber we had seen was gone. It could not be. The sun shone and the birds chirped. El Cap, enormous and neutral, was silent.

"Shouldn't we go over there?"

"No. Let's wait here, Dick. We can't do anything for him."

"Karl is probably over there anyway." Karl has just taken a twelve-hour bus trip up from San Diego to climb the Nose of El Cap.

A minute later, Karl walks out of the woods and says he has seen a body.

"Just one? Was he soloing?"

He goes away and comes back. There are three bodies. He feels sick from the sight and smell and does not want to do the Nose anymore. He looks close to tears. They hit so hard they broke rocks.

Later we learn that the three climbers were from Minnesota. We had met them the preceding night in the campground. They were not entirely inexperienced on big walls, but for some reason they were not going up, but rappelling. That seems to be the bad part, the most dangerous. Pam, a girlfriend of one, is now alone in this vacation paradise, surrounded by huge rock walls, swifts and violet-green swallows, by tourists with Winnebagos and cigars and poodles, alone with her misery. She has to drive home alone.

El Capitan just abides, perhaps waiting and listening for events of greater significance, such as an ice age, or a reversal of the earth's magnetic field, or the cooling of the sun. Rick and I plod on over to the start of the Salathé and leave Karl to his defunct dream. What can we say or do? We do not yet have a haul bag. Maybe we can borrow his. Idiots. Two specks, throwing it all to the wind.

Four days have passed since the accident. We have climbed to Mammoth Terrace and strung our ropes back to the ground from Heart Ledge. We are ready for the summit push. For one long day we jumar, climb, haul, and belay. We want to reach El Cap Spire (the twentieth pitch) by night; this will require ten pitches of climbing above the end of our fixed ropes. We hope to reach the summit with only two bivouacs. Eric Beck, the archetypal climbing bum (in the words of Chris Jones) now turned economics graduate student, says "speed is safety on a wall." To follow this dictum, we have diligently studied the super-topo he gave us.

The ground drops away and becomes indistinct. Huge cornfields spring up in our minds as we remember Eric's ascent of the wall with Keith Bruckner. Somewhere on the lower wall, Keith had remarked—out of the blue—to Eric, "One could easily grow corn here." A classic line, considering their elevation. Of course, I do not blame Keith for being infatuated with corn—but why corn? Why not alfalfa? Why not just say, "Man, it sure is wet and muddy here."

We move on up. The infamous Ear Pitch is not too wet, and above it I flail on aid up the amazing Double Cracks. We are now just a short distance below the Alcove, a blocky ledge one pitch short of El Cap Spire. It looks as if we can't make our intended bivouac site, but by now we don't even want to, since a party of two is already asleep there. Earlier, we had almost caught up with them; we wonder if we can slip past them in the morning. How fast are they compared to us?

Direct aid on overhanging rock is tiring beyond my comprehension, even using a sit-harness to rest. I am both startled and humiliated to feel my lips tingling from the exertion, my stomach muscles knotting, my fingers cramp-

Facing page: The southwest face of El Capitan; the Salathé Wall Route begins near the right side of the cliff. Crossing just beneath the enormous, obvious heart-shaped indentation, the route proceeds up and slightly left for about 400 feet until level with the midpoint of the Heart. Then the climbing line follows crack systems directly upward. *Ed Cooper.*

ing and useless after the long pitch. I sob curses at everything while tugging at knots, trying to set up the belay and haul. They can probably hear me from the Spire, but I cannot help it. I am grateful that I do not faint or lose my lunch via the technicolor yawn. Finally I get the rope tied off. Rick begins to jumar, and from somewhere I find the strength to haul. Maybe I should have been running ten miles a day instead of eight.

It is dark by now. By the light of his headlamp, Rick leads a 5.9 jamcrack-squeeze chimney to the Alcove. I recall the fellow who told us about popping out of this crack in the dark and plummeting forty feet, but Rick reaches the Alcove without incident. Once I arrive, I turn fetal, too exhausted even for a beer. Around midnight I awaken and slowly and painfully manage to drag most of my body onto a flat bench of rock.

In the morning I have recovered. Since our route lies on the southwest face, the sunrise is hidden. Nevertheless, faint strains of Mozart, Bach, Ravel, and Robbins are heard as the warming light creeps through the valley. We argue heatedly over the choice of composers and appropriate passages. A beautiful smoky mist from the controlled-burn areas on the valley floor slides along the Merced River. (The signs along the road read "Management Fire—Do Not Report," and I longed to acquire one for my office, where it would fit right in and be appreciated every day.) Eventually the party above us moves on, and with no excuse for delaying longer, we cruise up the giant chimney behind the Spire.

Late in the day I stare at the "Wet and Slimy Pitch." My new Goretex cagoule comes out, and I tape the wrists shut to keep the water out. It goes into my ears, eyes, and nose instead. We give this pitch a new, more explicit, name—several in fact—and are thankful it is the only mossy, ugly pitch on a thirty-six-pitch route.

We sleep on the Block. This sloping ledge is only five pitches above El Cap Spire, but we have fixed some ropes higher so that tomorrow we can jumar quickly in the cold early morning. The awesome landmark called the Roof is visible from the Block and looks quite interesting. Above the Roof we expect slow progress up the overhanging Headwall. It would be nice to be off tomorrow night, but ten pitches seem like a lot when they're mostly aid.

The party above us has become Gary and Rusty. They have stayed well ahead of us, and we will probably not pass them. Far below us, we can make out another party, or maybe two. We hope one pair are our friends Mike and Dewi, but we cannot communicate or see well enough to be certain. For luck, I tape a joint to a can of kippers and leave it on the Block with a "Mike" and an arrow scratched into the gravel of the ledge. (Later, sitting in the meadow below with a telescope, we saw two climbers ahead of Mike and Dewi. Oh, damn! We fear they scarfed the offering, as I would have done. But it turned out that the upper party perceived the spiritual depth of the gift. "It was really neat," Mike told me later. "They were two Frenchmen, and they yelled down, 'I theenk yore frehns 'ave leff you sometheen'.")

Gary and Rusty sleep on tiny Sous Le Toit Ledge, as if to expiate their routefinding error earlier, when an obvious-looking crack lured them right;

Two-thirds of the way up the wall, the climber cleans the hardware out of a dihedral. Overhangs and ceilings loom overhead; the notorious Roof Pitch surmounts the highest ceiling on the left. *Tom Frost*.

the route to Sous Le Toit is hidden as a short pendulum around a corner to the left. We tried once to warn them, then subtly cruised up to the ledge. We knew that Sous Le Toit is a one-man lie at best, so we soon returned to the Block. It seems, however, that Gary and Rusty *prefer* pain. They hauled their bags up the low-angled slabs beneath Mammoth Terrace, for example, whereas we cheated and merely climbed those pitches with a few extra ropes, traversed over to Heart Ledge, and rappelled to the ground, leaving the extra ropes. Later we jumared back to the ledge with our loads, a tactic which got us onto steeper rock sooner and thus eased the hauling problems immeasurably. This was Eric's suggestion; at first I did not grasp its wisdom, but Rick pointed out to me that at least half the work on a big wall is hauling—so why not make it as easy as possible?

Gary and Rusty have been on El Cap for four days already. Gary says, "Once I'm on, I want to stay on." I guess that's okay. As I examine my dry, cracking cuticles and sore googies (small flesh wounds on the back of the hand which result from poor crack technique), I inform our new friends that we actually followed the procedure of Robbins, Frost, and Pratt on their first ascent in 1961. Gary and Rusty are not swayed by this fact. I recall the Belgian party that we overtook low on the route because their haul bag was being torn to ribbons, but I keep this to myself. After all we are not here to compare methods, compete, argue, or criticize. We are here to get off as soon as possible.

Rick and I have a small, private party on the Block.

"Don't you think we ought to save some of this for the summit?"

"Hmmmm. No."

The third day dawns. Last night was very chilly, like the previous one, but passable. I discover that I did not roll over the edge in my sleep. From now on, though, I really should stay tied in. There simply wasn't enough extra rope last night. Several bars of Stravinsky whistle by; I catch a strain of the Firebird Suite.

"Yarrrgnm. Sigh. Waaummmmnngg. Shrtpz. Ahhhhh. Well, friend, let's cruise."

To judge from the noises above, Rusty and Gary have begun climbing. It is time to move, but it is still cold.

"Okay, I'm almost ready. Just let me get this extra gear packed."

"Let's boogie,"

"Cruise or bruise."

"Succeed or bleed."

"Top or chop."

"Summit or plummet."

"Make haste or tomato paste."

"Finger locks or cedar box."

"Consummate skills or heavy bills."

"Climb in style or fly a mile."

"Unravel the mystery or soon become history."

"Endurance or insurance."

"Keep your head or hospital bed."

"Lunge or plunge."

"Get the knack or face a smack."

"Underclings or angel wings."

"Nail the seam or giant scream."

Rick moves off the Block, jumaring toward Sous Le Toit Ledge. When he gets there, I untie the rope from its anchor on the Block, hook my jumars onto the rope, and swing out over the spectacular exposure. My oh my, this isn't just three times higher than my local crags. This is another world. The cord stretches . . .

Once on Sous Le Toit, we can see the Roof clearly. It almost begins to look reasonable and is even smaller than I thought. But the route goes around to its right. Why have I always assumed it went left? On second thought, it looks horrendous. Eric's topo indicates that the Roof is fixed but requires a long reach at one spot. We start up again, nailing two steep aid pitches while carefully watching Gary and Rusty as they climb and clean the Roof. When it is time for Gary to haul, Rusty cuts the bag loose. Rick says, "Now check this out, Dick," and I am immobilized as I watch it swing out from under the overhang. It takes a year. The Roof is indeed enormous. The scene calls for an ultimately personal phrase of self-expression: "Hoooooooooo Maaaaaaaaaaaaan!!"

During the morning, tourist buses stop in the meadow below to watch while I relieve myself. I hope they have a good scope, but for some reason—perhaps the complete irrelevance of anything on flat ground to our current state—I neglect to look over my shoulder and smile and wave at them. There must be a hundred spectators. Ants.

Last night I realized we had dropped nothing up to this point, and said as much to Rick. With typical foresight he pointed out the foolishness of the remark. Today I drop a carabiner and a pin. Bad. Then Rick drops a nut. They all make a pleasant, whirring sound, but it is so steep they fall beyond hearing before touching rock. We could scream "Rock! Rock!" all day long, but no one below could hear, for the wind is wrong. This is why one should not hang out at the base of El Cap when there are climbers above. Clip, clip, grab the haul line, swing out on the wall past Rick (good lead, Dad), and here at last is the Roof.

It starts out easily, and then I am standing in air in my aiders. This is almost fun. A little bit, anyway. Smile for a photo and try not to think how embarrassing it would be if one of these shitty old pieces of webbing were to . . . No, no, please don't think those thoughts, just the other kind, the pleasant ones . . . and concentrate on the moves. Move on. Eric's topo claims there is a place for a two-inch bong at the lip. Where, Eric, where? I search for long minutes, swinging in the breeze. Rick huddles shivering in the shade of the overhang. My spirits drag and so does the time. A fixed sling lurks just out of reach beyond the lip. All I need to do is grab it. Unngh. Shit, still too far.

Finally, in frustration, I lunge some fifty feet or so up overhanging friction holds, battle an avalanche of boxcar-sized blocks, hook a fingernail on the frayed wisp of rotten webbing, and clip into it only to find that the eighth-inch cord is attached to a may-pop stopper. A pop here would have a spectrum of consequences: psychological, physical, sexual, theological. For example, Rick might take over the lead. He tried once before, low on the route, but I drew a knife and threatened to sever his rope. My perspective returns as soon as I clip into the next fixed piece, a sturdy copperhead. Whew! Well, in all honesty, that was not too bad. A pretty simple pitch actually. Casual, even trivial. Look at that bag swing; easy hauling here.

Now we face the ninety-five-degree Headwall; six pitches remain. Rick nails and nuts onward, up the overhanging rock. There is supposedly a big ledge—Long Ledge—two pitches higher, but from here there is absolutely no sign of such a sanctuary. Across the valley, shadows on Middle Cathedral Rock mark the passage of time. It is growing late, almost 4:30. As I hang from my harness, I recall the overwhelming indifference of El Capitan. Toward the three boys from Minnesota. Toward us. I know this bears remembering, and I eye the anchors again and again. I am ready. The wind blows the haul line almost horizontally across the smooth, golden rock. We are climbing in the only crack for as far as the eye can see on either side. I want to stop time and absorb this forever. The insane swifts cavort in the wind.

The leader moves toward the Roof. Above it rises the wildly overhanging Headwall, with its solitary crack. *Tom Frost.*

I smear on glacier cream, face away from the hot sun, eat Starbursts, examine my anchors yet again, have a sip of water, and count the number of ways to sit in a harness. The pitch is long and strenuous, and I feel for Rick. The wall appears foreshortened since it overhangs so much. Soon the haul line is swaying fifteen feet out from the cliff. Finally Rick is done, and I come up, noting that several of his placements were tricky, if not tricky-difficult. Now I swing into the short aid lead toward the still-hidden Long Ledge. From the extreme right end of this narrow ledge, Rick nails and nuts up a crack which will bring us to a ledge only two pitches from the top.

As Rick climbs, the texture of the rock changes: knobs appear. For the first time in eight pitches, it is possible to make a free move or two.

My last lead. As the sunlight begins to leave us, I start up a crack in a big hurry, taking all the wrong nuts. Eric's topo says laconically, "Pretty pitch." I realize I have screwed up when nothing fits. I curse the crack into remote regions for being the wrong size. With practice, I have developed a ritualistic, five-word obscenity to deal with recalcitrant cars and cracks or nonlinear partial differential equations. Finally Rick stills my rage and attaches the necessary nuts to my haul line. Then I am free, jamming a gentle crack into the last belay stance, an alcove below Pratt's Crack.

Darkness comes, but a full moon dispells it almost immediately as Rick squeezes up the 5.9 summit pitch. So much of the climbing is good that I wish there were time for me to climb the pitch instead of jumar it. Exultant yell: "What a finish!"

"All reet!" I reply.

I can barely hear him now, but he is probably ready for me to jumar. I know that the end of the difficult climbing comes very suddenly and obviously he is there. Only one way to tell for sure: jumar. It is tight in the crack, particularly with a pack. Then we are together again and I feel weary, but only one trivial pitch remains. The holds are huge, and then I see a tree. The summit tree. Then many trees. Can it really be? It is very bright. Rick and the haul bag arrive safely. Since the slabs are low-angled, the hauling is difficult. I get a few more blisters and open up the old ones, but so what?

We are alone. Rusty and Gary have disappeared. The terrain is nice and flat here. We hang our equipment all over the big tree and I settle down for a few pipeloads. Always room for a little more elevation. There is very little to say. No sounds arise from the valley, but we spy an endless chain of headlights coming up the Fresno Road. We are both satisfied to be around trees, to have the harnesses off, to be silent.

Sleep.

Two climbers on the ninety-five-degree Headwall; the leader's haul line hangs far out from the rock. *Tom Frost.*

The Salathé Wall has seen at least one hundred—and maybe two hundred—ascents through the years. If any particular feature marked our climb, it was the absence of any remarkable features. We drove to the valley, hung out a little, did the route, hung out a little, and departed. But to paraphrase a famous mountaineer, adventure is a sign of incompetence. Not all climbers would agree, of course, but I feel that this simply reflects different opinions on what constitutes adventure, or maybe what constitutes incompetence. I was certainly satisfied and wanted nothing more. Our lessons were short and simple: prepare well, wear tape or gloves to spare the hands (it was three days before we could comfortably close our hands), and climb fast.

One afternoon, shortly after we had arrived in Yosemite, we drove to the meadow below El Cap to check out the route. I was staring at it—feeling vaguely terrified—when a tourist in a Hawaiian shirt asked if I saw any climbers on the wall.

"Yeah, I think I do."

The cliff was covered with parties. They were on the Nose, the Shield, the Dihedral, the Muir. Dale Bard and Ron Kauk could be seen working on a new line near the North American Wall.

"They gotta be nuts, ya know?"

"Right."

"You'd never get me up there."

I could hardly argue with that, and since I am agreeable by nature anyway, I said:

"I agree. I think so too. They're all just maniacs, hanging up there on the sheer face and climbing up ropes that could come loose any time or break. It's just like asking for death. Pretty sick, man. Hey, I mean no way, Ray."

As a rule, this type has a gigantic Winnebago, cases of beer, and daughters that stop your heart in midthump and provoke thoughts of . . . well, as I was saying, Rick wandered over and we chatted a bit. The tourist loaned us his binoculars to look at the madmen on the cliff. But as Rick and I quietly speculated about the route, the man fell quiet, and a look of confusion, suspicion, or possible awareness dawned on his features. He yelled across to his wife:

"Hey, Ruth! These guys are gonna scale that mountain!"

IN THE CONSTELLATION OF ROOSTERS AND LUNATICS

Jeff Long

For a few minutes after it landed, no one touched the body on the macadam street. Finally a New York City policeman pulled a card from the dead climber's pants pocket: "Harry F. Young. Work guaranteed on flagstaffs, church steeples, water tanks, and impossible places to reach. America's unique and original steeplejack and stuntist."

That one bare image of conceit collapses into a penny tombstone. Young had earlier wisecracked, louder than necessary, to a hotel detective, "If I do it, have the bath ready. If I don't, get a shovel."

At noon on March 5, 1923, Young approached the Broadway façade of the Martinique Hotel. It's not unlikely that he kissed his pretty, bob-haired wife of two months just before wiping his hands on his pants and grasping the masonry. One foot, then the other, left the ground. With the bustling 34th Street shopping district fat with shoppers, his audience was immediate, as anticipated. Young was a professional; the climb was a matter of contract: 100 dollars. The next day's *New York Times* reported the event:

Frequently, in order to give the crowd . . . an extra thrill, Young seemed purposely to let his foot slip, holding tightly to the coping. . . . Up, up he climbed, resembling a giant moth, but his figure growing less and less conspicuous as it faded into perpendicular distance.

He made the eleventh story. People stood thrilled, their heads thrown further and further backward. Young's foot slipped. They thought he was again making believe, but in an instant they learned their mistake. For an incredible moment Young seemed to stand in space, then his white form came crashing down . . . in a quick plunge to the sidewalk. A prolonged "Ah!" went up from the crowd.

Within five weeks the city aldermen had passed an ordinance forbidding human flies to climb the buildings of New York City. The fine was to be ten dollars, ten days, or both. Urban ascent was, for the first time, criminal trespass. Being in a place you're not supposed to be is also called other things: arrogance, stupidity, hubris . . . and no doubt the dead climber suffered further calumny that day. To an extent, the pejoratives will always apply; every time a climber enters the vertical world he's thumbing his nose at biological propriety. Human beings simply aren't built to live on a ninety-degree world.

Nevertheless, given a monolith that is taller than a man—whether it's made of granite, limestone, ice, or cement—twentieth-century humans will come and struggle to the very death with it. For all its sophistication and evolution in the past fifty years, ascent remains as old-fashioned and violent as ever, drawing at raw muscular thought and transforming it into a hole beneath your feet.

Even more antagonistic to the social order than people who crawl around on rocks and walls in the wilderness are people who crawl around on buildings, infiltrating those spaces which society has taught us men cannot go. It seems especially impertinent to go clambering around on cliffs made of steel

Facing page: Climbing "Ship of State" on the Student Union Building at San Francisco State University. *Robert Zipperer.*

and concrete, on glass waterfalls, and on marble and asphalt bergschrunds instead of the real thing.

A city, after all, is the very epitome of modern civilization, typified by regulation and technological achievement, and obsessed with the new and current. To have climbers reminding a skyscraper not only of its origin, but also of its artificiality, is to remind the rooster of the egg, an unwelcome pecking order. Harry F. Young must have expected the pejoratives. A letter to the *Times* editor chastised the police for permitting Young to risk his life for such a poor purpose: "The inclination to meet danger—to find a certain charm in it—is a valuable quality, *when reasonably controlled*." Citizens cried for control, *reasonable control*. Which, of course, is why Young made wisecracks about dying and why he was being paid 100 dollars on that day when he found himself halfway to the ground from a place beyond control. Reasonable control doesn't always lead to the place you want to be.

A hand traverse on "Ship of State." *Robert Zipperer.*

Take Joachim Richter, for instance, a young German lunatic who was internationally publicized in the 1920s because he climbed out of three asylums. In eluding the police on the second of those escapes, he climbed a smooth wall to the fifth floor of an apartment house in Berlin and entered a window. "Don't worry," he told the screaming woman who lived there. "I'm the Kaiser. I just came to wash my hands." He did so, then ate the bar of soap. The authorities recaptured him, but the same week Richter bolted for freedom again, taking to the prison wall . . . beyond control.

There was more substance to these early human flies than their circus courage and criminal modes of independence. Their portraits would be superficial cartoons if they depicted nothing more than roosters and lunatics. But there is always that constellation of reasons we call ego, and there were some big ones making the circuit half a century ago. An unemployed steelworker, a bellboy, a sailor, a half-baked boxer: proletarians without real access to the public nonetheless made themselves bigger than life, front-page material. Reading the accounts, one discovers that almost every one of these men proclaimed himself *the* human fly, *the* unique stuntist, the *one and only*. Some were fair athletes, no doubt, with egos like beacons.

After climbing the Woolworth Building and the tower of the *Chicago Tribune* building, Johnny Meyer ("The Human Fly of America") set off for Europe, where he planned to climb the Kaiserschloss in Berlin, the dome of St. Benedict's in Paris, and numerous tall steeples in England. His sole purpose, he crowed to the press, was to become world famous. "Everywhere I go, people will point me out." And as persistent as a shadow was the fairy tale of instant wealth: "I can sell my nerve tonic and my picture, then."

Because no legacy is left by a building climb, especially viewed from a distance of fifty and sixty years, people have forgotten some of the more spectacular ones: Bill Strothers' ("The Human Spider") ascent of the Brockway Building in Los Angeles (1919); Harry Gardiner raising money for war bonds on the Brooklyn Eagle Building (1918); and Steve Peterson, who fell three stories because he was past his prime ("It was a bum break," he said as he jauntily smoked a cigarette on the way to the hospital in 1928).

The penchant for provoking attention wasn't intractable, though. More daredevils cooled into ordinary citizens than didn't. A few fell, fewer still died, and as for the majority of human flies, the world simply ceased to hear about them. They became anonymous neighbors in neighborhoods without a literature to glorify them. Sometime in the early 1930s urban climbing quietly petered out.

Recently, though, urban ascent has regained a visible profile, catalyzed by George Willig's success on Manhattan's World Trade Center building on May 26, 1977. Building climbs had been on a number of climbers' minds before that, but quietly, like a masonic word. Willig's Trade Center climb would have taken me by complete surprise if it hadn't been for Ed Drummond, who introduced me to the Transamerica Building in San Francisco.

Wily and innovative, Ed had been considering skyscrapers for years before letting me in on the idea. He was thirty-two at the time, coincidentally the age of Harry F. Young when he fell in 1923. Without assembling too many similarities, I should add that Ed's pocket was rarely without his own business card, which advertised his Bulldog Construction Company, a fledgling organization that offered scaffoldless steeplejacking for such jobs as sandblasting and goldleafing. And the steeplejack's wife, Mrs. Drummond, like Mrs. Young, was pretty and youthful—just twenty years old.

Somewhere in his past, Ed had escaped to America from an unfriendly English climbing scene—something to do with his abrasive habit of renaming already-established routes and generally outraging the local lads. A tall and sturdy poet, Ed espoused a sort of bastard Jack Londonism, according to which extraordinary men are on fire, living so intensely that when they die, they disintegrate in a sudden furious blaze. His updated version of this character was the intellectually alert climber capable of one-arm pullups with either arm and able to survive for days without water. Ed had done that once, near the end of a twenty-day epic of stone. It was on the Trolltind Wall in Norway when he and his partner, Hugh Drummond (no relation), ran out of water and had to hang marooned in their hammocks until rain came. In the process, Ed's bladder closed off, creating the painful, dehydrated condition known as trench penis. Despite such adversities, the two men finished the ascent.

To silence any doubts about which of the two Drummonds was the animating force behind that ascent of the Troll, Ed later repeated his amazing survival act during a ten-day solo of El Capitan's Nose in Yosemite. It's important to concede solitude's brunt when you're soloing a wall. Three thousand feet above the ground, tied into knots that no one else can check, dependent on judgments that are either right or fatal, you become absolutely crucial to your own continued existence.

The exit pitch on the Nose consists of a line of old bolts angling up a blank, overhanging terrain of granite. As with so many dangerous sections on extended climbs, this final pitch has acquired a small history. In June, 1973, a pair of young climbers reached the bolt ladder after a week on the rock. One of the men led up to the summit acres; the other— a nineteen-year-old—made a small mistake in his jumaring technique. Climbers 2000 feet below, hearing the fluttering hum a rock or falling haul bag might make, turned to see the wingless boy. Months later, alone, Ed navigated the listing rock wall, finishing that terminal pitch in a gray autumn snowstorm. On fire, naturally.

The plan to climb the Transamerica Pyramid—an 843-foot skyscraper in downtown San Francisco—was more a civilized heresy than the conspiracy we pretended. In late November 1976, Ed invited me to join him on a special climb that had been percolating in his mind for a year. I'd never heard of the Transam, but the immediate thought of police and punishment made me reluctant to consider it seriously. There were far too many unknowns; yet I listened as Ed methodically spread out the contents of his plan, and we concluded by agreeing to survey the building. It was nearly Christmas when we met. The lights of San Francisco were powdered with a slow, colorless fog. Its windows glinting, the Pyramid jutted up forcefully from the city's atomized glow.

Urban climbing is not restricted to skyscrapers: here noontime shoppers observe a "builderer" in action. *Robert Zipperer.*

It has been said that the Pyramid is "too tall for its site, too unconventional for its surroundings and altogether unsuited for a city like San Francisco." Even before it was constructed, the thirty-million-dollar building was fiercely opposed by San Franciscans who feared for their skyline. Zoning authorities had, in fact, already declared that no new buildings could have a total floor space greater than fourteen times the ground area of the site. This edict was specifically aimed at excluding skyscrapers from the neighborhood.

Architect William Pereira—adhering to the standards for floor space—foxily tapered his proposed building into an elongated pyramid. People were outraged. The Northern California Chapter of the American Institute of Architects demonstrated that the same office space could be built into a structure 500 feet shorter. The Transamerica Corporation compromised by giving up ten stories, and when disgruntled protestors still showed up, there were well-groomed Transamerica secretaries on hand to serve tea and fortune cookies. The Pyramid was built.

Beginning as a gothic square occupying fully half a city block, the building tapers gradually to a needle point 843 feet higher. Windows dominate to the forty-eighth floor, where, along with two symmetrically opposed elevator fins, the building's sharp nipple builds itself out of mysteriously lit, louvered panels. The climb looked furtively possible as Ed diagrammed its three distinctive features: the columns at the base, the windows, and the louvered summit. By shimmying up the sixty-five-degree columns with the aid of webbing, Ed projected, we could get to the windows, where jamming, liebacking, or stemming would take us six hundred feet higher to the headwall of strange metal scales. His wife, Grace, would climb with us, Ed reiterated. In the spirit of joining the enterprise, I welcomed her as a partner.

Our research in the next frantic month was to belie that rudimentary strategy. Like any plan, ours required more and more knowledge as it developed, drawing on fields that were immediately useless, but in the long range proved relevant to our chameleon purposes. Detailed information was more significant—and more difficult to obtain—than we'd first thought. Exactly how far apart were the jutting window frames? Did they spread near the building or pout open at the outer lip? Or were they parallel? Were there anchors for window washers? Would pairs of window frames take a nut, a

piton, or a cam? How did the windows open—up and down, or in and out? How high would we have to climb before we were out of range of firetruck cherry pickers? Should a rope or carabiner accidentally drop, which wall would have the least number of spectators below? Would a Saturday or a Sunday be better than a work day? And in the likelihood of police action, was a large crowd better for us than a small one? The more questions we compiled, the less adequate our speculations and opinions appeared.

We toyed with various dodges and masquerades to glean dimensions and facts, lamely posing by turns as architecture enthusiasts, an aspiring window-washing team, assistant professors of engineering, and tourists from Kansas. Ed had already been denied permission by the managers to climb the building, so we had to be careful about raising further suspicions.

For the most part, each bit of solid information we acquired would satisfy an entire segment of the project. Once a single pair of window frames was calculated, all the pairs of window frames were understood. We had half a dozen oak wedges, five-and-a-quarter-inches wide, made up—an expression of certainty about that much of the building.

Other statistics gradually accumulated, but the key to that last portion of the Pyramid—the 212-foot spire of louvered panels, which seemed both solid during the day and opaque at night, both grilled (and therefore passable), yet smooth (and impassable)—eluded our studies. We visited the city building commissioner's office, applied for twelve microfilm slides of blueprints, and returned the next morning to peruse the vital data. Instead, we found that the slides listed only serial numbers for hundreds of individual blueprint slides, each of which cost twenty-five cents. With 500 dollars we might have found the right slide. We changed tactics, costumes, assumptions, and tried different approaches.

In the course of our research, the architecture of San Francisco—and architecture in general—started to take on a more fluid tone for me. I began to regard the exteriors of buildings as something more than basic geometric adornments of space. Among ourselves we envisioned—only half in fun—a whole generation of climbers who would someday grope about on these man-made houses of cards. We talked about all the strange new media involved—glass, metal, concrete—and how new styles of climbing would necessarily emerge.

In a sense we were challenging the architects, engineers, and builders by equipping ourselves with secret techniques to solve their secret techniques. In making skyscrapers, they had built external faces that were as physiologically inhuman (read "unclimbable") as anything nature has ever designed. Now it seemed that climbers as silent as *ninji* would creep out of the wilderness to paw the urban skylines.

In another sense, however, and one that I began to appreciate the more I read, our proposed climb shared affinities with the bold, intelligent architecture of the Pyramid and certain other structures. I came across many examples of architecture that dared as much censure as our climb would attract. Some of the boldest, most exciting designs have remained unbuilt, for the simple reason that they were *too* bold.

To my eye, Raphael Soriano's United Nations Tower—created in 1969, but never built—is one of the most elegant designs ever conceived. The all-aluminum, 110-story tower would have tapered in the center, creating, for the climber, a gentle but ever more insistent overhang above the seventieth floor. Thin, embellishing struts would have provided some intriguing climbing not totally dissimilar from that which the Eiffel Tower has offered alpinists in the past.

Bolder yet, Frank Lloyd Wright designed a mile-high office tower to be located in Chicago. At the time (1956), it would have been five times higher than any other building in the world—so high, in fact, that he designed its windows to be set four feet back under metal parapets "to afford a human sense of protection at such enormous heights." It would have housed 130,000 people and challenged generations of building climbers.

For the greatest height (a feather in the cap to some architects and climbers) none can top Siah Armajani, who designed what was modestly entitled "A Fairly Tall Tower." It was to be 48,000 miles high. At 24,000 miles above the site (somewhere in America) Armajani proposed a "synchronous joint." This is the balance point in space where the force of gravity equals the centrifugal force moving objects away from the earth. If it could be built, I daresay it could be climbed. Architecture that might have seemed aesthetically or structurally ridiculous on paper now exists in cities around the world. Similarly, climbs that at one time seemed utterly fantastic—Everest, the Matterhorn, or the Eiger's north face—by now have been repeated to the point of disinterest. Someday, no doubt, an expedition will climb the 60,000-foot dead volcano that Voyager spacecraft have discovered on Mars.

Our excitement in climbing manmade objects was not limited to skyscrapers alone. As we crossed the Golden Gate Bridge one night, Ed described the understructure to me, laying out a traverse that he hoped to accomplish someday among the gulls and iron shadows beneath the highway. Later he confided that, to celebrate his forthcoming American citizenship, he had considered climbing the Statue of Liberty.

Ed and I approached our project from quite different points of view. Intellectually, I was fascinated by the various architecture, but I couldn't really see making a career out of urban climbing. For Ed, the Transam beckoned not only as a climb, but as a manic vocation. In a way that he insisted was incidental, he wouldn't have minded making a quarter-million on a TV contract as well. Failure was highly possible, though, and as a way of dispelling his anxieties about this ascent of the Pyramid, Ed would speak of an even larger pyramid in Chicago.

On one foray to reconnoiter the Pyramid, Ed and I went to the Bank of America Center two blocks south of the Transam. After being reprimanded by a security guard for bouldering on an amorphous sculpture in adjoining Giannini Plaza, I put my sandals back on and insouciantly entered the building proper. As we walked in, immense panes of window glass reflected our images. It took us only a moment to project a manner of ascent for them. Glass clamps—the large suction cups used by glaziers—would certainly negotiate the long stretches of upright glass. It was dizzying to conjure a climber on vertical panes of fifty-foot glass, suspended from one suction cup which might loosen as he was setting a second clamp higher. Worse, a slight misstep would collapse the whole sheet. The glass climber, then, faced not only a fall-off but a fall-in, a fragile duplicity of elements that climbers face only rarely on certain kinds of waterfall ice.

One of dozens of high-speed elevators took us to the fifty-second floor of the Bank of America Center, where a plush restaurant and observation deck are fitted out with floor-to-ceiling windows, sod-thick carpet, and a handrail for the acrophobic. The *maitre d'* of the Carnelian Room made himself conspicuous, and with his most baleful glare reminded us that this was his domain. Exuding the nonchalance of realtors—though distinctly handicapped by our shabby clothing—Ed and I pulled binoculars and telescope from our daypacks.

Directly across from us, the Pyramid stabbed the misty sky at an altitude shared by few other buildings in the city. Set among lesser structures, the Pyramid swept up from its massive root in a manner suggesting that the building's sole purpose was to support a solitary red dot, the air beacon, on the skyline. We murmured conspiratorially when we saw it, for we hoped to be hanging our hammocks from that very beacon in a few nights. For a full hour we studied the upper third of the skyscraper, attempting once again to decipher the mysterious metal grill on the final expanse. We spied several new variations to our line of ascent as well as two or three blind spots invulnerable to police retrieval. But as the sun set, the upper louvers of the spire still eluded our understanding. With only a few days left before our secretly scheduled ascent, we could do no more than prepare for several eventualities.

As the ascent drew near, Ed became ever more inebriated with the project, loping throughout San Francisco for advice, mechanisms, free rope

The leader prepares to mantle
onto a small ledge on the Holy
Cross Church in San Francisco.
Robert Zipperer.

and slings, confidential talks with newspaper and radio people, and meetings with a group of amateur filmmakers who hoped to secrete themselves in neighboring skyscrapers. So much was riding on the venture by the last week of January that Ed went so far as to declare we should not surrender unless the police drew their guns, and even then that we should resist.

Compounding the hazards of ascent with guns and arrest didn't appeal to me, nor to Drummond's wife. The closer we got to the date of the climb, the more timid she became. The debates about how we should react to arrest exposed my own hesitancies, too. Each of us began to assess the commitments we were willing to make, aware now that the game was not entirely a game. Ed insisted that once we started, the police would let us finish the climb, especially if we showed an attractive bravado and style. He pointed to Phillipe Petit—the French aerialist who walked a tightrope between the World Trade Center towers in 1974—as an example of how a city loves its daredevil heroes. When asked to justify his stunt, Petit had explained, "If I see three oranges, I must juggle; if I see two towers, I must walk." He escaped with a slap on the hand and was ordered by the court to perform aerial tricks for children in Central Park. Ed assured me that we could exchange court leniency for instruction to police and fire departments on ways to snatch suicides and future climbers from building ledges. I did not share his conviction that we were going to be heroes. Finally Ed compromised, moderating his resolve to bluff police artillery.

On the evening of January 28, 1977, a cool and cloudless Friday, all the conspirators gathered at the Drummonds' apartment. What had begun as a modest trespass on the Pyramid had swollen to include an eight-person film crew, a photojournalist from the *San Francisco Chronicle*, a physics professor from Berkeley, friends with "program notes" to be handed out to spectators and policemen, and letters to be delivered to San Francisco's mayor George

Moscone, Police Chief Charles Gain, and Governor Jerry Brown. A helicopter with a camera mount was scheduled to make two sweeps of the building at 250 dollars per sweep. Miscellaneous gear included a rubber chicken, balloons to be released from the summit, and three clown's noses purchased from a local magic shop to keep things light.

Once the idea of a two-day spectacle had become fixed in our minds, each of us had begun to rehearse our performances. Ever ready to advance his Lone Ranger morality, Ed went so far as to write a pamphlet that condemned the Transam owners and portrayed the building as a showpiece for the Mafia. Less interested in grandstanding a cause, I decided to do street-theater program notes to offset Ed's ferocity with a little frivolity. Grace bashfully wrote nothing.

That night everything was prepared: the cameras were loaded; portable microphones were taped to our backs; and hammocks, parkas, piss bottles, food, tape for our hands, glass clamps, water, hard candies, and the rubber chicken were all packed into a tattered haul bag. Ropes and hardware were placed into smaller packs. Attempts at festivity were few and subdued. Whether we would even get off the ground was a matter for real concern; if the police or security guards were on their toes, the efforts and money of dozens of people would be wasted.

At two in the morning I retired to the bathroom for what might be the last relaxed chance for days. At 3 A.M. our tiny caravan drove to a spot two blocks east of the Pyramid and parked. The photojournalist from the *Chronicle* watched us heap the gear onto our backs and stealthily accompanied us from beneath an overpass. Our first misfortune occurred one block later when a second reporter suddenly materialized from the shadows.

Gambling that the police would be less likely to shoot first if a bona fide reporter was present, Ed had informed the *Chronicle* of our secret climb twelve hours earlier. By way of securing the paper's confidentiality, he had also sworn not to alert any other news agency; this would be their exclusive. The *Chronicle* reporter was predictably upset to discover a competitor on the scene, and she made several caustic accusations. (We later learned that her husband worked for the second reporter's radio station.)

As our attempts to pacify the two fuming reporters muttered to a close, a police car slid down the street. The officers didn't look at our tense cluster, or if they did, passed us off as innocent rabble. Startled by the sight of the police car, we mobilized. Ed sauntered toward the garden restaurant located beneath the east wall, stood atop the stair rail, and pulled himself onto the canvas awning that tunnels out from the restaurant. Grace was next, then I followed.

One by one, afflicted with the cold and anxiety, we balanced on the awning ribs and quietly relayed our equipment onto the restaurant roof before sliding up and over the lip ourselves. Grace was shivering, the only perceptible trace of her uncertainties about the climb. In the past few weeks, she had finally stitched together some formula of resolution. Ed caught her wrist; I pushed her foot. The Pyramid loomed above us.

Fumbling at the coils of rope as we slumped against a pillar, we realized for the first time that our line of ascent was directly in front of the guard's coffee room. The cubicle was well lit and illuminated our selection of pillars like a spotlight. We couldn't go left, for it would put us too close to the street; if we shifted to the right, we would be immediately above the restaurant's glass roof. A fall would mutilate the unfortunate leader. We could only hope that the coffee-room window would deflect the guard's vision until dawn equalized the lighting. By that time we were sure to be higher.

The pillars section, for which we'd prescribed half an hour in our timetable, instantly rebuked us. In trying to walk the pillar in the fashion of lumberjacks ascending a tree, Ed's loop of nylon webbing shredded and then stuck on the concrete. Had the webbing allowed more mobility, Ed might have risen twenty or thirty feet only to rocket backwards when the sling finally cut through. The cement was rough and sharp and had us all bleeding after a few touches. While I belayed him from the shadows, Ed next attempted to hug the steeply slanted pillar and scoot himself up. He could have gone higher, but the futility was apparent: thirty feet up and he would have needed to anchor himself in with slings—without a hand to spare. A half hour had passed.

Nervous whispers from the garden below informed us that the coast was clear, more a report of affairs at sidewalk level than for our benefit. The whispers did nothing but frighten Grace and me even more. It seemed very possible that the cement might have ears. Grace huddled in her green cagoule at the root of the monolith, her smallness emphasized by the immensity of the Pyramid. I considered surrendering to the night while we were still undetected. Some other time we could return with a mechanical answer to the pillar. Grace later told us she'd crawled off to a corner and peed in a trough of roofing gravel "like in a kitty box."

Left: The climber nears the apex of the notorious Banker's Heart, the obsidian-like "boulder" in San Francisco's Giannini Plaza. *Robert Zipperer.*

Right: Here a "builderer" encounters a friction ramp, a rarity in urban climbing. *Robert Zipperer.*

An attempt to solve the mysteries of rivet climbing on the Golden Gate Bridge. *Lanny Johnson.*

Besides holding offices in its neck, the Pyramid also contains a bank. The significance of this surfaced as we looked at the coffee machine that was bound to lure bank guards to our molecule of activity. Ed and I whispered with unsaid anger, strangely cocked to blame each other. The unnatural silence, the merciless concrete, and the threat of eventual arrest combined to create a sharper feeling of anxiety than I've ever met with on a mountain or rock. We were being beaten by magicians who really *had* made an insoluble architecture, but rather than admit it, we were daring each other to say the profane word "retreat." At the same time, angry as we were, we were racking our brains for the key to the pillars and glass. Then, abruptly and in perfect focus, I spied a way to continue. In pointing out the dubious possibility, I also realized that I was not good enough to perform the maneuver myself.

Before we lost all momentum, Ed snaked across a bridge of horizontal pillars and lodged himself at the bottom of my proposed route. With his rump seated against the pillar, he gently pressed his feet against the ribless glass that hung above him. The counter-pressure was sufficient for him to scoot a little higher, then reset his feet. One misstep concentrating too much pressure on too small an area of glass, and he would have shot his foot through, leaving one sheared leg on the second floor and his body dangling above the pavement. It was impossible to protect his ascent, so Ed gingerly continued with an even, apelike meditation. I watched horrified as other, equally deadly, consequences to Ed's motions occurred to me, but I didn't communicate this fear to Grace. She lay against a pillar, suffering Ed's boldness without a glance. Ed was halfway up the pillar when she finally admitted that she didn't want to be where she was. She then returned to muteness among the packs and the haul bag.

Ed's dare was the sleekest, fiercest act I've ever seen, and it worked. With ruthless happiness, he allowed himself to fool the sharp, massive contours of the building, glueing and unglueing his hands and feet and body across the glass as if exploring the genitals of a giant. At last he began to marionette two ropes into position, one on each side of a pillar. I clipped jumars onto these ropes, which by arrangement draped the pillar on either side, and then walked up in opposition to Ed's stance. Fairly quickly I was level with Ed, though fifteen feet distant from him. He peered at me from beneath the false ceiling he had arrived at. I looked up at the windows, elevator fins, and headwall as the sun started to paint them flamingo pink.

We'd lost two hours and still hadn't reached the windows. I hauled the sack of gear up to where I hung, then whispered down for Grace. Dawn was traveling down the canyoned streets, poisoning our cover. We were certain now that we'd be caught, though how high we could reach before the first alarm remained an open question. We still hoped that dangling in grotesque suspension from the skin of the building, we could persuade the police to let us make ourselves safe. If we had our way, that would not be until we'd topped out. Ed prodded Grace with the special language of married people, and silently she allowed him to haul her up.

Meanwhile, two janitors had appeared in the room just opposite our stance on the pillars. With an easygoing monotony they were changing lightbulbs; one man would hold a three-foot stepladder as the other jockeyed old and new bulbs. The first to see us, their sole reaction was to render us a friendly wave.

Calmed by this incident, we set to work gaining the windows. Failure again seemed imminent after a few attempts, and again retreat was on the tips of our tongues. I fastened a stirrup to what had become a cobweb of ropes and slings and stood in the highest loop. Ed then clambered up my leg and back and stood on my shoulders, then on my upstretched palms, but repeatedly the cliffhanger he was trying to hammer into a seam in the concrete popped out. The joint angled downward and spat out all the inventions Ed came up with. Each time he tried to stand in a stirrup his foot would come slamming down onto my shoulder or head, and I was seriously weighing the chances of a crooked neck if he continued much longer. Another effort and Ed managed to stack two tenuous cliffhangers in the seam. The stirrup held and Ed victo-

riously squeezed up into a downsloping window well. Like an animal, he surveyed the cliffs and linear gulfs from his private cave, delighted with his own audacity. It was nearly 8:30. The Saturday-morning city was still restive and hushed, but beginning to sparkle. Looking around, I saw a dozen office workers standing at a fourth-story window across the street. One, absolutely silent and insulated behind his plate of glass, toasted us with his cup of coffee.

As we'd hoped, the windows were only moderately difficult, and, of course, architecturally uniform. In minutes Ed was up to the seventh floor, anchoring himself to a window-washer's bolt. He cautiously backed up the bolt with several tube chocks and one of his special wooden pitons, then called for Grace to join him. Steeling herself, Grace repeated her wish to go down.

At that very moment a security guard, alerted by someone, dashed to the garden entrance and frantically scanned the wall above. It took him a moment to locate us—the perspective was unnatural—and then he exploded. Small and distant though he was, he looked tempestuously muscular in his rage. Luckily, the daylight exposed us as something other than tardy thieves or he might have drawn his gun. The guards, we later learned, were supposed to check the outer grounds regularly, but seldom did. They didn't fail to respond, however, once we were spotted. The Berkeley professor, a balding man with a look of husbanded wisdom, stepped up to the guard and tried to soothe him as per plan. This only provoked the guard; the professor's later dealings with the police landed him down at the holding tank. The guard ranted at us for several moments more, then disappeared to call in more professional help.

The stage was set for a race against arrest, but the situation was visibly remote from climax. We were still near the foot of the Pyramid, the climbing was slow, and we lacked dynamism. Again Grace relented and allowed herself to be pulled, hand over hand, up to the seventh-story windowsill where Ed was perched. As I watched Grace dangle upwards, a window far above and to my right opened. A white-haired head popped out, sighted us, and vanished. Moments later, a second window, lower and still to the right, repeated this sequence. Finally, triangulations focused and the window next to Ed opened. It was the head janitor. He proved to be a pleasant man; at first gruff, he became warmer after Ed's invitation to join us for the remainder of the climb, even agreeing to meet us ten floors higher with coffee and sandwiches.

Below us, reporters and television cameramen had begun to congregate, heralding the arrival soon afterwards of firetrucks and police cars. To my surprise, the crowd was dominated by professional media people and uniformed men—people who channel thoughts and control activity. The people we'd hoped would enjoy the climb with us, the common city dwellers, were uninterested or at best bemused, and definitely in a minority. The climb had not been created as a performance—we weren't climbing for publicity—but knowing that we would be climbing publicly, Ed and I had expressed a mutual wish to include San Franciscans in our sojourn. Instead, there were reporters and cameramen who would package us on the second page, display us on January 29 television, and sell us to the Associated Press. As for the law, one

Facing page: Ascending the architecturally uniform windows section of the still-unclimbed Transamerica Pyramid. *Mako Koiwai.*

While an officer looks on, Ed
Drummond liebacks the
vertical concrete labyrinth.
Mako Koiwai.

fireman was overheard volunteering to remedy the problem with a sharp
knife. It was obvious we'd anticipated something more (or less) than the urban
gestalt.

The moment Grace reached Ed she began crying, scared of the building
and yet exhilarated, but also disappointed in having to confront Ed with her
decision to go down. She was firm this time: she had faced the Pyramid and
now, facing Ed, there was nothing more to fear. Ed lowered her. As she spun
lazy circles downwards, Grace looked relieved. We exchanged salutations as
she went by, and then she looped gently into a tight circle of newspeople and
was gone.

Soon I began to join Ed, jumaring the line that hung from his intricate
anchor. Working around an overhang, I could hear the police before I saw
them. A young, articulate officer had set his call radio on the ledge beside Ed.
As I got closer, I could hear the static and verbiage of numerous murder, theft,
and fire alarms that were thronging the city's airwaves. Now and then the
officer would lean out and identify one of the calls as being from his district.
Normally, he pointed out, he could have responded to this or that genuine
emergency. He never went so far as to declare that we were directly responsible, but he did throw the burden of economic guilt on us. I counted six
firetrucks and eight police cars near the garden entrance. A fire alarm crack-
led through the radio and three casualties were enumerated. The officer
politely showed us which trucks should have been on the scene.

Nearly up to the seventh story, I could hear Ed busily trying to set the logic straight and have the firetrucks and police cars dispatched to their areas, but the officer was adamant. We were unknown factors in a map of hourly emergencies, and because we were outside the ordinary computations of crime and emergency, the authorities overreacted, then insisted on their overreaction without really justifying it. The argument would have lacked all force except for the radio that snapped off casualty numbers and calls for help. It affected both Ed and me, even though we knew the logic was fuzzy.

The police had chosen to react in absurd numbers; they flocked beneath us and milled silently inside the window behind Ed. With the radio imparting a heightened sense of urgency to each successive minute, our arguments for the climb as an aesthetic survey of the Pyramid—and as a climb in itself—seemed incoherent even to me. The idea had been to append ourselves to the Pyramid, to interweave our lives, for the duration of the climb, with the life of the building. Dangling from a rope beside the call radio, I thought that idea sounded very hollow.

And so the city won out. We were citizens, and despite our native instincts, we accepted the responsibilities. We were out of the woods, in a place where the objective hazards of climbing included a felony charge in addition to glass that was fragile and cement that chewed ropes. It startled us both, I think, and still does, that we surrendered so easily. By noon the architecture literally absorbed us. I went first, stepping in through the open window of the seventh floor where a dozen men, looking huge in their uniforms, were obviously pleased to have captured at least one of us. As I passed inside, Ed pursed his lips and histrionically confided that he'd be "soloing on then." For a few minutes I actually thought he might, too, infected with the conceit of Harry F. Young—the arrogance of the hermit.

His face was bright with the sun. As I watched him from inside the building, two happy policemen detailed the plan they'd readied for us if we hadn't surrendered. Ignorant of the fact that we'd been anchored to the exterior, they blithely described how, with a quick shove on the window behind Ed, they would have neatly tumbled us both into the room. In horror I imagined the likelihood of officers tumbling to the sidewalk instead.

Their ignorance of climbing, and even of the workings of a window, gave me an odd, retrospective feeling that I'd betrayed something. Their calculations were off, their knowledge was faulty. The "reasonable control" of citizens was not reasonable, and logically not even control. It was a trap of some sort, a sacrifice. For an instant I considered escaping outside on some pretext, or at least yelling to Ed to go ahead and solo. But with a metallic jangle of hardware, he had already unclipped his knots and freed the anchor. One step and he was inside with the rest of us.

ABOUT THE CONTRIBUTORS

Jim Balog worked for several years in his chosen profession, geomorphology, before succumbing to the lure of freelance writing and photography. He has written for *Outside* and is presently completing articles for *Geo* and *National Wildlife*. He took up climbing seriously five years ago and has participated in expeditions to Mount McKinley and the Stikine Icecap region in the panhandle of Alaska. Ascending frozen waterfalls was at one time his ruling passion, but the instability of those huge, hanging icicles has led him toward more "mundane" ice climbs such as the one described herein. Balog lives in Boulder, Colorado.

Margaret K. Berrier-Petranoff became interested in the dynamism of rock gymnastics while observing her husband working out on Colorado crags. Her sketches in this book, executed in pencil, were inspired mainly from photographs. Berrier-Petranoff has a degree in art education from Indiana University and is presently continuing her studies at Metropolitan State College in Denver, where she lives.

John Daniel is a freelance writer, climbing instructor, and poetry teacher. His work has appeared in *Mountain Gazette* and *Climbing*, and he is presently completing several nonfiction articles for *Mariah/Outside*. "The Way of the White Serpent" is his longest published piece of fiction, although he has other short stories in manuscript. In his spare time he punches cows on a ranch in southern Oregon.

Mike Graber began climbing in 1969, and after graduating from California's Claremont College with a degree in philosophy, joined the ranks of climbing and skiing adventurers who make their living in the mountains. His illustrious climbing career has encompassed several summers among Alaska's Cathedral Spires as well as challenging expeditions to Mexico and South America. In 1979 he participated in a skiing expedition to Antarctica's Forbidden Plateau with a group sponsored by the American Broadcasting Company. Graber, who lives in Mammoth Lakes, California, is currently involved with the Fall 1980 Eastern Sierra Himalayan expedition to Baruntse, a 23,700-foot summit near Mount Everest. He has written for the *American Alpine Journal,* and his photographs have appeared in *Powder*.

Tom Higgins has spent most of his eighteen-year climbing career in California. An exponent of free climbing and partial to practicing the sport unencumbered by heavy gear, he has for the past few years shunned the major climbing centers in favor of making difficult first ascents in unusual places. Higgins, who lives in Oakland, California, is a public policy analyst specializing in urban transportation. His articles have appeared in *Ascent, Mountain,* and *Climbing*.

Jeff Long has been writing professionally for six years, his evocative articles appearing in *Climbing, Mountain,* and the late lamented *Mountain Gazette*. One of his earliest published pieces was "The Soloist's Diary," a powerful and unusual work of fiction which came out in the 1974 *Ascent*. He cites as his most memorable mountain experience the 1977 expedition which attempted the west face of Makalu, the world's fifth-highest peak. Long's climbing—on both mountains and buildings—has suffered while he labors on two novels and pursues graduate studies in history at the University of Colorado.

Ron Matous has spent the last four summers working as a climbing ranger at Grand Teton National Park, a coveted job among mountaineers. Although most of his climbing has taken place in Colorado—where he lives—or in the east, his list of other successes is extremely impressive, including two climbs of El Capitan, the west buttress of Mount McKinley, and, besides the Eiger, several outstanding routes in the Alps. His articles have appeared in *Climbing* and *Mountain Gazette*. Matous is presently the Winter Course Director of the Colorado Outward Bound School.

Frances Mayes is Director of the Poetry Center at San Francisco State University, where she also teaches. Her poems have appeared in numerous publications, including *Mother Jones, The Texas Quarterly,* and *Women in the Wilderness*. Her latest book of poetry is *After Such Pleasures,* published in 1979 by Seven Woods Press.

David Roberts has been in the mainstream of Alaskan mountaineering and exploration for nearly two decades; his first major expedition, in 1963, resulted in a new route up the enormous north face of Mount McKinley. A bold ascent of nearby Mount Huntington two years later is described in his acclaimed book, *The Mountain of My Fear*. A second book, *Deborah: A Wilderness Narrative,* published in 1970, dealt with the fluctuating emotions he experienced during the course of a long, two-man Alaskan expedition. Roberts recently left his position as an associate professor of English at Hampshire College to concentrate on writing. His articles have appeared in *Horizon* and *Harvard Magazine,* among other publications, and he is presently finishing a book on exploration hoaxes for Crown Publishers. *Like Water and Like Wind* is his first excursion into the realm of fiction.

Alison Salisbury is an artist living in Seattle. Her illustrations for "The Way of the White Serpent" are all photographs taken of the same oil painting, which was partially masked with sand to isolate the various elements.

Dick Shockley learned to climb at Devil's Lake, Wisconsin, in 1969; soon thereafter he took up the sport on the granite crags of southern California. A decade later he visited the Shawangunks—a New York climbing area—and ascended, on sight and unroped, Shockley's Ceiling and the 5.8 Minnie Belle. Such daring feats are not unusual among today's superclimbers, but this one had the distinction of repeating routes established thirty years earlier by his father, the Nobel Laureate William Shockley. When not climbing, Dick Shockley plays jazz drums and works as a physicist at the Naval Systems Center in San Diego. His next climbing goal is the notorious Shield Route on El Capitan.

John Svenson is a climber and artist who spends his summers in the mountains of Alaska, California, and Europe. During the long, dark winter nights at his home near Juneau, Svenson, working from sketches made while climbing, alters the reality of mountain scenes by "thinning the distracting clutter." His sketches have appeared in many North American and British climbing magazines.

Ed Webster took up rockclimbing at the tender age of eleven, when his mother—the only climber in the family at the time—introduced him to local climbing areas on the east coast. Later, while obtaining a degree in anthropology from Colorado College, he fell in love with the spires of the American Southwest, making nearly twenty trips to climb and photograph them. Webster is one of that rare breed who, while at grips with the complexities of extreme routes, takes the time to photograph his companions; his striking shots have graced the covers of *Mountain* and *Climbing*. At present he is a guide for the International Mountain Climbing School in North Conway, New Hampshire. Between climbs he serves as the American editor of the new British magazine, *World Rock*.